THE
APARTMENT
BOOK

THE APARTMENT BOOK

by the editors of *Apartment Life* magazine

Text by Rick Mitz

[H]

Harmony Books/New York

Editor: Harriet Bell
Designer: Ken Sansone
Design Assistant: Wendy Cohen
Production: Murray Schwartz, Celie Fitzgerald
Illustrations: Janet Sutherland

Published simultaneously in Canada by General Publishing Co., Ltd.
Printed in the United States of America.

Library of Congress Cataloging in Publication Data

Mitz, Rick.
The apartment book.

1. Apartments. 2. Interior decoration. I. Apartment life. II. Title.
NK2195.A6M57   1979   747'.8'831   79-17077
ISBN 0-517-53699-4

Second Printing

Contents

Acknowledgments

his book comes not from one author's head but from the shared sensibility of a community; it is really the life's work of a magazine staff and their like-minded friends. Through most of the seventies, this group struggled to invent and interpret a way of life that did not follow the old patterns. For the first time, because of the radical changes of the sixties, young people were not automatically following their parents' paths to marriage, children and a house in the suburbs. Rather, they were searching, alone or in pairs or in groups, for a place to live that would express their own values. And that place was most often the city; usually an apartment, but increasingly a loft, a garret or a rehabilitated house. *Apartment Life*, the magazine, did that searching with them, because *they* were *us*. The community of people who made the magazine were part of the group that the magazine was edited to: young people who were, by God, going to live their own brand of life, their way—even if they weren't so sure what it was yet. From its beginning in 1969, the magazine has been a laboratory to test ideas against a sample peer group; to sort the real ideas from the "magazine-y" ones; to

throw out a project because it was too hard for one of us to do.

Because we come from various persuasions and backgrounds, we approach our subject matter—real home service—with new eyes. The only discipline is a shared commitment to making real ideas happen, without decorator hype or the tyranny of status names. Indeed, on most of the pages that follow, you will see no specific design credits, a sign that means this "community at work"; a team of editors and photographers (often at work on hands and knees) put together the ideas, the rooms, the photographs and the pages.

If this group is especially talented, it is certainly without pretentions. In an industry where pictures often are made when an editor just happens to look up from his/her pate and Perrier to move the Breuer chair six inches to the left, ours is more the lash-and-dash school of burgers and bagels, ordered in; the instant blitz of a photo location, whether it is an empty studio or some celeb's bedroom. Ideas come from dial-a-design or call-a-concept: frantic inter-editor phone calls to fill the need for a fast coffee-table project or an instant-window treatment. We lug props in bags with "Apt Life Editor/Shlepper" emblems

and are never anywhere more than five minutes without moving the furniture (homes, apartments, restaurants, shops). Occasionally we become "contractors to the stars" and have to search for lost cats, clean under beds, iron pillowcases and suffer tantrums graciously. We travel the country in ragged bunches, always with more shopping bags than hands; and always with a willingness to push for the better idea, the better solution and the better picture.

Who are the people in this community? First, those who put the pictures together, *Apartment Life* editors like Carol Helms and Ben Lloyd; Donna Warner and Steven Wagner; Peter Bocour and friends including Wonsook Kim; Bobby Miles; Mike Jensen; Nick and Bruce; and the photographers, Tom Hooper, Bradley Olman, Bill Helms and more. There are those gone-but-not-forgotten types: the daddy of us all, David Jordan; Jim Hirsheimer (T.B.J.); John Baker; Allison Engel. Then there are editors who make sense of these pictures and cloak them in words, chief among them Marcia Andrews, Emily Freeman and Art Director Bob Furstenau.

None of the above could have happened without an entirely

supportive, if sometimes bemused, management at Meredith, especially Jim Autry, Editor-in-Chief; and of course Ted Meredith, Bob Burnett, Wayne Miller, Bob Phelps and of course, our publisher, Harry Myers.

If these people made the magazine, who made the book? The ever-devoted, agile writer Rick Mitz; Harmony's incredibly industrious and generous Art Director Ken Sansone; Bruce Harris, who calls himself publisher but has as astute an editorial mind as exists; Harriet Bell, our super-competent editor-in-relief; our dear publicist and friend Bobbi Schlesinger; and a whole *Apartment Life* support group of fast-talking and fortunately (for them) fast-acting facilitators led by Mary Didio and Charla Lawhon with Carolyn Holland, Pam Hanks, Francine Matalon-Degni and Mell Meredith.

But if this book belongs to anyone, it is to Joanna Krotz, *Apartment Life's* Articles Editor, whose clear vision (never without a twinkle) and professionalism molded this book with the same wisdom and insight, time and devotion she brings to the magazine.

Dorothy Kalins
Editor, *Apartment Life*

Introduction

First, what this book isn't: It is not a book that tells you what Designer Look the penthouse people are pursuing this season. It is not a book of just pretty pictures—swell to look at but with no relation to your rooms or life. You will not read the authorized story of how the Ten Best Decorators of the Twentieth century turned some perfectly marvy hall into the Taj Mahal.

The Apartment Book is about fact, not fantasy. On page after page these rooms break outmoded design traditions and offer new realistic solutions that are in step with today's space and problems. This *is* a book about Dream Homes, and these dreams can be realized. It is a book about sizing up your needs, solving your space dilemmas, and providing comfortable choices for your personal style. And it is a book chock-full of pretty pictures.

Apartments do, of course, have problems. Usually, there are too few rooms with too little space. You do need to maneuver in close quarters for storage, paper work, parties, and plants. In addition, just a few years ago, every piece of furniture simply had to match. Sofas were either pushed against the wall or sat face to face in a living-room showdown. End of alternatives. Industry manufacturers and retailers assumed that apartment furnishings meant scaled-down pieces for scaled-down living, as if apartment dwellers were a race of Lilliputians. If furniture was hard to find it was not because of size—it was limited

function that made the choice so difficult. Each distinct room had its own four-walled purpose—dining, cooking, sleeping, living.

Living? We believe all rooms should be designed for living. The care and feeding of an apartment does not require outside surgery. With thoughtfulness, perhaps an eye for the unexpected, it is easily possible to set up an apartment that works for the way you live. And that is accomplished by using ordinary space in unusual ways. Bedrooms can double as offices, dining places, gyms or second living rooms. This book is loaded with ideas for setting up work spaces at home—even in "useless" hallways. Surprising storage solutions, dynamic uses of color, clever screens at the window that move up and down —these are just a few ways to turn awkard rooms into attractive and functional ones.

If there is any leitmotiv here, it is Trust Yourself—sung to a chorus of hundreds of different rooms, settings, and situations that help you to stamp your own style on your own space. *Style*, not as in Early American or Mediterranean. But *Style*, as in the style you like.

Over the last decade *Apartment Life* magazine has been working full time to destroy some antiquated notions about apartment living: Apartments are no longer holding patterns for people waiting to move to the Permanent House in the Suburbs. Apartments are ongoing homes for real people; "borrowing" space does not mean not *living* in it.

At *Apartment Life* we have dedicated ourselves to redefining the vocabulary of possibilities for apartment living. You can see that in the photographs on the pages that follow. Much more than a collection of pretty pictures; every one, in fact, is a visual composite of several ideas in action. *Apartment Life* has developed a new kind of photojournalism, where the picture is the medium that transmits ideas and information. It is all in the setup. We do not just walk into an apartment, plunk down a tripod and begin shooting. Rather, before we photograph any story, we analyze the real problems that must be solved to make the story work. Then we come up with tailor-made solutions that can be adopted in other places. After that, we show up at the photography site and set up a living situation from scratch. Like a classic essay, our photographs have a central thesis and many supporting facts—ideas that provide service and solve problems. *Apartment Life* has moved into more new apartments than anyone in the world.

Our criteria have been vigorous. Beyond overall good looks, all furnishings have to work hard—a table must fold away when it is not needed. A desk must also serve as a dining table. Extended kitchens. Convertible living rooms. And, when the circumstances demand custom design, we design furnishings that can be assembled quickly—from lamps to shelving units to coffee tables. We take you through each project, step by step, so you

will not need a degree in shop.

A word about the organization of *The Apartment Book*. It is different. We have tried, wherever possible, to discard many traditional labels just as we have discarded many traditional design rules. "Living rooms," therefore, becomes rooms that live; "dining rooms" becomes eating places (because how many apartments actually have separate rooms for dining anyway?). "Work spaces" are hardly leather-bound dens but are areas that are integrated into other rooms. Most pages have quick-access legends at the top that capsulize the ideas that each room offers. So if you are looking for solutions to a window problem, you need only flip through the pages for the word "window" on the upper right side. At the back of the book you will find a comprehensive source list of manufacturers, suppliers and retailers who provide the furnishings and wares found in the room photographs. The *Apt Information* section details the basics of equipment and demystifies how-to skills, like track lighting and when to use a Molly bolt. We have included an extensive section on tenants' rights, from how to read a lease to how to get more heat. Finally, the index will direct you to specific ideas and information scattered in each chapter.

This, then, is a book designed for living, a companion to apartment life that will help you turn ordinary space into your own place with style, personality, imagination and a pride of home.

A MATTER OF STYLE

TONGUE IN CHIC

Yes, there is a way to fight Creeping Chic—those expensive styles and looks that designers generate and magazines regenerate. With imagination, you can find alternate sources and materials—minus the initials—that put it all together. With elan and ingenuity, you can approximate designer creations without paying name-brand prices. There are ways of getting around the magic names by using a little magic of your own. Improvise, don't imitate.

It is not just antisnob appeal. If you admire the aesthetic quality of a look but do not want to make an emotional or financial commitment to something that you might not want to live with for the next decade, you will be glad to know there is an alternative.

Of course, certain objects are expensive because of the handcrafted workmanship and fine materials. Some things are pricy because they are priceless —old or rare. Others are simply in vogue, thanks to status, initials or the cachet of the source. We show you both ends of the scale—the high and the low— not only to amaze but to illustrate the point. It is our design one-downmanship. A tongue-

-chic approach that is there
 r the taking: at the Salvation
 rmy, thrift stores, restaurant
 uppliers, drugstores and the
 ve-and-dime. Looking around
 ts you have your look, and af-
 rd it too.

USICAL CHAIRS
 reaking rules is what it is all
 bout. Old Fashion dictated
 hat you must—*simply must*—put
 period piece in a period set-

ting. Period. For example, that
Early American wing chair *must*
flank an Early American fireplace. And that streamlined
chrome lamp *has to* enlighten a
marble-topped table.

   Nonsense. Musical chairs
mean furnishings that work in
all environments. Yes, you can
put a camelback sofa in a space-
age space. Sure, a chrome and
glass table can live amicably
next to a golden oak breakfront.

The rules have been broken; it
is open season for options.

   To unlearn these old habits,
see how the same setting can
work for two quite different
styles of furniture. Stretch rigid
standards of what is appropriate and what is "now." Give
yourself permission to mix and
match, to take some design
risks and to trust your instincts.
The following pages show you
some examples.

TONGUE IN CHIC: Sleek Italian

Sleek, slick, sophisticated, Italian design has emigrated to stylish settings all over the world. The Italian look seems to speak any language. Its innovative design, revolutionary styling, its architectural shapes and methods of construction, have made this style reign supreme everywhere. Although the manufacturing processes and the quality materials of the authentic objects cannot be rivaled, you can approximate this design for a lot less money.

Art: An original Vasarely, painstakingly created by hand from hundreds of plastic shapes. With a signed edition of 30, the wall mosaic costs $2,600.

Headlights: Magnificently engineered Toio flos lights are designed by A. G. Castiglioni, $550 each.

Seating: Another Italian import: Le Mura modules are designed by well-known Mario Bellini. Upholstered in alpaca, each costs $1,450.

Pillows: The real thing from Ambience. The large calfskin is $125; broadtail pillows (one on each side) are $150 each; and the small calfskin is $50. Total $325.

Table: Franco Fattini designed this sleek chrome and mirror coffee table. A piece of sculpture at $720.

Boxes: Exquisitely finished and still fashionable. Karl Springer, innovative creator of custom-made, unique accessories, offers these marvels: the hand-lacquered goatskin parchment box, $525; African tappa cloth (bark) domed box, $375.

African Art: The Guro mask is $585 and the Senufo mask is $600. On the table the Bambera antelope sculpture is $650.

Tree: Ficus gives a lush look, $150.

Accessories: The chic coffee table demands the best. Chrome ashtray from Karl Springer, $300. Here, heavy equals good in a crystal ashtray from Steuben Glass, $200. Cottontail is $250. Crystal bud vase, $50. Orchid spray, for the utmost $8-a-bloom elegance. Silver tray for simplicity itself, $395.

Food: Pâté en croûte is flown in fresh from Paris by Ideal Cheese Shop, $6 for a four-pound loaf. Garnished with canned truffles from Maison Glass, $10.95 and cornichons (pickles), $3.25.

Rug: Carefully handwoven from the finest wool it will last a lifetime. From Stark carpets, $630.

Photos: Armen Kachaturian

TOTAL: $12,579.20

...oster: Trust your eyes ...d forget about the sta-...s of "owning" an origi-...l. This Vasarely poster ...ves much of the punch ...thout the price. Framed, ...5.

...mps: Adjustable height, ...ivel head, two say more ...an one. From five-and-...ne, believe it or not. $25 ...ch.

...ating: The same now-...ssic Italian lines, with a ...ore palatable price tag. ...orner piece is $155, side ...$120.

...lows: Make your own ...fake fur and pillow ...rms. Forms $2 to $4 at ...e-and-dime; fabric (½ ...rd each) $4 to $7.

...ables: For cheap sleek, ...ild or buy four cubes of ...rticle board (12" square ...d 15" high). Glue on ...ashable Moccaskin by ...rings Mills, top with ...irrors. Cubes, $8 each; ...occaskin $27, (2 2/3 ...rds at $10 a yard); ...oolworth's 12" mirror ...es, $7.50 for six.

...ccessories: The African ...owls are excellent, af-...rdable reproductions. ...he tripod bowl is $42, ...e shorter bowl is $30. ...he ginger jug is a Chi-...ese staple, $6.25.

African Masks: These copies exude ethnic chic. Top mask is $45; bottom $35. Antelope headdress sculpture on table is $42.

Plants: Instead of a tree, group a couple of fat Swedish ivies, $15 each. Import store stools, $20 and $32.

Accessories: Functional things made of good ma-terials: camping store stainless plate, $5; jug (vase), $5; with gladiolus, $1.25. Plump glass bird, $3.50. Auto shop hood ornaments would cost a mint if they were made for coffee tables. Fish, $12; side mirror, $15. Bamboo stool, oriental import store, $6. Chinese earthenware casserole, $10.

Food: With this food who needs a silver platter? Res-taurant supply tray, $6. Homemade pâté en croûte is a cut-off loaf of white bread, scooped out and filled with a "meat loaf" of ground pork, veal and hard-boiled eggs, $5 a four-pound loaf.

Rug: Actually, it is hand-some, heavy yard goods (54" x 72" including fringe you add yourself), about $50.

TOTAL: $886.50

TONGUE IN CHIC: Island Wicker

Casablanca meets south-of-the-border in these settings that are alive with naturals of all kinds. The fabrics, colors and materials are all pure and fresh and add an extract of exotica to any setting. It is an easy atmosphere to re-create because wicker is one of those things you can either spend a fortune on or very little indeed. We show you how to do both.

Plants: Elegant hanging Boston ferns add a cool touch to the room, about $12.50 each.

Lamp: Each of these beautiful Akari lamps is an individual work of art, $135 each.

Table and Chairs: Hand-woven rattan for a sophisticated interior. Table, $1,000; chairs, $500 each.

China: Flora Danica from Royal Copenhagen: Soup tureen with flowers, $2,350. Dinner plates, $355 each. Smaller but more expensive salad plate, $365. Elegant butter dish, $310.

Floor Matting: Made of strong, hand-spun coir, similar to hemp. Comes in squares, a cinch to put down. $5.40 a sq. ft. Total $378 for 70 sq. ft.

Fan: A Caribbean cooler for a balmy night, $275.

Paintings: Lush pastoral landscapes. Two rarities, $850 and $325.

Lattice Window Panel: The finest craftsmanship goes into these attractive wooden panels. The one shown is 36" x 60" and retails for about $100.

Water, Wine and Champagne Glasses: About $24 each.

Goblets: Sterling silver and a pleasure to sip from, $350 each. Scotch tumblers, also in silver, $225 each.

Silverware: The "Classic" line from Royal Copenhagen. A five-piece sterling silver place setting, $450.

Salt and Pepper Shakers: Sterling silver, $45.

Napkins: Soft to the touch, ecru linen, $24.50 each.

Wines: A great red, this '71 Romanée St. Vivant goes down like velvet, $87.50. Corton Charlemagne, $22.49.

Flowers: Fragrant Destiny lilies, $6.75 a stem. Alstromeriums, $3 each. Total $67.45.

Photos: Thomas Hooper

TOTAL: $9,850.94

Plants: A similar look to the Boston fern but almost half the price. Asparagus fern, $7.50 each.

Standing Lamp: Build your own using an import store shade, about $15.

Table Base: Really a basket, the lid is inverted so you can rest the glass on it. Sandbag the base for balance, $50. Glass cut to measure, about $85.
Chairs: Wicker and inexpensive, $90 each.
Cushions: The import store variety, $4.25 each.

China: Our version of Flora Danica Porcelain from Royal Copenhagen: Pillivuyt china painted with Vogart pens. You can fire your own work in the oven and though they are not dishwasher resistant, the color will not fade if washed by hand. Soup tureen with flowers, $37.75; dinner plates, $6.50 (the total bill for pens, $10).

Floor Matting: Lake grass, $13.95 for a 3' x 6' mat. Total $56 for 72 sq. ft.

Fan: A motorless Victorian version in wicker, $49.95.

Paintings: Really poster reproductions from museum gift shop, $25 for both.

Window Panel: A stairway safety gate painted white. Most hardware stores, $12.

Glasses: Water, wine and champagne, about $1.25 each.

Goblets: Elegant pewter, $14.95 each.

Scotch Tumblers: The look says silver but they are really plastic, $1.35 each.

Silverware: Five-piece place setting, stainless steel, $12.50.

Salt and Pepper Shakers: Chic luncheonette variety, $1.25 each.

Napkins: Import store, $2 each.

Wines: B. V. Pinot Noir, $5.75; Sterling Vineyards Chenin Blanc, $5.99.

Flowers: Pink carnations, 60¢ each. Daffodils, 90¢ each. Total $15.

TOTAL: $644.04

TONGUE IN CHIC: The Decorator Look

Prissy and precise, the quiet little table in the corner has become a collector's classic. The diminutive painted enamels, the understated birdcage and other accents hold court on a draped table of the finest fabric. Top designers charge a fortune for this trendy look. You can have the same symbols of status by substituting affordable collectibles for expensive ones.

Lamp: The very "right" ginger jar with fluted linen shade, $430.

Birdcage: Of slimmest bamboo, $160.

Painting: Enamel floral on stand, $375.

Boxes: One, cut velvet, two, leather with gold leaf, $250.

China: Oriental blue and white pedestal bowl, $375; teapot, $210.

Shells: The chambered nautilus, still "in," each $15.

Tablecloths: One simply *must* sleep and eat off Porthault. From France. The rust undercloth, $210; the hand-scalloped overcloth, $140.

Wall: The requisite and original tortoiseshell, $300.

Decanters: They are status if they are crystal and Baccarat. These are. $180, $110, $95. Wineglasses too, $97 each.

Sterling Silver Tray: Vintage, $200.

Chair: Chinese Chippendale updated, lacquered, $350.

Photos: Bradley Olman

TOTAL: $3,609.00

Lamp: The ginger jar. At five-and-dimes, $38.

Cricket Cage: A delicate oriental import, $2.

Painting: Cardboard print, import store, $1.

Frame and Box: Pseudo shells, or pasta shells to be exact. Frame, $1.50; box, $4.

Other Boxes: Some covered with adhesive paper, $1. Others, tea boxes, $1.50.

Teapot: Terra-cotta oriental import, $8.

Shells: The kind used for Coquilles St. Jacques, two for $1.

Tablecloths: Top, one square yard of fabric, $2. Beneath, a sheet of course, $15.

Wall: Simple small fans make a statement. Not too weighty, perhaps. But nice. And cheap. Fans each $1.

Decanters: Real liquor and liqueur bottles, free if you drink the contents. Or if you buy them full: left, Anis Del Mono (Spanish anisette) $8; Amaretto di Saronno $12; rear, Gilbey's Vodka $6; right, Pippermint Get (crème de menthe) $7.

Corks: Each, 10¢

Straw Tray: Oriental, $3.

Chopsticks: Rich-looking tortoiseshell finish, eight for $3.50.

Chair: Imported leather and slats, $65.

TOTAL: $182.90

TONGUE IN CHIC: Palm Beach Patio

Like a summer breeze, this light and airy, white-and-white look seems to float in any room it graces. It is a luxurious mixture of outdoor/indoor furnishings, plus plants and pristine fabrics, adding up to a cool flavor—whether the price tag is high or surprisingly low.

Umbrella: Not restricted to the outdoors, this sturdy, natural 8' umbrella fits into the most elegant surroundings, $600.

Plant: Raphis palm. Requires a great deal of attention and care, $450.

Lamp: A gorgeous glazed ceramic shell lamp from Mediterranean shores, $560.

Tablecloth and Napkins: Lovingly hand stitched by women on the island of Murano, near Venice. Rare organdy, $650.

Plates: Four-piece place setting of this delicate "Corail" china, $135.

Floor Tiles: This cool, lily-white tile is $2.15 a sq. ft. Total $107.50.

Curtains: Elegant Swiss eyelet, $11.85 a yard. Total for fabric before sewing: $187.50.

Silverware: From Victorian England, handmade, round-tip silver. Five-piece place setting, $300.

Salt and Pepper Shakers: Three sets of silver-plated shakers in an elegant gift box from Cartier, $55.

Figurine: For true collectors, a delicate Capo di Monte violinist, $405.

Glasses: All from Waterford Crystal. Wine and water, $23.50 each; champagne flutes, $24.25.

Table and Chairs: The finest workmanship has gone into these wrought-iron works of art, table, $1,100; each chair $650.

Photos: Thomas Hooper

TOTAL: $6,722.50

Umbrella: Not as tall or thick as its high-end counterpart but just as effective, $250.

Plant: A beautiful bamboo. Requires a lot of love but minimal attention, $140.

Lamp: A beauty in brass: the shell lamp, $124.

Tablecloth: The lacy look, $20.

Plates: A common lotus shape available at many import stores, $3.75 small, $4.75 large.

Napkins: Pure cotton from import stores; $1.79 each.

Floor: Brush on a new coat with easy-care deck paint, $12.95 a gallon at most paint stores.

Curtains: Cotton muslin, $15.95 a pair.

Silverware: Five-piece stainless steel place setting, $6.99.

Salt and Pepper Shakers: Just like the ones you find in a roadside diner, $1.25 each.

Figurine: Since the real thing is unavailable, how about this 7" replica of David to camp up your table? Available in many novelty stores, $5.75.

Glasses: Wine, water and champagne come in sets of six, $10.50 a set.

Table and Chairs: A handsome five-piece outdoor-indoor living room, $410.

TOTAL: $1,031.72

TONGUE IN CHIC: Pattern-on-Pattern

Blue-and-white, pattern-on-pattern, collector's chic—this luxury look has always been "in." The custom version at left is filled with one-of-a-kind antiques, fragile porcelains, intricately patterned rugs and fabrics and oriental accessories. You can put it together for less—much less—with ethnic finds, plastics, wicker and a sense of style and humor.

Photos: Armen Kachaturian

Fabric: Hand-screened and shirred on brass rods, it makes a luxurious backdrop, $300.

Plant: Elegant palm, $75.

Chair: The white plaster look is very Southampton. This chair is molded from a special composition of plaster, polymer and Fiberglas, reinforced with steel, $3,600.

Pillow: A made-to-order treasure, $45.

Lamp: The base is a nineteenth-century Chinese porcelain vase, $200. Shade and wiring adds $55. Total, $255.

Side Table: Beside the chair is a graceful John Rosselli drum-shaped porcelain piece, $1,200.

Table: Oriental inspiration, twentieth-century craftsmanship. David Barrett's straw table is $900.

Goose: It is porcelain and might well cook your budget, $595.

Rug: Intricate geometrics, and subtle, muted colors. This custom 6' x 9' Canton dhurrie, $975.

Etagerè: Museum quality, antique display, $2,295.

Accessories: Top shelf, bamboo box, $225. Here is an ironic twist—Karl Springer's $600 box is inspired by the look of everyday Bennington pottery. It is lacquered, suede lined, with silver inlay. Rabbit from shards of antique Ming pottery, Karl Springer, $225. Blue and white platter, John Rosselli, $150. Matched Chinese vases, John Rosselli, $135 each. Smaller box, Karl Springer $435. Bottom shelf treasures: nineteenth-century Fu dog, $900. Smaller pair, $225.

Dishes: Royal Copenhagen means quality. "Blue Flowers" cup, saucer and dinner plate, $73. For the pattern-on-pattern look, a John Rosselli platter under all, $38.

Food: Coquilles St. Jacques —lobster, shrimp, crab and scallops in a rich cream sauce—makes the perfect after-theater supper, $27 for four. China shells, $2.50 each. All on a Royal Copenhagen platter, $48. Total $85.

Elephant: Handwoven from split bamboo, then lacquered, Boxer and Ashfield's hollow box, $300.

TOTAL: $13,763.50

Fabric: Indonesian cotton from Fabrications is stretched over three Fome-Cor panels. These took 5 1/3 yds. at $9.50 a yd., plus $25 for Fome-Cor.

Plant: Fat asparagus fern, $20.

Chair: Bamboo director's chair with lots of class, for $55.

Pillow: Cover a form ($2) with a handsome dish towel, $2.

Lamp: The same whited-out look for less. At department stores, $25.

Side Table: Import store basket ($30), topped with glass ($28), stacks up to the custom-made kind.

Accessories: More oriental lovelies: fan, 65¢, coral, $2.50, cup and saucer on stand, $3, small and medium plates, $3.50 and $1.25, butterfly, $1.50. Larger Mikasa plate, $11.

Goose: Gladys glows with 25 watts. Whimsical and functional, one or a gaggle, $35 each.

Rug: 6′ x 9′ multicolor cocoa mat rug from import store, $50.

Etagerè: Smooth and plastic for display or books, $38.

Accessories: Take another look at everyday stuff: goblets, $7 each. Restaurant supply plate ($3.50) and tureen ($10.50). Ersatz objets d'art from import stores or a Chinese grocery: China bird, $3.50. Elephant, $8.50. Ring of geese, $12.50; stand, $7. Stacked baskets, $15. Frame any handsome fabric scrap, 11″ x 14″ frame, $7. Chinese soup tureen, $9. Super sake bottles, $2.50 each, $1 for each stand. Rice bowls, $1 each. Bottom shelf holds carved wooden box, $7. Basket/tray, $8. Five-and-dime lion frightens away the evil spirits, $20. Hiding underneath, dime-store tureen, $9.

Dishes: A trip to Chinatown never hurts the wallet. Saucers, $1 each; ginger jar, $5; chopstick holders, 50¢ each. Then hit restaurant supply houses: oval dish, $7; platter, $7.

Food: No need to use high-priced fresh shellfish for Coquilles St. Jacques. Frozen or canned (fillets, clams, shrimp) stir up quickly. $13 for four servings. In natural scallop shells from Katagiri, $2 for four.

Elephant: Wicker and sculpture in one. Oriental import store, $50.

TOTAL: $611.08

TONGUE IN CHIC: Thirties Deco

Nothing was more modern than Moderne—wood and chrome, sharp edges and zigzag curves. Called Art Deco, it represented a machined streamlined style that appeared in European design. Its development—about 1910—continued until the mid-thirties. Characterized by a developing technology, stylized motifs, often Egyptian, and other geometrical patterns, Art Deco got an added boost in the early 1920s following the opening of Tutankhamen's tomb. In the early seventies there was a resurrection of the Deco look— retro Deco, really—and it came out of the attic and came back into fashion. It is now all quite pricy but, as we show you here, it is possible to approximate the look of the Moderne mode.

Wall: Gray vinyl car upholstery fabric, 8 yds. at $13 per, trimmed with auto chrome strips, 50¢ a foot, $112.

Framed Piece: Painting by Robert Flinn, $100; frame $85.

Floor Lamp: Chrome torchère with glass rims, $185.

End Table: It is marble all around, $125.

Table Lamp: Vintage chrome with enamel stripes, $135.

Statue: New Lalique crystal, $290.

Candy Dish: Cobalt glass, chrome, $40.

Candy: Imported bonbons, $5 lb.

Sofa: Chrome and wood— super S-curve arm—upholstered in Ultrasuede (7 yds. at $37.50 per yd.), $600 total.

Rug (on sofa): Geometric area rug, $125.

Animal: Gazelles epitomized the strength and grace of the period. In plaster, $150.

Magazine Rack: Chromed steel, Bakelite handle, $65.

Plaque: Plaster cast of Diana and the Hound, $125.

Pedestal: Lucite column with illuminated base, $190.

Vase: Cobalt glass slips into sterling base, made by Kensington, $100.

Flowers: Silk magnolia blossoms, $235.

Table: Metal designed by Ray Patten for International Nickel Co., $125.

Glasses: Ruby glasses with antelope motif, $13 each.

Sugar and Creamer: Chrome from Manning-Bowman, $25.

Clock: Cobalt mirror surrounds face, $75.

Pitcher: Chrome with black wood trim, $45.

Cocktail Set: Cobalt glass, chrome details, $65.

Bottle: Cobalt glass again, $30.

Coffee Table: In fact, the birth of the coffee table. Lacquered bow base with cobalt mirror top, $240.

Glass Balls: Cobalt thingamajigs, $20 each.

Lamp: Frosted glass cube by Sabino, $175.

Animal: German ceramic antelope, $40.

Vase: English pottery by Carter, Stabler and Adams, $90.

TOTAL: $3,676.00

Photos: Thomas Hooper

Wall: Just gray latex paint —with wood molding —rips wrapped in Mylar —pe, $15.

Framed Piece: An Icart re-—roduction (on mirror), —45.

Floor Lamp: Shower rod, —ass shade (painted black) —d more, $17.

End Table: Quick as a —ash, plastic and glass, —35.

Table Lamp: Great look —r a stack of plastic parts, —lver paper and stars, —15.

Statue: Harlow likeness in —aster, $37.

Candy Dish: Formerly an —e bowl, $8.

Candy: Good 'n Plentys, —0¢.

Sofa: Sweet and simple —ut of questionable line-—ge (maybe from a bus —tation), covered in good —ray denim (7 yds.at —3.99 per yd.). Frame, —25, from Goodwill. —otal, $52.93.

Rug (on sofa): From new —ug remnants and sam-—les, cut and fit, $15.

Animal: New plaster yard —rt, $10.

Magazine Rack: Two hub-—aps ($10 each) blocked —ogether, $20.

Plaque: Large photocopy made from a drawing, $30.

Pedestal: Three Plexiglas tubes, two Plexiglas disks, $60.

Vase: An old cocktail shaker, $14.

Flowers: Plastic, $16.

Table: Thrift shop kitchen table, polished and painted, $14.

Glasses: Woolworth's, cir-ca 1955, 25¢ each.

Chrome Cups: Plastic, $1.89.

Clock: Runs a little late but has a kind face, $2.

Pitcher: 1950s hammered aluminum, $5.

Blue Bottles: New from Bromo Seltzer, Noxema . . .cost $5.

Coffee Table: An unfin-ished wood Parsons table, $45 (lacquer it black) topped with blue Plexiglas mirror, $36.

Glass Bulbs: Lightbulbs and porcelain sockets (all new), $6.

Lamp: Glass brick with bulb, socket and wire un-derneath, $4.

Animal: Plaster dog, sold white, $5.

Vase: White with blue flamingos—no pedigree, $5.

TOTAL: $519.92

TONGUE IN CHIC: Turn of the Century

Take a turn on the Turn-of-the-Century—cozy and patterned. Grandmother's looking-glass look—Early Room-at-the-Inn—has lived on as an interior institution. What were common everyday furnishings in the 1900s (brass beds for $11) have become valuable and expensive today—(brass beds, $500), carved oak rockers, beveled pier mirrors and oriental rugs. By using similar patterns, replicas and ornamentation, you can make Granny still feel at home.

Wallpaper: Pattern is "Suzann" from Fashon, $12.95 a single roll, total $77.70. New.

Framed Print: Maxfield Parrish's *Daybreak*, original, $225.

Frame: Gilted gesso on wood, $50. C. 1900.

Picture: T. Roosevelt campaign poster, $35. C. 1900.

Commode: Solid oak, perfect condition, $250. C. 1895.

Lamp: Green tinted glass, $75; handpainted shade, $100. C. 1892-1910.

Clock: Single bell alarm, black face with moving eyes, $225. C. 1905.

Jar: Crystal with sterling top, $65. C. 1897.

Comb and Brush Set: Celluloid, six pieces for $65. C. 1908.

Dresser Cloth: Linen with drawn thread embroidery, $30.

Bowl and Pitcher: Staffordshire ironstone from England, $210. C. 1898.

Rug: Kerman, Persian, hand tied, 9' x 12', $1,300. C. 1924.

Curtain: Handmade lace, $160. C. 1890.

Curtain Rod: Spiraled oak $40. C. 1897.

Pier Mirror: Oak with beveled mirror, a buy at $550. C. 1888.

Scarf: Gentleman's, embroidered silk, $60. C. 1906.

Hat: A straw boater, $35. C. 1890s.

Portrait on Shelf: Admiral Dewey on celluloid photo album cover, $55. C. 1898.

Packages: Four rare tin containers, $225. C. 1895 1928.

Bed: Classic simplicity in brass, not a nick, $550. C. 1912.

Quilt: Lonestar pattern, all handwork, $350. C. 1920.

Pillowcases: Lace trim. Check fabric boxes in thrift and antique shops. Two for $50. C. 1890.

Pillow Sham: Embroidered cotton with applique, $30. C. 1908.

Pillow: Silk sewn into a heart shape, $25. C. 1922.

Tray (and contents): $300.

Rocker: Oak with pressed carving, Sears' finest, $185. C. 1896.

Cushion: Needlepoint in ten colors, $60. C. 1900.

TOTAL: $5,382.70

Photos: Thomas Hooper

Wallpaper, $35.

Framed Print: Maxfield Parrish's *Daybreak*, $20; frame, $25.

Frame: Plaster, from a ceramics shop, painted gold, $5.

Picture: Take a portrait of a pal, print it sepia, $15.

Commode: New unfinished pine cabinet, $50; hardware, $5.50; stain, varnish and wax, $7.

Lamp: Reproductions are everywhere. Base $15; new shade, $35.

Clock: Big Ben, $25.

Jar: Cotton dispenser from medical supply, $3.

Comb and Brush Set: Pseudo tortoise (new), four pieces, $8.

Dresser Cloth: Salvation Army, $1.

Bowl and Pitcher: Greenware, paint it yourself, $11.

Rug: 6' x 9', rayon/cotton, $115.

Curtain: "Machine-made" lace tablecloth, $6 at Goodwill.

Curtain Rod: New spiral dowel and two finials; stain and add curtain rings, $9.

Pier Mirror: An old oak door, mirror trimmed with new molding (stained), a small shelf and brass coat hooks. Total $55.

Scarf: A five-and-dime special for 89¢.

Hat: Costume shops have hundreds, $3.50.

Portrait on Shelf: John Philip Sousa on sheet music, $3.

Packages: New powders, soaps, fancies, all for $10.50.

Bed: It is iron; manufactured for three decades, very findable, painted with Illinois Bronze #236 Metallic Brass Spray Plating, $35.

Coverlet: A project: Collect thrift shop doilies, pot holders and other crocheted pieces (about 85 for double bed) and sew them to an open-weave fabric. Total $65.

Pillowcases: From Sears, $5 a pair.

Pillow Shams: Antimacassars ($7).

Tray (and contents): $26.

Rocker: Made yesterday, $55.

Cushion: Thrift shop doily (50¢) over a small pillow, $3.

TOTAL: **$659.89**

MUSICAL CHAIRS: Swapping Sofas

The sofa/sleeper used to be a luxury—a place to put extra guests when the guest room was occupied. Guest rooms? Today, sofa beds *are* our guest rooms. And—thanks to technology and a heightened sense of style—we now have hideaway beds that give us night-after-night comfort—for ourselves, not just for our guests.

Two classic sofa designs have been successfully adapted to sleeping and combine high style with high utility—plus, they are attractive and convertible enough to fit into any setting. The traditional Chesterfield sleeper at left is covered in soft corduroy, handsomely designed with deeply buttoned back, rolled arms and beechwood bun feet. A rattan convertible? Sure. The bright print at right—riding on top of a rattan-paneled frame—lets a most contemporary style work double time.

Photos: Bradley Olman

MUSICAL CHAIRS: Shuffling Chaises

The chaise—whether it was in Marie Antoinette's boudoir or Bette Davis's bedroom—used to be for swooning and resplendent relaxation. When homes got smaller and budgets got tighter, the chaise was one of the first pieces to go. Now it is back—but for different reasons than the first time around. Chaises are now an alternative or addition to the sofa—they combine high style with high comfort.

These two stellar versions come from similar traditions but got separated en route due to updating. The one at left—a classic version with old-country charm—disarms a setting that mixes traditional with contemporary. The chaise at right—complete with bun feet and a madcap modern print—makes a more fun-loving impact in the same setting.

As for the rest of the room, the fabric shutters and curtains shed light while ensuring privacy. The natural wood and light fabric complement the soft lines of the chaises.

Photos: Bradley Olman

28

MUSICAL CHAIRS: Changing Seats

Two extremes work extremely well in the same setting. And what two styles could be more disparate than low and modern, and tall and traditional? Both chairs fit well in this environment. Just as blue jeans are now appropriate with quilted smoking jackets so too these chairs.

The low-slung foam chair and ottoman at left has a zip-off, dry-cleanable cover. Well priced and chameleon in character, they work anywhere. At right, a traditional wing chair is "easy" and comfortable.

The setting comes together with primitive patterned paper, marble plant-stand-as-end table, Victorian shelf, large palm and a lamp made from an inexpensive oriental parasol and a bamboo pole.

ROOMS THAT LIVE

The apartment living room has to act like many other rooms—the garden and utility room, the guest room, the workroom, the backyard. And sometimes all at once. Plus, it has its own life to lead.

Such demands could give any room an identity crisis. But with a sense of challenge and a little common sense, today you can let your living room live the way you do.

We are no longer defined by the possessions that once possessed us. We are augmented by them. We have been finally exorcised of mandatory color coordination and everything-must-matchness. Now fun and function are as important as pure aesthetics. We put up a picture over the sofa not because it "goes" but because it "pleases." And that coffee table has to do more than serve coffee. It has to support: dinner? feet?

And as the way we live has changed, so has our furniture. We call it "furniture that works," and that means furniture that lives right along with you. In days past it seemed that the living rooms of our childhoods should have been set off with velvet cords —*look, but don't touch*. They were Drop Dead chic—the Urban Cathedral, the Subur-ban Sistine, into which guests filed, paying homage to each venerable object, price and bloodline duly noted. Museumlike.

Now we do not want our friends to come in and Drop Dead. We want them to drop in. And we want the living room to communicate that welcome.

But how? The chic design publications tell you that home happiness will come your way if you only use the requisite prints and patterns, coordinated colors and this season's hottest decorator. They would be out of business, though, if they said

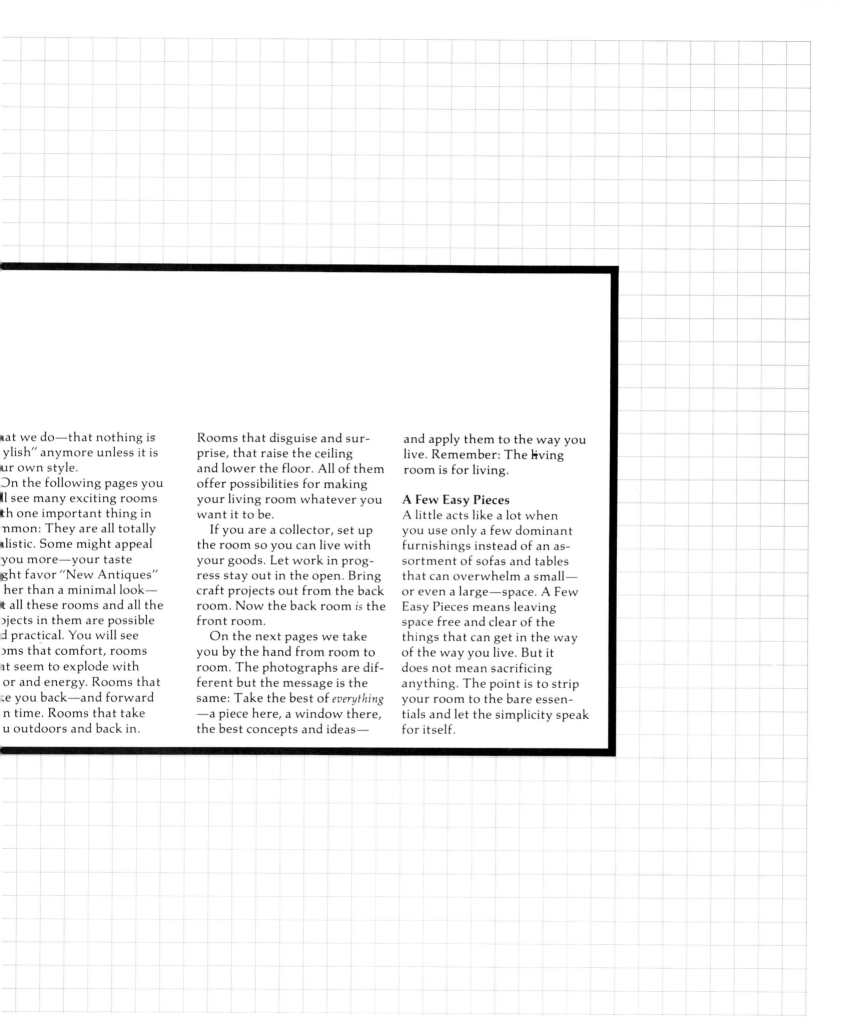

at we do—that nothing is ylish" anymore unless it is ur own style.

On the following pages you ll see many exciting rooms th one important thing in nmon: They are all totally listic. Some might appeal you more—your taste ght favor "New Antiques" her than a minimal look— t all these rooms and all the jects in them are possible d practical. You will see oms that comfort, rooms t seem to explode with or and energy. Rooms that e you back—and forward n time. Rooms that take u outdoors and back in.

Rooms that disguise and surprise, that raise the ceiling and lower the floor. All of them offer possibilities for making your living room whatever you want it to be.

If you are a collector, set up the room so you can live with your goods. Let work in progress stay out in the open. Bring craft projects out from the back room. Now the back room *is* the front room.

On the next pages we take you by the hand from room to room. The photographs are different but the message is the same: Take the best of *everything* —a piece here, a window there, the best concepts and ideas—

and apply them to the way you live. Remember: The living room is for living.

A Few Easy Pieces

A little acts like a lot when you use only a few dominant furnishings instead of an assortment of sofas and tables that can overwhelm a small— or even a large—space. A Few Easy Pieces means leaving space free and clear of the things that can get in the way of the way you live. But it does not mean sacrificing anything. The point is to strip your room to the bare essentials and let the simplicity speak for itself.

The New Classics

This living room has a mind of its own. The attitudes of the past are the antecedents of the new pieces—a comfortable sofa, lounge chair, traditional table. All of it has an updated twist and a tip of the hat to technology. The result is a pure and fresh living space that is airy without putting on airs.

The focal point is clearly the sofa, a super easy chair that lounges the way you do. This kind of fat upholstery abounded in the thirties. It worked then because it was comfortable. The new classic version is still voluptuous, but now svelte.

The lighting in this room is notable because it is hardly noticeable. Whereas yesterday's lamps were permanently planted in place, these new ones travel, moving around as your needs do. Clamp-on, flexible lights combine pared-down beauty with high function. Our lighting aesthetic has expanded in recent years. The beauty of lighting is not only what it looks like, but what it does.

Adding or hiding more light are the curtains—not dreary draperies that turn a living room into a hideout, but fresh fabric on attractive wooden rods that make an open and shut case.

At right are storage cubes (which use overlooked floor-level space). The clean lines of the square box, plus the add-on options of doors, drawers and shelves greatly increase storage possibilities. They look built-in —and, in a sense, they are, since you arrange them yourself.

The dining table serves work as well as dinner. This one is butcher block, combining the best of nature and science. Around the table are molded plastic chairs. Easily used with a myriad of styles, they can stack, come in many colors, are inexpensive—and are engineered in a shape that could only happen in plastic, which is no longer imitation anything.

The lounge chair, combining metal and canvas, is a logical extension of the classic director's chair, another outdoor piece moved inside.

The storage unit (at left) comes from commercial sources and was originally used as retail display. It is easy to assemble, and creates a grid that adds interior dimension. Made of chrome tubes with masonite shelves, the unit is easily added to or knocked down.

The oversized poster is accessible, affordable and, when blown up big and hung alone, is a grand option to little clusters of pictures. These days our finest contemporary art often comes printed large on paper with someone else's message. Communication is the new key.

A kilim rug sits confidently on a white tiled floor.

The Convertible Living Room

Because the new family portrait is often children with interchangeable parents, the everyday living room and occasional office must also be the weekend bedroom. You can take custody of a room quickly and deliver yourself from lagging delivery dates with mass-market furnishings that have longtime durability, plus style that will stay put as long as you do.

The pieces that make this room so adaptable are the sofas —one that quickly converts to a bed while the other groups and regroups, thanks to lightweight, high-quality polyurethane modulars. With a forward flip of the back panel, the bed-sit-sofa serves for sleeping. The molded plastic tables are coffee tables by day, bed stands by night.

The windows represent another instant option: Shades are retractable art, with contemporary chintz fabric adding color and character. When the shades are down, the room is filled with light from fixtures around the room. Lighting that consistently works best happens to be lighting that worked first to shed light. The green glass shade from offices past, the Luxo lamp, late of artists' drawing tables, track lighting and some recent fixtures are all elegantly simple.

The table at the back is a modernization of the seventeenth-century trestle base in chrome with an ash wood top for durable dining/desk space.

Underfoot, a sisal rug—originally summer mats for porch rooms—comes indoors. Supertextured (like diving-board mats), sisal rugs come in a variety of styles, always well priced.

White on White

Minimal is the maximum in this room. Because it is small, furnishing with a few functional yet high-styled pieces is better than crowding it.

A few overriding principles help transform this room from a space to a place:

When using only a few furnishings, multiple-choice pieces like these modular units give you greater flexibility. These are covered in plain white canvas, making their simple lines even cleaner.

Leave the modulars out in the open—not jammed against the wall—for breathing room.

Like any good graphic design, this room needs a strong focal point, and that is what it gets with the striking fabric mural hung over the fireplace. Leading up to it is a practical fiber rug, readily available at many oriental import stores.

Bare windows give the room a sense of lightness. Those boxes hung above each window are really stereo speakers, cov-ered with loose-weave fabric and mounted onto the wall.

Because this room is small, the floor should remain as un-cluttered as possible to give the illusion of space. Rather than floor lamps, all lighting has been hooked up to a track so that no cords show. Track lighting offers both uniformity and flexibility. Those austere white industrial lamps are avail-able at hardware stores and are easily hung. The track lights over the fireplace throw spots in any direction, and each has separate circuits that can be controlled individually.

Graceful, white molded plas-tic pieces are both light looking and lightweight for easy mov-ing. The table and magazine rack have origins in high Italian design but are now being man-ufactured in affordable ver-sions. The piece at left doubles as a serving cart that can roll into the kitchen or bedroom (the holes below are for wine and liquor bottles).

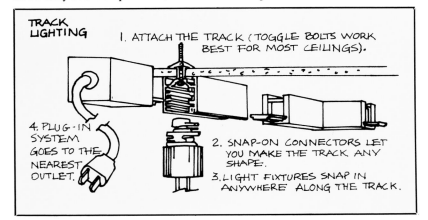

TRACK LIGHTING

1. ATTACH THE TRACK (TOGGLE BOLTS WORK BEST FOR MOST CEILINGS).

4. PLUG-IN SYSTEM GOES TO THE NEAREST OUTLET.

2. SNAP-ON CONNECTORS LET YOU MAKE THE TRACK ANY SHAPE.

3. LIGHT FIXTURES SNAP IN ANYWHERE ALONG THE TRACK.

Design: Stephen Habiague

Seeing Double

Trust your eyes: Unusual discoveries are found in the most unexpected places. Stalking the bins of hardware stores, the shelves of dime stores or the racks of salvage yards can yield things made for one purpose that will adapt to another.

Old can be made to look new. The sofa is created from three hassocks that were about to be thrown out. Rescued along with two armchairs, the hassocks are transformed by new slipcovers and a few pillows into stylish seating.

White paint turned a clunky packing crate into an unusual base for an outsize plant. (Although many shippers today use cardboard, there is an alternative: rough-sawn boards nailed together and painted white.)

The long, low table at left was always of the Parsons variety—but it got a lot more chic after meeting up with some snakeskin vinyl paper (apply with vinyl wallpaper paste).

A mighty pair of hinged screens—for height and color contrast—are more imaginative than draperies.

The wicker laundry basket—long hidden away in the closet—goes from hamper to coffee table, simply by placing it in front of the sofa. Its texture and natural tone make it a glad addition (and it is still good for storage).

Even a building supply store can yield art. The instant wall sculpture at right is aluminum flashing rolled into an artful shape, then held together with pop rivets and spray painted.

A star is born anywhere with a theatre spotlight.

HOW TO DO IT
Screens: These canvas screens add simple elegance to a room; they also add height and dimension, while—with the push of a panel—assuring privacy. Stretch artist's canvas over 2" x 2" frames, then paint with vinyl latex (or buy the canvas already primed with gesso). Hinge the panels as shown. Adjust dimensions to fit any window size.

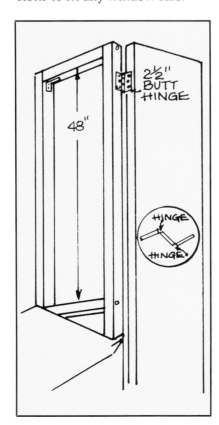

Photo: Elyse Lewin/Design: Pasquale G. Vazzana

A Touch of Tradition

An original elegance reigns here as miles of styles have been combined with a simple scheme. The modular seating is a flexible system of foam cubes that become chairs, sofas and ottomans, easily moved around as you need them.

Slick modern meets country provincial, and the common meeting ground is color—a terra-cotta red in French-inspired "chintz" wallpaper, the seating units, floor, lamp, accessories and blinds. Neutral baskets add natural texture, nestling as an end table/storage trunk at right and as magazine and plant holders. A Formica wall unit is discreet enough to fit into any style room—and here it stores stereo equipment as well as books and collectibles. With adjustable shelving, you can customize to accommodate both record albums and paperbacks.

Instead of fussy draperies (the towering corn plant is enough), the windows have been covered with easy-to-mount venetian blinds.

The two modern lamps—elegant and streamlined stand-up at left, updated thirties fan on the wall at right—provide indirect light that casts a warm glow. Carefully chosen accessories, from the duck decoys atop the bookcase to the contemporary-shaped telephone, provide the proper punctuation.

Looking at rooms through rose-colored glasses is not the key to color coordination here. The foundation for all the glow is the floor, actually an easy homemade remedy for an originally ugly foundation.

HOW TO DO IT

Floor Treatment: Cover an ugly floor with a new (and inexpensive) permanent covering by using sheets of masonite cut to fit.

Measure the area to be covered. Have the lumberyard cut masonite into tiles (2 x 2 tiles were used in this room).

Paint each piece with at least two coats of deck paint. Polyurethane makes floors washable, long-lasting and scratch-resistant.)

Glue tiles onto floor with wood flooring adhesive (the same kind that is used for installing parquet floor tiles). Over rug: use long nails.

Minimal Modular

A new rule: Furniture that works is designed for the way people live today—for good looks and multiple functions. Modular systems are especially flexible and are available in many styles. Here the sofa makes the whole room. Its simple lines, extra comfort and overscaled (yet graceful) design allow it to live happily in a modern studio as well as in a Victorian town house.

These particular pieces are all part of the same seating system—wave-quilted with a matching end table and coffee table. It all happens in three basic shapes (see diagram): a square, a square with a back and a square with a back and an arm (the corner piece). The ottoman (partially visible in the fore-ground) is made of two matching pillows stacked together.

But minimal is not the end of it. There is a striking balance of Victorian and sleek modern in various round-the-room pieces: Light comes from a streamlined metal sculpture lamp and a well-priced paper Japanese hanging shade. Natural light comes from the windows, hidden only by plain, natural-finish shutters with the louvers open to let in the light. A horizontal strip of natural wood molding tacked on the walls just below window level adds classic wainscoting quickly. A few bold plants, prints, pots and pillows fill out the room. A handsome kilim flat-weave rug projects softness and warmth. This room is not modern; it is classic.

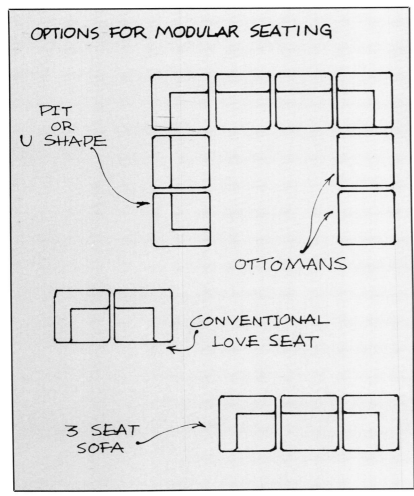

OPTIONS FOR MODULAR SEATING

PIT OR U SHAPE

OTTOMANS

CONVENTIONAL LOVE SEAT

3 SEAT SOFA

Walls: Natural wood molding
Lighting: Simple and sculptural
Windows: Natural-finish
shutters

An Unexpected Mix

It is up to you. Almost any choice works as long as it is made with a consistently inventive eye.

The colonial hutch at center is unfinished pine, and that is just how it stays. The slatted, natural-finish park bench at right has been transplanted from outdoors; it is comfortable, and the strong natural structure fits in well.

And another little trick: It may not look like there is a tablecloth in sight but that is exactly what the modern, straight-lined rattan sofa is covered with—French tablecloths. The pillows are covered with matching napkins.

The red table of hefty, molded Italian plastic is sturdy enough for serving dinner as well as a great gathering place for favorite collectibles.

A green clamp-on lamp hangs from a handwoven rattan screen (portable, practical, pretty) and, across the room, a bright yellow apothecary-style stand-up lamp adjusts the light to any direction. A well-priced and well-wearing handwoven dhurrie rug anchors the coffee table.

The accessories are equally available and well designed: a bold Milton Glaser poster, the low-hung contemporary clock, the red lanterns. The high-hanging ivy and handsome ficus tree complete the picture.

The New Mechanic

Floor: Woven sisal area rug

Window: Wicker screen

Walls: White molding, warm walls

Two-Piece Suite

Instead of the usual facing sofas, this room works by exchanging one sofa for a chaise. Both are exquisitely upholstered and formally flank the fireplace. Other surprises: The sofa conceals a double bed and the chaise doubles as a single bed. Pushed together, the units make a deep seating island, an L or any other configuration that pleases.

In the past, furniture—especially sofas—had to point the way to a room's focal point—usually a fireplace, étagère or window. Here the seating units are flexible and stylish enough to offer several options—and changeable focal points: a steady, sturdy, white molded plastic Italian table; a wicker screen as window treatment; an overgrown (but not overbearing) palm tree; and a simple, but substantial, woven sisal rug. Pillows are thrown around for comfort.

The New Traditional

In the late sixties anything that was not old enough to be "antique" was put down as "bad." Plus, many interior designers seemed convinced that Good Taste came only from the sleek and modern, from chrome and leather, from fantastic plastics and the austere white-on-white. A whole heritage of furnishings seemed to disappear right out the door—the classic curves and fine old lines as well as the vintage pieces of our near past: the wooden hutches, the curly-backed chairs with cabriole legs.

Well, we have gone around yet again. But this time—and this is the key to the New Traditional—we haven't thrown out the new as much as we have readmitted the old. No longer is it either the cold industrial look *or* grandmother's parlor. It is a way of living that combines the comforts of old with the trendiness of today, saying that old style does not have to mean old fashioned; that anything goes if you like it enough. The New Traditional spells comfort and a sense of home that welcomes you with furniture that is faithful in reproduction of authentic versions.

The New Traditional apartment has all the advantages of today without turning its back on all the good things from yesterday.

The Drawing Room Updated

Traditional design and furnishings are reinterpreted and reshaped in this room as some very new principles—variations and updates on old themes—prevail. Here is the new line on old looks in a room that does not take itself too seriously.

The comfortable camelback sofas—inspired by English Chippendale and Hepplewhite—are redefined by an overstuffed fatness and made today.

The Louis XV armchairs are left with a natural finish, making them seem contemporary without discarding their classic eighteenth-century French lines.

Holophane lamps make elegant hanging light fixtures.

Coffee tables were an invention of the twenties (before that all tables were higher), and this one is a modern adaptation in a light finished French Provincial style.

The Welsh sideboard is for all kinds of display, not just dishes. The birds on top are not folk art but new wooden ducks used for découpage.

Near the windows: Modern lacy curtains and wooden rods and rings dispense with the heavy draperies usually expected in a period room. The geometric fretwork of the Chinese bamboo screen suggests the imports used in eighteenth-century England—but it is new.

The rugs are only semi-antique (and from Iran), but more available and better priced than Persian models.

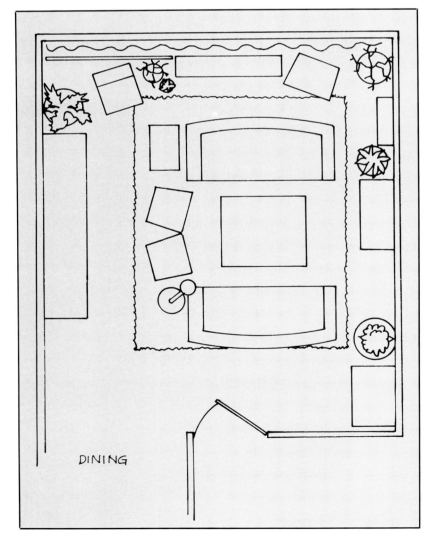

DINING

The Drawing Room Updated

On the wall a Metropolitan Museum reproduction of Oliver Tarbell Eddy's *The Ailing Children* is framed with decorative molding. Use a miter box to cut the frame's corners and then leave it unfinished.

And more new antiques: the country English pine blanket chest, Scandinavian hurricane lamps (on the coffee table), and new American fern stands. The green-shaded brass lamp on the blanket chest is a fine reproduc-

tion of an old classic. In the back of the room, a rococo English baker's rack (green painted metal instead of the traditional wrought iron and brass) gives stereo equipment an elegant housing.

In yet another corner of the room, the indoor palazzo has terra-cotta figures and tile designs so timeless that they can not be labeled. This small area, set off by the tile, makes a room within the room.

Photos: Bradley Olman

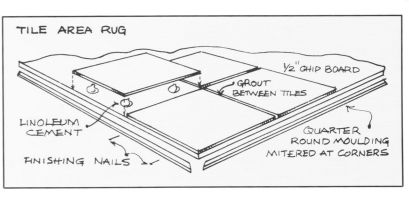

TILE AREA RUG

½" CHIP BOARD

GROUT BETWEEN TILES

LINOLEUM CEMENT

QUARTER ROUND MOULDING MITERED AT CORNERS

FINISHING NAILS

HOW TO DO IT

Tile: Cut chipboard to fit tile size. Glue on tiles, then grout.

Edges are finished with ¼"-round molding nailed to the chipboard.

Vintage Relaxation

Straitlaced rules of living do not apply here. This room tilts toward the traditional but its message is Relax. It is okay to put your feet on the coffee table or pull up any chair.

While many of the furnishings have a rich traditional look, they have been updated for function.

The camelback Chippendale sofa is no longer stiff or foreboding because it is covered in natural canvas. The slick and serviceable coffee table is strictly modern. Unlike dainty models of another day, this one is roomy enough to serve dinner for four.

Conventional wisdom might restrict these Italian-inspired light sculptures to a strictly modern space but they work well here. They are easily made by seaming stretchy white fabric; slipping it over a wire frame and fastening both to a plywood base. Screw a porcelain ceiling socket to the plywood base. The fabric can be secured with drawstrings to change bulb. A pair can divide a room or provide soft lighting anywhere.

Instead of wallpaper, a fabric-covered wall or two does the job —and camouflages bumps, cracks and the old peeling wallpaper that afflict many older apartments. First, the walls are padded with polyester batting. Then the fabric is stretched around a lightweight vinyl frame that is tacked to the wall's edges.

Two painted metal outdoor chairs are covered in easy canvas. A pair of ottomans stretch the comfort.

Home Is Where the Hearth Is

Everything here is clearly a period piece—yet the period is *now*. All these classics are new reproductions—modified a bit but always true to the ideas that made these furnishings great in the first place.

The pieces—not the room—are overstuffed. Borrowing from the "white and light" school of decorating, the room maintains white walls, several well-chosen large plants and sheer dotted Swiss fabric over the windows.

The sofa is an overstuffed version of its thirties ancestor, with ruffles around the pillows, as well as a gathered skirt on the bottom—a plushy and cush-iony place to flop. Covered in pale blue velvet, at left, is a Lawson chair whose familiar lines have been around since the late twenties. Even the new leather recliner is surprisingly good looking.

Two substantial pieces of golden oak give solid dimension to the room. Yes, you can find a reproduction rolltop desk, complete with nooks, crannies and cubbyholes. Made today too, the turned oak coffee table still displays fine detailing.

Highlighting the prevailing blue is an American-made oriental rug. Other accessories include an oak framed mirror and a brass fireplace screen.

Country Comfort

You do not have to live down on the farm to have the charm of it. Here are some homemade homespun ideas.

In the corner the Hoosier cabinet (the kitchen pantry of old) is used as a bar and serving piece.

That picture frame is really an old window sash. Old photographs, seed catalogs, botanical prints or anything that looks right to you works.

An old bed becomes a sofa with comfort provided by fat pillows made from feed sacks. Just iron and stuff (polyester fiberfill works well) to make the pillows.

That end table is a pickle crock with a pine top cut to fit. If you add a plywood disk to the underside of the pine top, it acts as a "lip," or wedge, to prevent the top from slipping.

Barn boards, picked up on a scouting expedition, were used to build that sturdy corner unit at left. It is made to look like an old corner cupboard but lacks a back. Make it by cutting shelves at 45-degree angles on both sides. Screw wooden cleats into the vertical sides, spaced to support the shelves. Then add wood strips top and bottom; everything unscrews to move. You will need 50 clean feet of boards.

Other country comforts: a cobbler's bench coffee table; a new, reproduction gas lamp; a round cheese box as end table; and a hickory branch settee handmade by southern craftspeople (available by mail order).

Walls: Old window sash as picture frame

Window: Dishcloth curtains; old house shutters as screens

Floor: Dime-store rugs sewn together

Storage: Barn-board corner cupboard

Unexpected materials can cover a window inexpensively and attractively. These are squares of dishcloths, sewn together and clipped with drapery rings.

A braided rug is really a shortcut patchwork of small, inexpensive dime-store rugs joined together. Machine sew together, join the strips with heavy cord.

A Place To Come Home To

This room is home—not so much as we remember it—but as we want it to be. It is warm and wonderful, an inviting place that gives you permission to relax. One secret of this welcoming comfort is the fabric, descended from English drawing rooms through early American homesteads. The tricks are a basic two-color scheme and all-new furnishings, though they look vintage.

The softly rounded, modular sofas and chaise are upholstered in fabrics reminiscent of William Morris's nineteenth-century English patterns—reinterpreted by Laura Ashley. They restate the romantic feeling prevailing for years in fabrics, with one important exception: These new fabrics are not pompous like their predecessors. They are old in style but contemporary in every other way.

The wallpaper and the fabric on the screens near the window complement each other in design and color.

The originality of this room comes from the way traditional design has been reinterpreted and mixed with contemporary styles. Look at the details: the bark chair (made of hickory) could have been lifted from the front porch of a house in the Blue Ridge Mountains a hundred years ago. Actually, it is made today in North Carolina. The Queen Anne table, covered with lace cloth, is also a faithful reproduction, down to its gracefully turned legs.

The hanging lights in the corner are only half old. Made from antique glass shades that have been wired to new fixtures and hung from the ceiling, they fill the corner with a cluster of charm. The window, treated with a wooden molding frames the lacy tablecloth. Screens, covered in a compatible fabric, provide a setting without hiding all the light.

Homemade wainscoting is achieved by painting the lower walls shiny burgundy, tacking on natural-finish chair-rail molding and wallpapering the wall above. A Matisse poster and a striking geometrical rug finish this room.

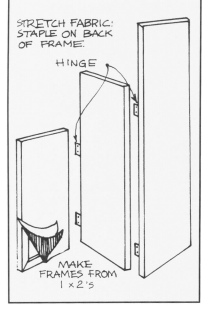

STRETCH FABRIC: STAPLE ON BACK OF FRAME.

HINGE

MAKE FRAMES FROM 1 x 2's

HOW TO DO IT

Screens: Make frames from 1 x 2s or canvas stretchers. To prevent light leaks, stretch black fabric over frames before you staple on the finished fabric. Stretch the fabric and staple onto the back of the frames. Hinge where shown (see drawing).

A Place To Come Home To

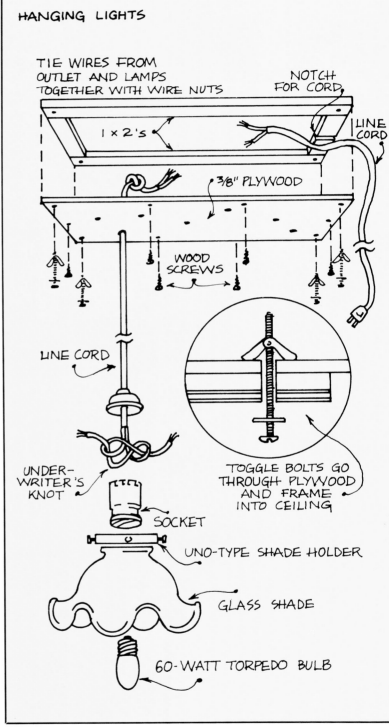

HANGING LIGHTS

TIE WIRES FROM OUTLET AND LAMPS TOGETHER WITH WIRE NUTS

NOTCH FOR CORD

1 x 2's

3/8" PLYWOOD

LINE CORD

WOOD SCREWS

LINE CORD

UNDER-WRITER'S KNOT

TOGGLE BOLTS GO THROUGH PLYWOOD AND FRAME INTO CEILING

SOCKET

UNO-TYPE SHADE HOLDER

GLASS SHADE

60-WATT TORPEDO BULB

The updated Victorian lamps above prove, once again, how we can rummage through the past and find new solutions. Hiding among the old are lots of brand-new ideas. For example, these turn-of-the-century lampshades are updated by using a display window trick and hanging them in a cluster. And at right, a very modern white-lacquered chest and glass shelves take a turn on an old farm dresser arrangement.

Walls can be papered, painted or paneled or, as here, all three. Wainscoting used to mean a lot of expensive wood paneling, often hand carved. You get the same look (above and right) by gloss painting the bottom three feet of wall, papering the top, then finishing the divide with chair-rail molding that is left natural. The Matisse print (above) is framed with scallope gingerbread wood molding, le unfinished.

Photos: Thomas Hooper

A Singular Collection

Venerable rooms are often made, not born. This comforting space is the result of careful collecting—rugs, fabrics and a special new/old coffee table made for an era that had none.

The coffee-table trick: Simply take an old wooden five-panel door and cut it down to size.

A kilim rug warms the floor and the Saltillo woven Mexican rug enriches the back wall. Needlepoint, Pennsylvania Dutch patchwork, old photos and vintage paintings all have a place. Soft peach-colored walls are romantic and warm, making an otherwise unremarkable space something special. The lines of the fanback rattan chair (with yet another pattern covering its pillow seat) and the rich wood of the great-great-grandfather clock balance all the cozy patterns.

HOW TO DO IT

Door Table: Find a wooden five-panel door from an old house or salvage yard. Saw the door into three pieces so that the three center panels become the tabletop and the two end panels make the sides. (Sometimes the lower panel is a little longer than the others but you can cut it down a bit to match the other end, which is usually about 16".) Four shelf support brackets hold the panels together underneath. Sand the door and stain it—or if the original finish is beautiful, go over it with fine steel wool and add a coat of wax.

Systems

Furnishing by system is more than an organized arrangement of sofas and chairs. It's a single grand gesture—one principle that will solve most problems. The answer can be modular seating that is lightweight and flexible. Or it can be a wall unit that serves for dining and work space. It could be arrangements of bookcases and mattresses that sleep, sit, store and serve. Most importantly, a system is a psyched-out space plan that fits the style of the people who live there.

Success on Many Levels

Most people change their living space by rearranging furniture instead of attitudes. Start discovering diverse ways to make the room fit into your life. Think of the space as a canvas—paint your own needs on it.

That is exactly what has happened in this room. The standard apartment fare—white walls, shag carpet, predictable windows—were transformed into a many-leveled room, simple and spare, with exceptional flair. Here's how:

The multilevel landscape raised the seating level to the view, making the outside cityscape visible from every part of the room. Platforms were covered in the same heavy-duty industrial carpet as the rest of the room, for visual uniformity. Each level was built to fulfill a function—dining, sitting, working.

With the spaces now so varied, white walls seemed all right again. The raw pine, baskets and natural earthy tones warm up the room.

Easy-to-build multi-use table surfaces make for high function in this room. The tables are sturdy and have a uniform look. (Except for the dining table, they are all easily made.)

Bare windows further heighten the airy lightness. At night, standard venetian blinds assure privacy.

The soft, modular furniture can be shuttled around at any time. That slatted bridge connecting the two living-room areas is fun but not essential. The slats are nailed to a piece of plywood and then the bridge is bolted to wooden 2 x 4 strips underneath.

In a room as minimal as this one, the accessories must be especially well thought out. Several substantial plants were chosen for warmth and color contrast. A simple industrial lamp overhanging the table combines clean lines with good light. A basket of fruit creates an artful still life. There are no pictures or posters—just several simple hanging baskets.

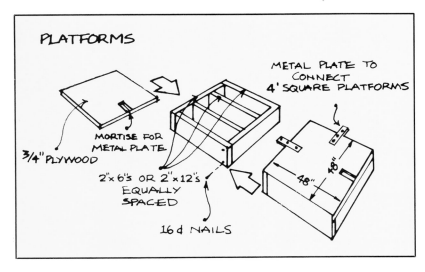

PLATFORMS

METAL PLATE TO CONNECT 4' SQUARE PLATFORMS

MORTISE FOR METAL PLATE

3/4" PLYWOOD

2"x 6's OR 2"x 12's EQUALLY SPACED

16 d NAILS

48"

18"

HOW TO DO IT

Platforms: The drawing shows the general construction method for platform plans tailored to any situation. Keep the platform units no larger than 4' x 4'. Make 4 x 4 boxes fit the system that fits you, then custom-make smaller ones to fill in. Join the boxes together with metal mending plates, recessed into the surface of the plywood. A sharp wood chisel and a hammer make short work of it. When the boxes are all joined, staple on carpet or use self-adhesive carpet squares—or have the carpet installed.

Windows: Uncovered windows for open space

Walls: Basket for simplicity

Floor: Platforms and industrial carpeting

Photo: Armen Kachaturian/Design: Jerry Ross

Success on Many Levels

HOW TO DO IT

Modular Seating: There is a wide range of modular seating now available in all price ranges and styles and fabrics, but you can also build it yourself. Use simple cubes padded with foam (footstools made the same way double as extra seating). Add backs to the others. Group the units to make a sofa.

Materials:
   3 1 x 12s 28"
   2 1 x 12s 26½"
   1 ¾" plywood 26¼" x 26¼"
   4 6" x 6" triangular corner braces of ¾" plywood
   2 metal straps ⅛" x 2" x 16"
   6 yards 48"-wide fabric
   1 piece 5" high-density foam 26¼" x 26¼"
   1 piece 5" high-density foam 26¼" x 12"
   2/3 yard 1" foam 36" wide
   2 yards ½" foam 36" wide

The secret of the softness and comfort here is to wrap the wood box construction with foam. A nubby loose-weave fabric cover wears well and hides any mistakes because of the built-in irregularities of the fabric. Hand sew the corners as shown on the base and the back. Wrap and staple the corners of the seats. Also cover 5"-thick foam forms for back pillow chairs.

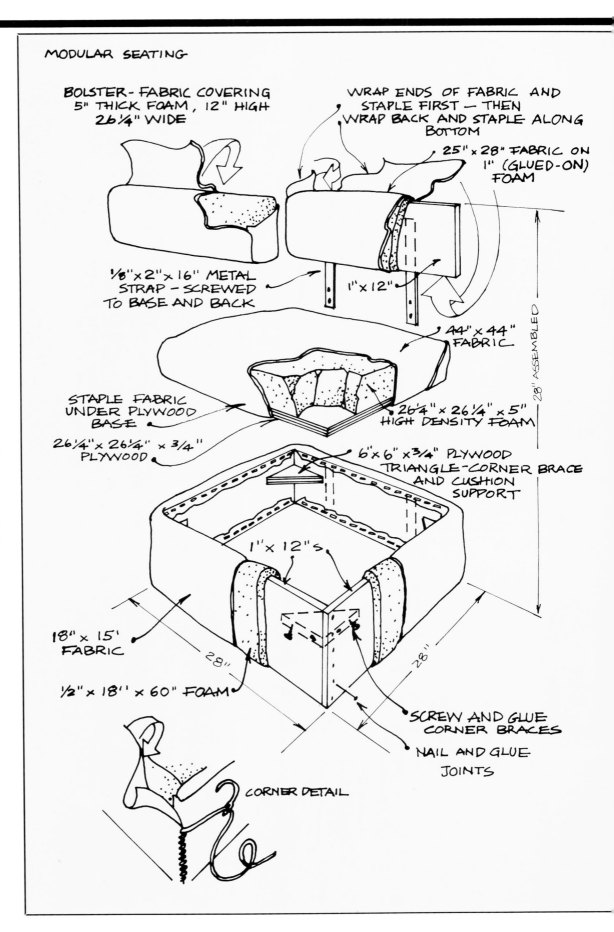

MODULAR SEATING

BOLSTER- FABRIC COVERING 5" THICK FOAM, 12" HIGH 26¼" WIDE

WRAP ENDS OF FABRIC AND STAPLE FIRST — THEN WRAP BACK AND STAPLE ALONG BOTTOM

25" x 28" FABRIC ON 1" (GLUED-ON) FOAM

⅛" x 2" x 16" METAL STRAP - SCREWED TO BASE AND BACK

1" x 12"

28" ASSEMBLED

44" x 44" FABRIC

STAPLE FABRIC UNDER PLYWOOD BASE

26¼" x 26¼" x 5" HIGH DENSITY FOAM

26¼" x 26¼" x ¾" PLYWOOD

6" x 6" x ¾" PLYWOOD TRIANGLE-CORNER BRACE AND CUSHION SUPPORT

1" x 12"s

18" x 15' FABRIC

28"

28"

½" x 18" x 60" FOAM

SCREW AND GLUE CORNER BRACES

NAIL AND GLUE JOINTS

CORNER DETAIL

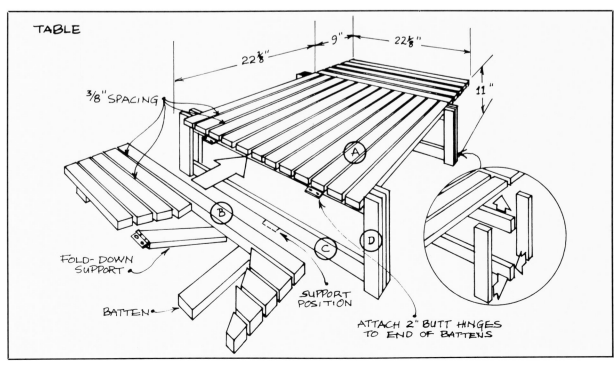

HOW TO DO IT

Coffee/End Table: This table is built by gluing all the joints together.

Materials:

- 22 1 x 2s 22⅛" (As and Bs)
- 4 1 x 2s 25⅛" (Cs)
- 8 1 x 2s 11" (Ds)
- 4 1 x 2s 9" (battens)
- 2 1 x 2s 13" (fold-down supports)
- 4 2" butt hinges
- White glue

Buy several small C clamps to clamp the joints while the glue dries. Put the two leg frames (Ds) together first (legs are set ½" in from edge of tabletop). Then glue on the tabletop pieces (As and Bs). Glue on the end flaps and attach with hinges as shown.

TABLE

3/8" SPACING

22⅛"   9"   22⅛"

11"

FOLD-DOWN SUPPORT

BATTEN

SUPPORT POSITION

ATTACH 2" BUTT HINGES TO END OF BATTENS

A   B   C   D

Room Within a Room

Think in broad strokes when planning a room. This super system—with its seventeen working parts—shows how one overall solution applies to all problems.

Here in yellow and white is a system for sleeping, sitting, eating and storing. Eight store-bought bookcases (painted yourself) frame nine foam slabs (75″ x 30″ x 5″) and inexpensive bed pillows. These slabs have been covered in cotton so they can be easily changed and washed. Hinged shelves were added to the bookcase fronts; when they are down, they work for closed storage; in the up position, they can be used for

eating and working. By removing the pillows, guests have a comfortable place to sleep.

Everything else in this space has been planned with the system in mind. Formica Parsons tables can be moved around for eating and are sturdy enough to put your feet on. Against the wall: a white table, which doubles as a desk and buffet area. The white folding chairs become functional art when hung on the walls for storage. The windows are framed with 1″ x 6″ boards, with fabric stretched and glued around them. Even the white carpet—supplied by the landlord—helps highlight this ingenious system.

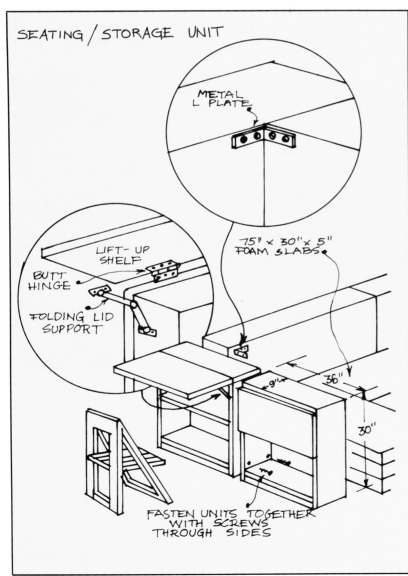

SEATING / STORAGE UNIT

METAL L PLATE

LIFT-UP SHELF

BUTT HINGE

FOLDING LID SUPPORT

75″ x 30″ x 5″ FOAM SLABS

9″

36″

30″

FASTEN UNITS TOGETHER WITH SCREWS THROUGH SIDES

Windows: Fabric-covered frames, inset shades

Walls: Hanging chairs are artful storage on a painted wall

Graphic Design

This design system is squarely suited to any small, plain white box. The idea is to go for a few simple—yet highly sophisticated—graphic effects.

That said, remember that any design problem has an infinite number of solutions. There are no right answers, only interesting possibilities.

Here are some guidelines for plotting a small, boxy room according to functions: The super graphic: It is a tape-on-the-wall grid that is the perfect canvas for setting off clearly defined shapes of simple furnishings. Adding a pattern on the walls can relieve small space awkwardness and pull all the pieces together. The furniture is on the square too—seating is provided by channel-quilted modulars that fit the room's compact size. As a bonus, these well-upholstered foam units do a quick conversion to lounging and sleeping platforms. Tube-framed director's chairs have rounded squares that look intriguing against the right-angle grid.

The two small laminate tables —used as a coffee table—mimic the latticework walls and the Raynaud poster. Also, the draperies echo the quilted seating units. These channel-quilted "window blankets" keep the cold out from ceiling to floor; the blanket lets a small window reach new heights. Lighting that makes a counterpoint: Vary the pattern and add high-rise lighting—from photographers' umbrellas mounted on shiny metal light stands. Both

found in photo supply stores, they convert in a flash with porcelain sockets and standard bulbs. Storage on display: Classically styled cabinets of warm honey pine are slim enough to give you room to move while still providing open and closed storage space. Plastic triangle shelves at right show off glassworks. Heavily textured sisal matting is neutral and wears well.

You can tape a room in a few hours even if you cannot draw a straight line (get someone to help you with the measurements).

To mark a horizontal across the middle of the wall, hold a spirit level against a straight edge. Then draw your guideline above the straight edge in light pencil.

Cover the pencil mark with 1"-wide duct tape, also called gaffer's duct tape. You will find it at hardware stores and photo supply shops.

Repeat the procedure for all horizontals, spacing the lines 9" apart.

For verticals, start in the middle again. Use a ladder to draw a line from ceiling to floor. After marking, cover with the tape. Repeat the procedure, spacing verticals 9" apart.

Note: To avoid taping yourself into a corner, remember to work your grid from the middle of the wall toward the edges. That way, you can adjust for possibly sloping walls at the corners instead of repeating a slanted line across the wall.

Windows: Quilted "blanket" draperies

Walls: Duct-tape grid

Lighting: Photographers' umbrellas

Floor: Textured sisal matting

Photo: Bradley Olman

Here is a closer look at the graphic design elements at work. Two small laminate tables have a pattern that complements not only the grid wall and poster but the heavy channel quilted material on the sofas and rounded director's chairs.

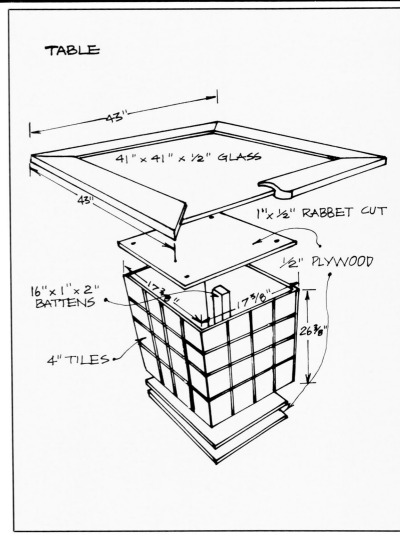

TABLE

43"

41" × 41" × ½" GLASS

43"

1" × ½" RABBET CUT

½" PLYWOOD

16" × 1" × 2" BATTENS

17 3/8"

17 3/8"

26 3/8"

4" TILES

HOW TO DO IT

Tile Table: The square root of this versatile table is merely bathroom tile glued to a wooden box. Build a box—have the lumberyard cut four pieces of ½" plywood to length for the sides after you have decided on your dimensions (figure a multiple of the tile dimension plus grout or 4" for a standard tile): three plywood squares (the double bottom and top); and four 1 x 2 battens for bracing (see drawing). Nail and glue the sides, battens, top and bottom as shown.

Tile it: Secure 4" tiles with tile adhesive, spacing tiles ⅛" apart. Grout after adhesive has dried.

Top it off: A 41" square of ¼ glass will do the job, or build a mitered picture frame for the glass with four 1 x 3s cut to length. Cut a groove along the lower edge (called a "rabbet") that is ¼" deep and 1" wide. Miter the corners and fasten with white glue and mending plates.

Finishing touches. Place felt circles at each corner of the base to protect the glass. Rest glass on base and place frame over it.

Photos: Bradley Olman

Quick Assembly Room

A sophisticated seating and storage system does not require sophisticated prices. Nearly everything in this room can be made in several hours—not merely the seating and storage units but even the tables and lamps:

The eminently adjustable storage wall system has pine handrails (for upright posts), held in place by furniture levelers so no nails go into the walls. The shelves rest on regulation metal standards and brackets screwed to the back of the handrails. The built-in desk is supported by the bookcases.

The store-bought pillow system was designed to sit on the floor but for a heightened effect you can raise the sofa with easily made plywood boxes.

The coffee table is really just a pile of 1 x 4s, stacked Lincoln log cabin style. Dab white glue between each layer. Cut ¼" thick glass 3" larger than the base.

The lamps are simply lights hidden under baskets.

High-style bamboo end tables can be made at home too.

That original-looking American Indian area rug is a beach towel with a carpet pad underneath.

Colorful fabric—an update of an Imari china pattern—hangs loosely to cover the window.

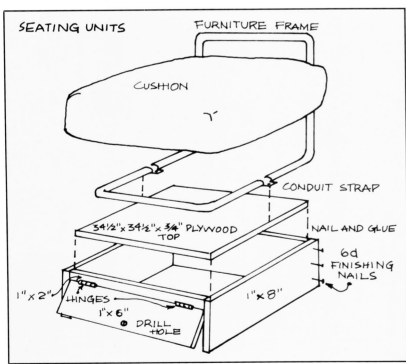

SEATING UNITS
FURNITURE FRAME
CUSHION
CONDUIT STRAP
34½" x 34½" x ¾" PLYWOOD TOP
NAIL AND GLUE
6d FINISHING NAILS
1" x 2"
HINGES
1" x 6"
DRILL HOLE
1" x 8"

HOW TO DO IT

Seating Unit Platforms: There are three parts to each of these store-bought units: a pillow, bolster and metal frame. Arm units have two frames and two bolsters (they double as corners). Adding plywood bases raises the cushions off the floor.

How to make base boxes: Cut three 1 x 8s to the desired dimensions for each box. Then cut a 1 x 2 and a 1 x 6 to the same length as the back piece: The box front is hinged to create extra storage space under the seat. Cut a 1 x 2 and a 1 x 6 to the same length as the back piece. Nail the box using the 1 x 2 as the top of the fourth side. Set the hinges into the top edge of the 1 x 6 door, then screw to the 1 x 2. Paint or stain, then attach the frames to the top with 2½" conduit strips.

Floor: Towel as area rug
Lighting: Basket lamps

Window: Imari fabric on big rings
Storage: Quick shelving

Quick Assembly Room

HOW TO DO IT

Wall Unit: The uprights for this project are wood stairway handrails (from a lumberyard) that are flat on one side so the metal brackets can screw right in. The number of shelves you use and their dimensions depend on your needs. The shelves can fit between two uprights or run the distance across the whole unit. The shelves are fir 1 x 10s, finished on the edges with optional ¾" half-round molding. Drill a hole in the underside of shelves for each bracket tip; this keeps the boards from slipping.

To fill any triangular corner with a small desk, support a ¾" plywood shelf on L brackets screwed to the wall.

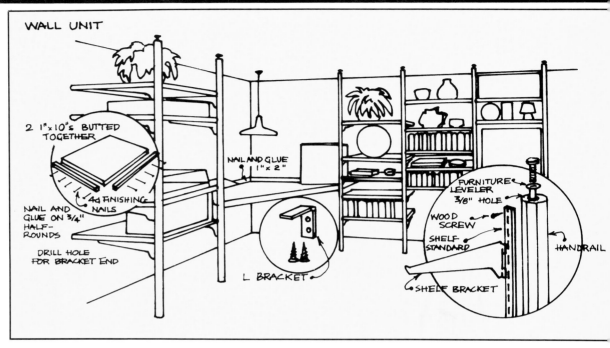

WALL UNIT

2 1"x10's BUTTED TOGETHER

NAIL AND GLUE ON ¾" HALF-ROUNDS

4d FINISHING NAILS

DRILL HOLE FOR BRACKET END

NAIL AND GLUE 1" x 2"

L BRACKET

FURNITURE LEVELER ⅜" HOLE

WOOD SCREW

SHELF STANDARD

SHELF BRACKET

HANDRAIL

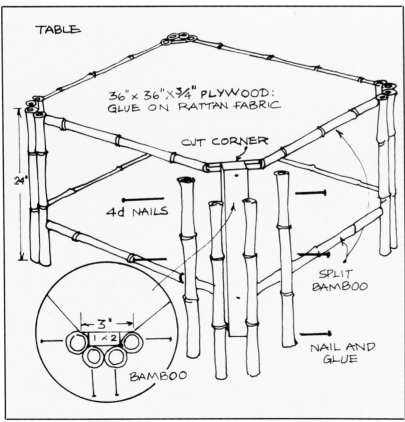

TABLE

36" x 36" x ¾" PLYWOOD: GLUE ON RATTAN FABRIC

CUT CORNER

24"

4d NAILS

SPLIT BAMBOO

NAIL AND GLUE

3"
1 x 2

BAMBOO

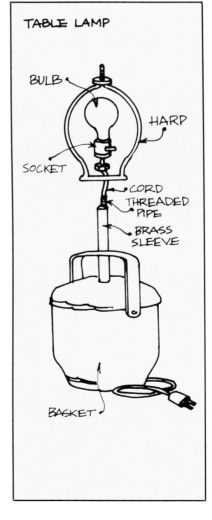

TABLE LAMP

BULB

HARP

SOCKET

CORD THREADED PIPE

BRASS SLEEVE

BASKET

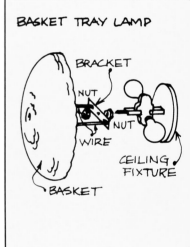

BASKET TRAY LAMP

BRACKET

NUT

NUT

WIRE

CEILING FIXTURE

BASKET

HOW TO DO IT

Bamboo Table: This is made of two pieces of plywood (cut from a single panel) with 1 x 2 legs. It is the covering that makes the difference. Put rattan-by-the-yard fabric on the plywood top and add lengths of bamboo edging to the 1 x 2s. Split bamboo finishes off the edges.

HOW TO DO IT

Table Lamp: Find a large covered basket. Drill a hole through the handle, then down through the lid and basket bottom. Use the hardware indicated in the illustration, and assemble as shown.

Basket Tray Lamp: This wall-mounted lamp (see illustration) is easy to put together and makes for dramatic mood lighting. Attach a dimmer switch to the lamp cord.

Vienna 1900
Union St. Graphics : San Francisco

The Bookcase System

An engineered maze of walls and living spaces—all within one large room—grew out of five unfinished bookcases in a 12′ x 23′ living area. This special system turns four plain walls into twelve efficient walls, with three multifunctioning areas. Rather than close up the space, they open it up to a number of possibilities: sitting, storage, dining, office, even a child's room. A quick tour:

In the sitting area at right, two leather sofas are placed face to face. Walls are kept white to offset the painted panels of the bookcase system, and the floor is covered with sturdy industrial carpeting. The Luxo lamp mounted on the wall and the chrome apothecary lamp are efficient, high-function lighting for this kind of space. Bookcase backs are used for color and to hang pictures. The cube table to the left of the sofa was custom made but store-bought ones are available.

All cases are fastened together with screws. With the turn of a screwdriver, it can all be changed, depending on your needs. The children's room can become a study, the middle area can be used for dining or working or it can all be newly set up when you move.

The Bookcase System

Here is the sitting area from another angle. Notice the bright blue color that is on the back of the bookcase at left, breaking up the wall of books by adding a patch of color. The dining area/office can be seen peeking around the corner at right.

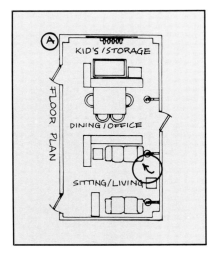

This yellow wall—a graphic gallery—divides the sitting space from the dining area/office. There is a pass-through space at right in the bookcase under the top three shelves (made by the placement of the cases). The dining table/desk is butcher block (with a coat of varnish) and there are cane bentwood chairs.

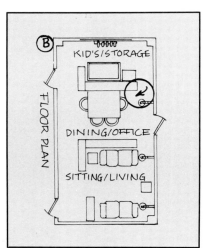

The same table (from another angle) is being used as a desk here, leading the way into the baby's room on the other side of the partition. Once again, the flexible lamp works both ways.

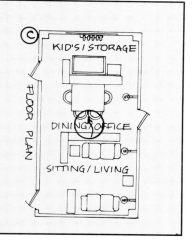

This bright yellow baby's room doubles as storage space, thanks to the many drawers and shelves built into the system. The bentwood chairs can be moved into this space for seating—everything works with everything thanks to light wood and light weight. Even the crib adds natural wood lightness.

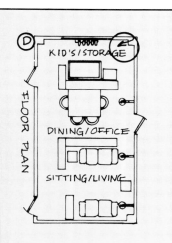

Photos: Bill Helms

The Bookcase System

HOW TO DO IT

The back should be durable, made of ¼"-thick plywood or hardboard from matching veneer. It should be set into the back edges of the cases. Lower-quality cases have ⅛"-thick hardboard backs, without veneer, just stapled to the back edges of the bookcases.

Adjustable shelves offer more choices than fixed ones but cost a bit more.

The bookcase should be sanded smooth. Less expensive ones often take some crack filling and sanding before finishing.

How they stack up: Stack the bookcases, side by side, facing opposite directions so there will be open storage on both sides of the wall. Make an L or U shape, which gives the system more stability. Leave a couple of open spaces in the new "wall." Connect the bookcases, side by side, with flathead wood screws; these wood screws will hold a lot of weight, even shelves loaded with heavy books. Use a screw a bit shorter than the total thickness of the two sides you are connecting so the point does not go through the other side. To countersink the screws, use a combination bit (see drawing at right) to drill the holes.

Bookcase backs: Cover the backs of the bookcases with painted ½" insulation board. Attach with brads. This surface can then double as a bulletin board.

Bookcase buying: There are some things you should know about buying unfinished bookcases:

The case should be made from ¾"-thick plywood or particle board (for sturdiness), covered with wood veneer, or from solid hardwood such as birch or maple. Cheap ones are made from thinner, glued strips of pine, often knotty, which is not as sturdy or good looking.

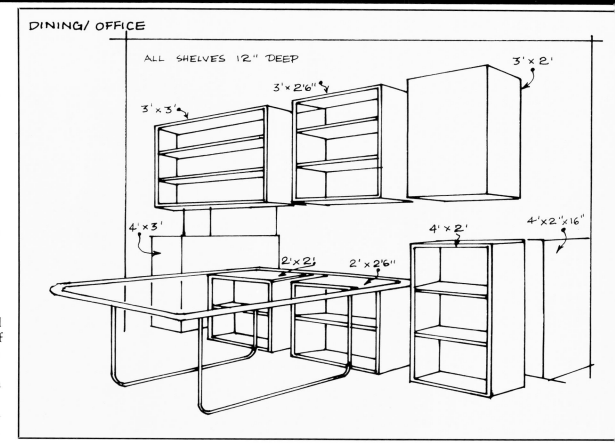

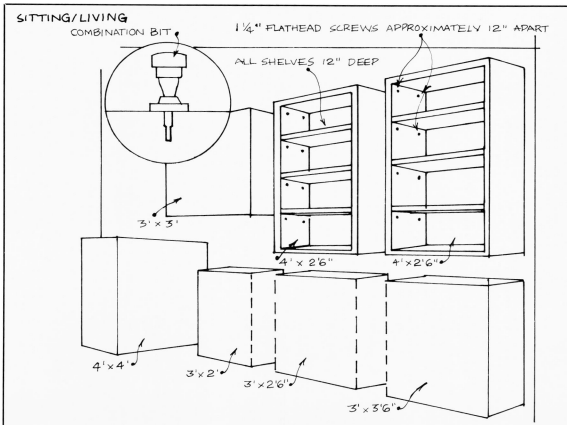

The Indoor Patio

The Indoor Patio is a style of furnishing that is much more than one windowful of plants or even a big tree in the corner. It is an attitude about the outdoors—and an attitude about the indoors—that suggests nature without trying to imitate it. This can be done with fabrics, colors, organic and natural furnishings. Too often, apartments—not just high-rise and not just urban—are victims of the shut-in blues. Here we show you how country greens can give your place a feeling of the Great Indoors. You'll see wicker and rattan, bamboo and sisal mats, plants and clever lighting—all working as useful furnishings. The Indoor Patio—like other styles—is also about breaking boundaries. It's about setting up the atmosphere you like. You can hang a hammock in a living room—or any other room—because, although at first it looks "unexpected," it does add grace and a natural feeling. Wicker, rattan and other straw-woven materials traditionally have been relegated to the veranda and porch. Now they are being updated and upholstered and are comfortably stylish indoors.

The Sunshine Room

You do not have to remain in the dark if your living room does not have plenty of natural light. Careful furnishing can turn it into an indoor sun porch —with a little help from golden colors, light rattan and wicker furniture.

By day, sunshine takes the place of pictures, draperies, rugs and heavy furniture. Wicker and rattan pieces give an atmosphere of elegant informality while underscoring the casual flavor of the space. A wine crate becomes an end table here when it is placed between two porch-style chairs.

The light bamboo and glass table at right is a desk during the day, a dining table at night. Cardboard file boxes stacked beside the table are camouflaged with the same coordinating East Indian fabrics that cover the cushions in the seating area. The "Casablanca" fan chair also is used as a desk chair. The basket hassocks (some of which double as plant stands) can be pulled up for extra seating.

Above: Even without natural light, this room glows at night. White floor spots illuminate the corner pots and the tree fern.

Lush bromeliads, each enthroned on its own basket hassock, define this corner of the room. Strategically placed lights cast weird and wonderful shadows on the screen and wall.

The Great Indoors

This apartment substitutes a view for draperies: clouds and high rises seem to waft by this inside-out room. Roller skating, biking, kite flying, all these signs of outdoors are proudly displayed.

Ignore all the old rules about window treatments; here the view is the window treatment —plus a curtain of greenery. Making the most of the outside view is the low-scaled furniture. A custom-made rainbow rug makes everything fit exactly into place; the curve of the rug echoes the curve of the windows. Extra color is provided by the great big African pillows.

The little touches have not been overlooked: a "four-poster" is created by four apothecary lamps; the classic chrome and glass coffee table is loaded with objects that reflect the happy tone. At left, a television and an antique clock are held up by a simple white wooden shelf (courtesy of wall brackets)—left low, in keeping with the rest of the room.

Photo: Tom Ebenhoh

Tilling the soil does not have to take place only outdoors. This foliage display adds green grace to ordinary space. Holding it together are three vertical 2 x 4 uprights. Fasten the uprights to the ceiling with metal L brackets. The shelves here are lengths of clear cedar 1 x 10s resting on 2 x 4 wood cleats. (You can, of course, use pine shelving too.) The front shelves —ladderlike—rest on short 2 x 4 uprights that are nailed to 2 x 4 cleats and to the tall upright supports.

Crate Expectations

Here the unexpected takes a turn for the terrific. Crates— the kind that oranges, melons and pianos come in—become fun and functional furniture. These contemporary primitives make sense with their no-nonsense looks and high utility.

All it took was minor reconstruction to get these sturdy, knotty-pine pieces ready for living-room use. So what if the joints do not exactly dovetail? That is part of the charm. Here is how it happens:

The coffee table took no reconstruction at all; it is just a big wooden skid, cleaned up and given a few coats of polyurethane (but you can paint it instead).

The end table is a larger skid, cut down, sanded and again coated with polyurethane.

The bar is simply a packing crate with a couple of alterations. A little quick work with a saw created a door, and a plywood shelf set inside doubled the storage space.

Crates created the little love seat, but with a painted finish this time for variety (the dimensions of the piece have been stenciled on). The cushions came from an old sofa, with quick slipcovers made from new yard goods. Bed pillows and cases can also be used.

The sofa is a found oldie given a quick make-over with a lace tablecloth tucked over the old upholstery.

A long pine board has been placed over the radiator as a holding platform for plants.

The wonderful blue-sky window shades are just lengths of fabric stapled to wooden shade rollers. Narrow hems are sewn along the sides, plus a deep hem along the bottom for a length of wooden molding.

A hammock (at right) swings from the ceiling to the wall.

Crate Expectations

A. BAR

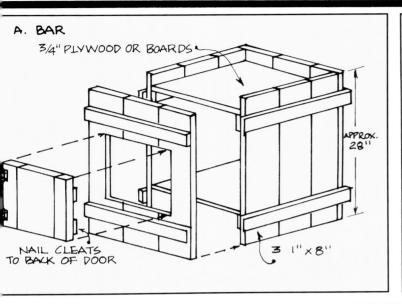

3/4" PLYWOOD OR BOARDS

APPROX. 28"

NAIL CLEATS TO BACK OF DOOR

3 1"x 8"

B. SOFA

ADJUST ANGLE OF THE BACK TO SUIT YOUR BACK

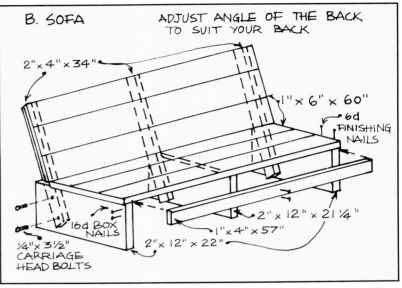

2"x 4"x 34"

1"x 6"x 60"

6d FINISHING NAILS

16d BOX NAILS

2"x 12"x 21 1/4"

1"x 4"x 57"

2"x 12"x 22"

1/4"x 3 1/2" CARRIAGE HEAD BOLTS

HOW TO DO IT

A. The Corner Bar: Buy construction grade pine or fir. If you can hunt around, pick the pieces with sound knots and lots of grain. Cut the door opening with a saber saw.

B. Sofa, So Good: The dimensions for this sofa are shown in the illustration but you can adjust the overall size to fit any cushions you already have and want to use.

C and D. Tables: Both tables are built the same way, except that the coffee table has a couple of 2 x 6 cleats across the bottom to make it a little taller and stronger.

E. Hammock: Sling a big hammock across the corner of a room but measure first to make sure you have the space. Hammocks are always longer than you would guess—a fact of life. Make sure too that you find all studs to anchor both ends. Drill a pilot hole in the stud. Hang with a sturdy screw hook.

E. HAMMOCK

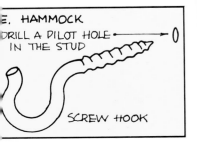

DRILL A PILOT HOLE IN THE STUD

SCREW HOOK

C. TABLE

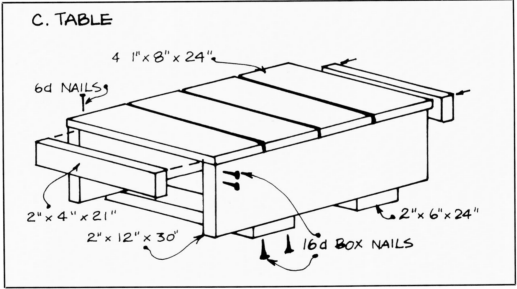

4 1"x 8"x 24"

6d NAILS

2"x 4"x 21"

2"x 12"x 30"

2"x 6"x 24"

16d BOX NAILS

D. TABLE

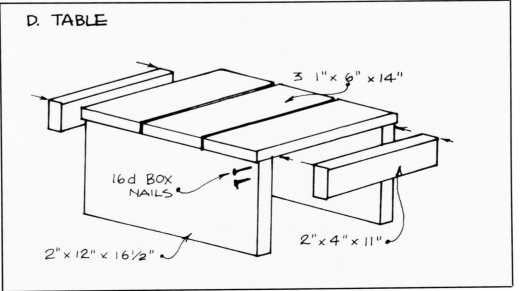

3 1"x 6"x 14"

16d BOX NAILS

2"x 12"x 16 1/2"

2"x 4"x 11"

The Upstairs Backyard

Feeling boxed in by your plain white box apartment? It is all a matter of mind-over-matter-of-fact. Let fantasy and flair make an unexpected gazebo right there on the wall-to-wall.

The look of this nook—the graceful bamboo, the plants, the whole indoor porch—comes from an easy-to-assemble trellis. This space gets definition by the white vinyl tile on the floor. Wicker, rattan, baskets (including one topped with a slab of glass for a coffee table), all add up to indoor exotica.

On the floor, a well-heeled and well-priced sisal mat is easy to look after. The bold bamboo wallpaper wraps up the room. Even the storage is in keeping with the atmosphere: Wall shelves are tied to bamboo poles.

Another view of the canopy is shown on page 96.

Photo: Thomas Hooper

Windows: Lace fabric shade

Floor: White vinyl tile on plywood and sisal squares

Walls: Bamboo wallpaper and shelving

Lighting: Dresser scarf shade

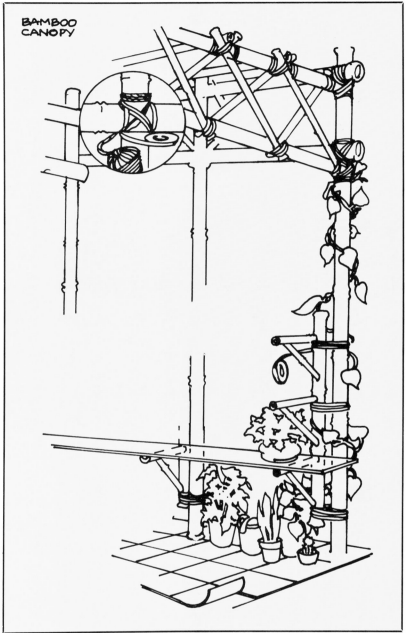

HOW TO DO IT

Bamboo Canopy: This simple canopy takes one handsaw, strapping tape, twine, bamboo poles and another person to help you. Measure the ceiling height and cut the vertical supports a bit more than the height of the room. The poles are wedged into place so trim them to get a tight fit. Cut four horizontal poles the width you want the canopy to be (this one is just under 4' x 8') and cut thinner crosspieces to lash as the Xs. The horizontal poles with strapping tape as shown. (It is a two-person job: one to hold, one to wrap.) Then cover the tape with twine for extra stability and camouflage. The bamboo shelf brackets are attached just like the canopy pieces: wrapped with tape, then twine. They support glass shelves cut to fit. Trailing plants hang from the canopy and big pots of philodendron send climbers up the vertical poles. To train the plants upward, secure the vines loosely to the pole with wire plant ties.

New Antiques

An antique is usually considered to be any object more than a hundred years old. New Antiques, however, are different sorts of relics—things from the turn of the century, from the twenties and thirties, even from the fifties. And along with these new discoveries comes a new philosophy: Just because they are old and not aged does not mean they are not as beautiful or worthy as their ancestors. Plus, New Antiques can be functional; never thought precious enough for showcases, there is no reason why collectibles should not work too.

Art Deco chrome, Fiestaware dishes, golden oak pressed-back chairs, Hoosier cabinets—these are just some of the finds that flourish in thrift shops, garage sales and attics. Collecting furnishings that work makes a lot more sense than living with a museum full of nonfunctional things. Another plus: investment value. Someday they will grow up to be Real Antiques.

Fabrications

The blaze of warmth in this room comes from a lot more than the fireplace—it emanates from the fiery colors of the fabrics and fancywork from the thirties and forties.

Two sofas sit on both sides of the fireplace in the traditional manner—but mend their ways with a lot of hanky-panky pillows. Pillow forms are covered with lush, floral pillow covers in bark cloth and polished cotton. They are inexpensive and easy to find in secondhand shops; some even have zippers. Old drapery panels have the same vintage charm. Just cut the fabric for round or square pillows or stitch around the design for a one-of-a-kind shape.

What to do with the pillows? Try displaying them on a single bed (at left) with wedge-shaped bolsters at the back. Plants, prints and new antique collectibles make the pillows feel at home.

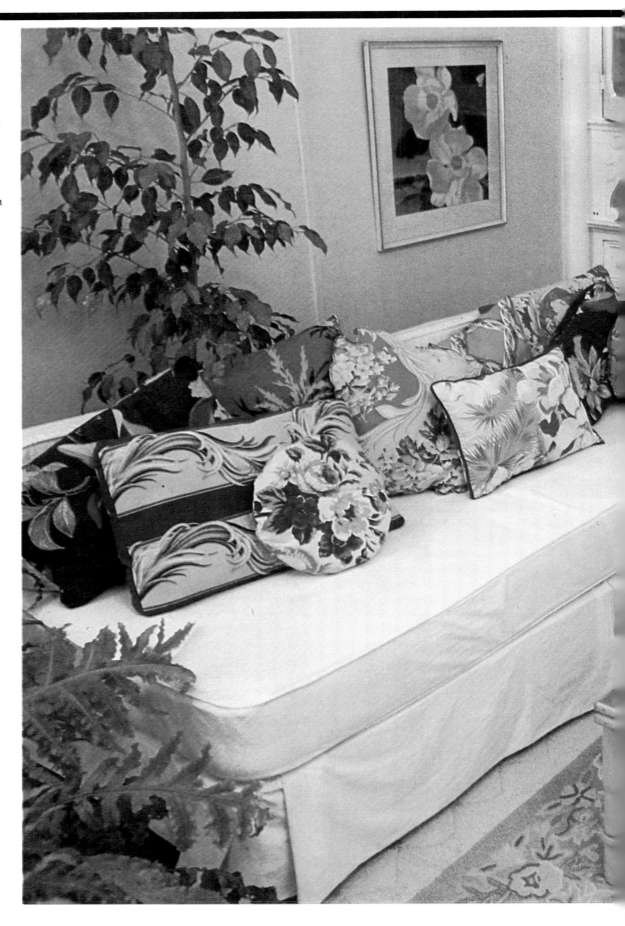

Putting Collectibles to Work

Give collectibles a job; hire an heirloom. Do not let your period bits and pieces hide under glass looking pretty—let them work for you as well. That will give you space for more of them too.

This room combines twenties to forties design with comfort and utility. All the new antique pieces are readily available today by scouting flea markets and shops and have been made livable with old fabric pillows and new covers. The rundown:

Both 1920s chairs in the foreground are of durable reed construction, comfortable enough to sink into.

The framed mirror was salvaged from a thirties oak dresser.

Rich velvet draperies came from an estate sale, and are hanging on new fat wooden rods and wide rings, stained dark.

The sofa and table bases are well-crafted rattan. New pine boards were added for the table.

A much-worn oriental rug was cut up and used for pillow covers. The four stained-glass window panels were salvaged from a house that was being demolished as was the old leaded, stained-glass valance hung from the ceiling.

The lamp is a recent marriage of a bronze base and a silk-lined metal shade.

Unique curves, period details, humor, architectural bits—even the oversized rubber tree—all add humor and personal style.

Photo: Erik Arnesen

Instant Heirloom

In a roomful of bamboo and oak new antiques, the newest—and brightest—is an irresistible rag rug, made today to look like yesterday. In the truest sense, this rug is a case of rags to riches. Once make-do floor coverings, rag rugs have become American folk art and, nowadays, you are lucky if you can unearth one for less than $600.

But by using the old potholder principle, you can turn your own rags into rugs. Recycled materials—old bedspreads, draperies, tablecloths, shirts, slacks, towels, flannel bathrobes—are the strips.

HOW TO DO IT

Rag Rug: Building the Loom

The only tools you need are a screwdriver, tape measure and hammer.

Materials:

    4 6′ 2 x 2s
    300 3″ finishing nails (get some extras in case you bend a few)
    8 3″ wood screws

First screw together the 2 x 2s into a square. Then reinforce the corners with braces. Mark off each inch (72 per board) with a pencil. Drive the nails into the marks, about 1″ deep.

Tear or cut your fabrics into 4″ or 5″ strips. In all, you will need about 50 yards of 45″-wide fabric. Half the strips should be sturdy, nonstretchy fabrics—cotton, flannel, corduroy, upholstery material—to make the warp. These strips are strung on nails to make a base to weave through. The weaving strips should be stretchy fabrics such as nylon, acetate, double knits or matte jersey.

To make the strips easier to handle, sew the ends together to make 8 to 10-yard lengths. Roll up the strips as you go along, folding under the edges.

You will need about 30 10′ long rolls of the stretchy fabric and 35 8′ rolls of sturdier fabric (it gets too bulky if the rolls are too long). Tearing and rolling the strips is time consuming, but it is better to have them ready before you begin.

Begin to weave. Warp the loom with the sturdy fabrics. Loop the fabric, going back and forth around each nail, sewing on each new strip as you need it. (Be sure the raw edges are turned under.) One important rule: Do not pull the fabric too tight—it should be slack enough to lie along the floor. Also keep your eye on the rug as a whole. The warp is the pattern of the rug so plan the colors and textures before you begin.

When you start weaving, it gets a bit tricky—the stretchy strips go through double. To measure the first double strip, lay an unrolled strip of stretchy fabric across the loom, grabbing it a few inches beyond the edge of the loom. Hang onto this loop and take the strip back to the other side; start weaving. Hook the loop on the nail when you finish each row, then measure and weave again. Sew on new rolls as you need them. If a row bulges too much in the middle, skip a nail on each side.

Finish off the edges by pulling a doubled strip of fabric through a series of loops. To get started, unfasten a loop from one of the corner nails; either tie or hand sew the end of a stretchy fabric strip to it. Then use a crochet stitch: Taking off one loop at a time, push the edging strip through this rug loop and make a new loop (about the same size). Push it through the loop you have just made. Take the next rug loop off its nail and start over again. Continue around the rug. Hand sew the tag end.

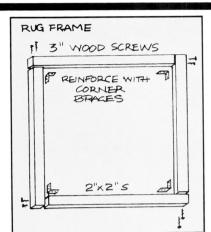

RUG FRAME
3″ WOOD SCREWS
REINFORCE WITH CORNER BRACES
2″x2″s

Deco-rated

Below: Hotels and theatres about to be demolished are two more places where you can salvage old furnishings at old prices. Because so many public places were built or remodeled in the thirties, they are especially rich sources for finding the highly decorative, overstuffed, solid furnishings and accessories of the Art Deco period. For example: The chenille rug here came from an old movie house lobby; the sofa, recovered in red, purple and brown cotton suede cloth in a typically Deco pattern, used to hang out in a hotel lobby; the end table is an archetypal thirties nightstand from a hotel room. The hotel lobby coffee table's distinctive rounded legs spell thirties.

But not everything is old. The lamp on the nightstand/end table is new but descended from Deco tradition. The sleek neon standing lamp behind the sofa is made from a circular fluorescent fixture with a round base. The narrow slat venetian blinds are a modern version of the old wooden ones. Other accessories, on the windowsill and coffee table, are a discriminating mix of contemporary and secondhand finds.

Opposite: Along with a sense of wit and humor, collectibles can easily become part of your living room. The chairs, the tables —even the clothes hanging like art on the wall—are yesterday's funk and flash that have become another alternative for today's furnishings.

This offbeat mixture of Deco and forties findings breaks rules as it breaks with tradition. No thick velvet sofas with matching side chairs here. In- stead, a delicate pastel mural painted on the wall, three one of-a-kind chairs, pulled together by color, surrounding a modernistic fifties blond wood and glass table. The pillows on the floor—covered with discarded fabric remnants—now become their own seating.

The overstuffed chair is slip covered in forties bark cloth, found in a thrift shop. The fifties rattan chair moves inside from the old front porch. The thirties standing ashtray—originally for trips on ships and trains—rolls around.

Untiques

Legally, antiques must be over a hundred years old. But untiques—those American golden oldies that were machine or hand crafted within the last century—are still less expensive and more available. Treasures like these—found in salvage yards, estate sales, junk stores, attics, basements and points in between—can turn the most modern room into a collector's paradise.

The first task is to set the groundwork. Lay a new cotton import rug over the wall-to-wall carpet. New, lacy curtains, a 1910 steamer trunk, an old, stained-glass window (hung from screw eyes attached to the window frame on top), and an old auto sign camouflage a sliding glass balcony door.

A rescued, well-seasoned sofa from the forties has a colorful afghan on top hiding its bald spots. Next to it: multipurpose spool cabinet like the ones found in general stores. (The "O.N.T." drawer stands for "Our Newest Thread.") Behind is a handmade folding screen (which helps round out the room's sharp corners), a cast-iron lamp and other second-hand finds.

A round-back wicker rocker nods toward its country cousin, a farm house oak rocker that cost $7 in the 1905 Sears catalog. You can still find them today. The secretary-desk unit to the right has everything: drawers, plenty of glassed-in shelf space, a drop-door writing surface, a mirror and fancy pressed carving.

Other collectibles provide imaginative accents: a 1900 trike, new folk art for warmth and whimsy. The metal and wood shoeshine parlor chair is quite at home here. The coffee table is really an old type-setting tray with letters still intact, set on a wicker table.

Windows: Lacy curtains, stained glass and collectibles camouflage the balcony door

Floor: New cotton carpet hides a wall-to-wall carpet

Photos: Bradley Olman

RICHARD DREYFUSS: A Home of One's Own

Ever since he played Everyboy in *American Graffiti,* Richard Dreyfuss hadn't had a living room to call his own. Having suffered the anonymity of at least 200 hotels and resisted the temptation to acquire some old-time Hollywood star's monument to himself, Dreyfuss rented an apartment—with bowling-alley rooms. "Plus," he added, "the problem with this place is that the rooms eat up the view. I want the view to eat up the rooms."

The answer: Do not lower the windows; raise the floor. With the addition of ingenious platforms that put everything on a new level and defined new living areas, the view comes right in and makes itself at home.

With graceful curves, the two-step platforms lead you forward by way of a seating area that is both intimate and inviting. The two levels add new shape to the large but ungainly space.

After the platforms were built, they were carpeted in a rich synthetic. The furnishings have comfort in common and, too, are modern interpretations of traditional pieces. The lines are straighter, cleaner than their ancestors, extra large and covered in velvets. Near the window, chaises predominate so Dreyfuss can stretch out while checking out his new-found view.

The track lights illuminate pictures on the walls but also throw enough indirect light for the seating area. The mirror over the mantel, the Deco hanging lamp in back on the left, the tapestry-covered footstool and the kilim area rug are all old.

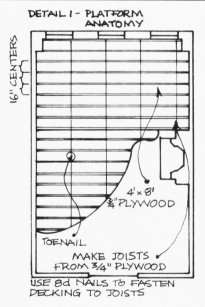
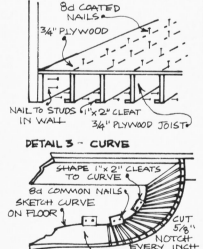

LIVING ROOM FLOOR PLAN

16" HIGH PLATFORM

8" HIGH PLATFORM

11'

11'

12'

11'

5'

17'6"

DETAIL 1 - PLATFORM ANATOMY

16" CENTERS

4' x 8' ¾" PLYWOOD

TOENAIL

MAKE JOISTS FROM ¾" PLYWOOD

USE 8d NAILS TO FASTEN DECKING TO JOISTS

DETAIL 2 - UNDERSTRUCTURE

8d COATED NAILS

¾" PLYWOOD

NAIL TO STUDS IN WALL

1" x 2" CLEAT

¾" PLYWOOD JOIST

DETAIL 3 - CURVE

SHAPE 1" x 2" CLEATS TO CURVE

8d COMMON NAILS

SKETCH CURVE ON FLOOR

CUT 5/8" NOTCH EVERY INCH

¾" PLYWOOD

HOW TO DO IT

Platforms: A split-level room like this one can be a bit overwhelming—just how do you build all those mysterious things? But the philosophy is basic-box simple.

Think of each platform as a system of modules: each module is a box made of ¾" plywood —with the open side down. (The crosspieces underneath are also ¾" plywood.) If you do not want to cut all those plywood strips for the bottom supports, you can get by with construction grade 2 x 6s or 2 x 12s.

If the platform covers up electrical outlets, you can move the outlets higher on the wall or install them in the platform. (Check with an electrician if it is necessary to extend wires or conduits.)

Staple carpeting (over padding) to the platforms. You can also use carpet squares, vinyl tile or two or three coats of polyurethane.

Photos: Thomas Hooper

Used to running his life from a hotel room, Dreyfuss needed a place in his bedroom for meals and bill paying. This long narrow space suffered one of the living-room's ills—invisible windows. Platforms let him sit on the bed and see the view too. This time: one major level for the bed with a built-in headboard that divides the bedroom from the entry/office (at right). The wall has cantilevered shelves as night tables on both sides of the bed and an entryway shelf on the study side. The continuity of the two separate but equal areas is courtesy of the enamel-painted bittersweet walls and a steady stream of warm textures from the rug, carpet, bamboo and dark, burnished wood.

Other specifics: the bookcase only looks old; the Chinese Chippendale bamboo chair and mirror add unexpected light touches.

EATING PLACES

The dining rooms of our childhood were not exactly places to eat in. More often, they were stage sets—backdrops with props that came to life for role playing with relatives, acting out special scenarios or recurring family dramas. The dining room was a static formality of table proper and chairs reserved for company and holidays. And while waiting for that next occasion, the dining room was just a very fancy passageway to the warm kitchen.

Our eating habits have changed considerably. We snack and we eat on the run. We cook with a crowd and we taste-test as we go—which is as much a part of the meal as the sit-down courses afterward. We order in pizza and serve it on bone china plates. In homes everywhere, formality for meals and service is a choice, not a given. It is not that we have rejected the old for the new—we have simply synthesized and acknowledged our options.

Just so, our eating surroundings have changed dramatically too. Very few people can afford the space for a room that does just one thing, a room that sits around waiting for the next occasion. When space became a premium in apartment architecture, the dining room was the first to go. Some were replaced by euphemisms such as nooks, alcoves, ells, but these were swiftly transformed into guest rooms, children's rooms or offices.

Today's apartment dining rooms are defined by where you eat, not by the furniture, and it is never just one place. If friends arrive to watch a special television program, you simply turn the bedroom into an eating room by piling on the trays and pillows. If dinner is served in the living room, you wheel over a movable feast on a rolling cart. Instead of a table that just sits there and looks pretty, we have adopted the supertable: by day, a mild-mannered desk, additional work space or even a wall hanging; by night, faster than a speeding dustcloth, it becomes a flop-down, drop-down, fold-up, drop-in and sit-down eating surface for eight, buffet for sixteen or intimate dinner for two. These well-priced, functional eating units are today as universal as the old mahogany dining ensembles.

New materials have kept pace with our changing needs. Furnishings made from chrome, vinyl, wood or plastic are serving meals nowadays right alongside the more traditional setups. Simultaneously, stainless steel utensils are placed next to sterling; plastic plates mix with china and glass. Edibles turn into the new centerpiece.

With our developing flexibility and our growing demand for hardworking good looks, the contemporary dining room is a state of mind, not a room waiting in state.

New World Splendor

Whoever said "Don't mix light and dark wood" has never seen this dining-area setup that runs the gamut from dark walnut to natural pine.

Those hand-carved shellback chairs (made-today imports from Italy) are comfortable with the glossy Parsons table or as extra seating anywhere. Plus the table is a clean, well-lighted place to work.

Stack-up storage units sit in front of an awkwardly placed kitchen door to add architectural interest. Another character builder is the wraparound cornice of embossed sheet steel.

Another natural, the lattice-work grid, deals with a no-view window.

HOW TO DO IT
Instant Architecture Cornice: Purchase the sheet steel from an industrial supplier (look in the Yellow Pages under "Metal Ceilings"). The metal is quite sharp and should be handled with work gloves. Cut the strips with tin snips.

Then attach the cornice to the wall, nail the sheet steel to two furring strips (1 x 2s nailed around the ceiling and walls). Seams should be overlapped. Mitering the corners can be tricky so allow an extra piece or two for errors. Tip: When you fit the miter, you do not have to work at ceiling level. Try it out in the corner at a more reachable height.

HOW TO DO IT
Hanging Lamp: Cut 30° grooves in two 12" 2 x 2s and two 18" 2 x 2s. (If you do not have a table saw, have a lumberyard cut it for you.) Miter corners and assemble frame with glue and L brackets as shown. Glue in centerpiece. Mount and wire porcelain sockets. Staple wire alongside vertical 2 x 2 (or rip the 2 x 2 in half and cut a groove down the center with a rabbet plane or table saw. Conceal wire inside groove and glue boards together). Secure pieces of Plexiglas to frame with epoxy glue. Hang lamp with eyebolts and S hooks and connect wires to ceiling fixture.

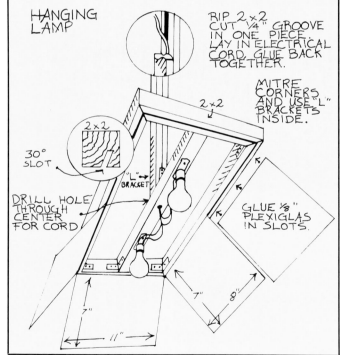

HANGING LAMP

RIP 2 x 2 CUT 1/4" GROOVE IN ONE PIECE. LAY IN ELECTRICAL CORD, GLUE BACK TOGETHER.

MITRE CORNERS AND USE "L" BRACKETS INSIDE.

30° SLOT

2 x 2

"L" BRACKET

DRILL HOLE THROUGH CENTER FOR CORD

GLUE 1/8" PLEXIGLAS IN SLOTS.

7"

7"

8"

11"

Walls: Embossed sheet steel ceiling molding

Lighting: Plexiglas hanging lamp

Windows: Latticework screens

Photos: Bradley Olman

Grids for Dining

Below: Grid—this one for style, not storage—gets the wall-to-wall treatment with the application of 1" duct tape (available at hardware stores). A chrome hanging lamp lights this unusual pedestal table—made from a tiled box covered with a framed slab of glass. A surprising seating solution: chrome tractor seat stools.

The table, seating and lighting fixture define the space, making a dining area in the small space outside a kitchen that the architects had labeled "living room."

Right: When you have no room labeled "dining," mandate one. An empty wall just inside the front door or adjacent to the kitchen can be all the dining room you need. This space was transformed from no place to showplace, thanks to the hanging industrial railroad lamp, the plastic stacking baskets (at left) and the checkerboard floor tiles.

The real secret is a contemporary version of a pegboard—an ingenious wall-hanging grid that comes in sets of four stainless steel parts, shelves, all necessary hardware (two sets are shown), and hangs up anything.

All that color gives straightforward, functional furnishings (bought right off the department-store floor) bold, cheery interest, showing once again how you can zap a room to life with minimum effort/expense and carefully selected accessories.

A few extras—the unexpected ceramic masks as sitdown "favors," well-placed baskets, copper molds and the hanging artist's model.

Photo: Bradley Olman

Photo: Thomas Hooper

Table Topping

With the mere swing of a table-top, you can turn any foyer or entryway into an eating room. Just add a side table that flips.

After a tabletop transplant, this small Parsons table gives you two tables in one: a working side table in the entryway, or enough sit-down seating for up to eight.

The other pieces in the room are just as inventive as the flexible table. Even with the apparent formality of a wall sconce, traditional drapery and a gilt mirror and picture light, the casual pieces fit in. Dishes and silverware are all high camp gear. Dish towels were pressed into napkin service. An institutional pitcher displays flowers, and plant pot saucers hold bread and fruit.

HOW TO DO IT

The Tabletop Transplant: Find a Parsons table (finished or unfinished). Take two plywood pieces, each the same size as the top (the one pictured here is 24″ x 48″) and hinge them as shown. Be sure to place the hinges so they will not scratch the tabletop. Cover the edges with wood tape. Finish the new top like the original table. Double the tops over on the tabletop (hinges hide in the back). For a sit-down meal, unfold the top, turn 90 degrees to create a 48″ square table.

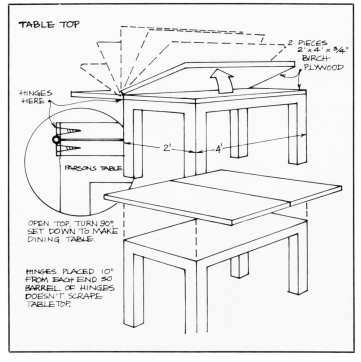

TABLE TOP

2 PIECES 2′ x 4′ x 3/4″ BIRCH PLYWOOD

HINGES HERE

PARSONS TABLE

2′   4′

OPEN TOP, TURN 90° SET DOWN TO MAKE DINING TABLE.

HINGES PLACED 10″ FROM EACH END SO BARREL OF HINGES DOESN'T SCRAPE TABLETOP.

A Room in Bloom

Thanks to inexpensive lunch cloths—those colorful cotton tablecloths from the forties with wide borders of cherries, apples or flowers—this dining room bursts with color. Everything in the room—except for the plants and the food, of course—is a secondhand find. The old-time charm has been enhanced, stretched and assembled in new ways.

With some imagination and a little luck at the thrift shop, you can get a similar rich look for rag prices. Use several cloths layered as has been done here, and do not be troubled by contrasting patterns.

Of the same vintage: the embroidered tea cozy, dish towels and napkins. At the windows are starched, hand-embroidered dresser scarves, hung from tension rods. Wide hem tape has been sewn to the backs to make a casing for the rods to slip through. Everything on the tabletop—all still manufactured today—carries through the room's forties flavor.

The Short-Order Dining Room

The eating/serving area is a colorful island at the end of a typical white box living room, just to the right of a galley kitchen. This roomful of tricks turns a drab corner into a showplace.

In a masterful stroke the back wall has been painted black, adding interest and drama to the space and unifying the living and eating areas. The simple plywood buffet shelf, also painted black, blends right in while offering a counter for serving and display. Pillows covered with inexpensive but elegantly simple unbleached muslin are stored below, ready to be used for extra seating.

Anything can go on the wall —even if it was originally intended for the floor. The hanging over the buffet is a handcrafted sisal rug. That rooster presiding over the table is a large square of fabric stapled over canvas stretchers. It lends focus and picks up the color in the room.

Any flat surface can become an eating table. This one is simply a plywood cube with plate glass on top. It can be stored away at will and another like it can be added for extra dining space.

Rules about old-with-old and modern-with-modern were meant to be broken. Although the overall design here is contemporary, traditional chairs with turned spindles provide contrast. Left natural, the chairs are instantly updated.

Votive candles placed in inexpensive bar glasses and spread out on the table replace the old candelabra. For a thoroughly modern centerpiece—scallions tied with monofilament.

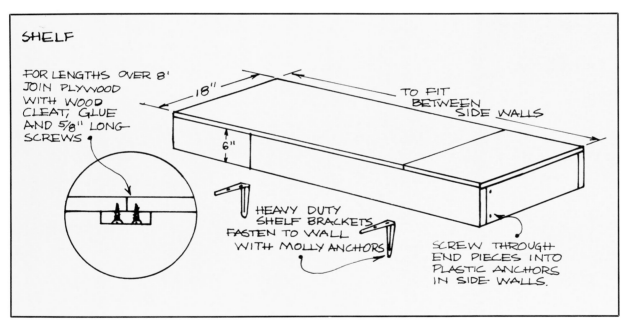

SHELF

FOR LENGTHS OVER 8' JOIN PLYWOOD WITH WOOD CLEAT; GLUE AND 5/8" LONG SCREWS

18"

6"

TO FIT BETWEEN SIDE WALLS

HEAVY DUTY SHELF BRACKETS FASTEN TO WALL WITH MOLLY ANCHORS

SCREW THROUGH END PIECES INTO PLASTIC ANCHORS IN SIDE WALLS.

HOW TO DO IT
Buffet Shelf: Build from ¾" plywood, then paint with semi-gloss enamel or cover with Formica.

HOW TO DO IT
Dining Table: The table is made from four equal-sized panels, ¾" birch or maple plywood. For a finished look: 1) Apply matching edging tape with contact cement. 2) Fill over nailheads with wood color crayons. 3) Rub with finishing oil. Top with 48" x 48" x ½" plate glass; have the edges of the glass finished when you buy it.

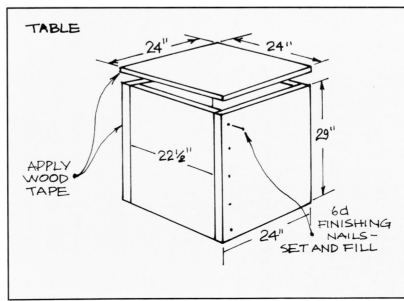

TABLE

24"   24"

APPLY WOOD TAPE

22½"

29"

24"

6d FINISHING NAILS — SET AND FILL

Photo: Thomas Hooper

Table Talk

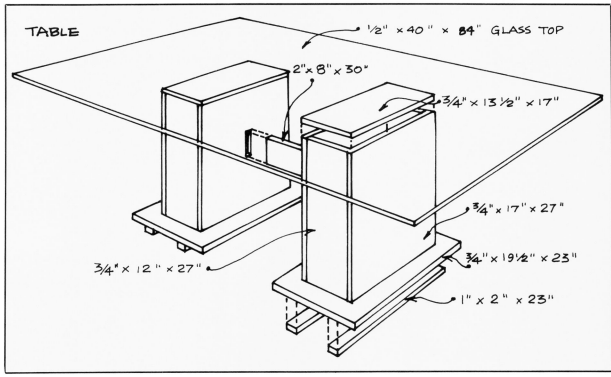

TABLE

½" × 40" × 84" GLASS TOP

2" × 8" × 30"

¾" × 13½" × 17"

¾" × 17" × 27"

¾" × 12" × 27"

¾" × 19½" × 23"

1" × 2" × 23"

posite: Anything with a leg to
and on can be the basis—and
e base—for a dining table.
Plywood boxes and smart
ovincial fabric update the tra-
ionally stalwart English
estle table. This one, unlike its
cestor, has a glass top, but a
llow-core door or a slab of
tcher block can also effect the
ansformation. Chippendale
airs finished au naturel are a
itable update. The bar in back
is originally an unfinished
easure chest—available from
aft stores.

OW TO DO IT

estle Table: All base pieces
e plywood, nailed and glued
gether. Stapling or gluing the
bric is much easier if you
oose a pattern that does not
ed to be matched. Use white
bric glue.

ght: With one unexpected
ea, an ordinary table can be-
me surprisingly special. In
is case, using chrome bar
ool bases to hold up an over-
zed tabletop changes a white
x space altogether. This table
s a copper top but plywood
ould work as well.

r Right: A dining area does
t need to be an alcove: Any
all can be used to provide a
ble-shelf. Mount the table on
rner brackets screwed into
e wall.

Photo: Bill Helms/Design: Demetrios Kontopoulos

Photos: Bradley Olman

Off-the-Wall Dining

This dining/wall unit, complete with storage space, includes its own nook for serving meals. The drop-down table is part of a four-stack bookshelf/drawer system that is easy enough to build over a weekend. There is even a perching place for out-of-use chairs; they are stacked behind the table housing.

The simple natural wood keeps the system contemporary and light while the blue tabletop adds strong color contrast.

HOW TO DO IT

Dining/Wall Unit: Get all the supplies at a building supply dealer. Pick out a good grade of pine if you intend to leave the wood natural; it can also be painted. Have all pieces precut.

What to Buy: This list is for a unit 7' tall, 8'6" long and 14" deep (shelves are 11½" deep). The chest of drawers is a stacked set of three, each 28" high.

2 x 2s (actual size–1¼" x 1½")
8 pieces 7' for uprights
4 pieces 8'6" for top and bottom
7 pieces 14½" for crosspieces
1 piece 35" for tabletop crosspiece
2 pieces 30" for table legs
1 x 2s
1 piece 24" for table legs
34 pieces 11½" for shelf supports
1 x 12s
17 pieces 32" for shelves
Plywood
1 piece ¾" x 32" x 48" for tabletop
Plastic laminate for tabletop
1 piece 32" x 48" (optional)
Hardware
34 3½" x ¼" hex head bolts
5 5" x ¼" hex head bolts
Nuts and 2 washers each for the bolts
30" continuous hinge (for table)
1 pair 1½" butt hinges (legs)
1 cabinet catch
1 pound 4d finishing nails
1 pint contact cement (optional)

Bolt together the four uprights and the crosspieces (7'-long 2 x 2s and 14½" crosspiece 2 x 2s). C-clamp the pieces in position, drill (with a ¼" drill bit) through both at once and bolt them together before removing the clamps. Then bolt on the 8'6" lengthwise 2 x 2s.

Stand the whole unit in place and nail on the 1 x 2 shelf supports, spacing the shelves at the best heights for your storage needs.

Make the table legs and hinge them to the tabletop. Bolt the 2 x 2 crosspiece on the front of the unit and attach the table with a continuous hinge. Screw a cabinet catch under one of the shelves to keep the tabletop folded up. Cover the top with plastic laminate or paint.

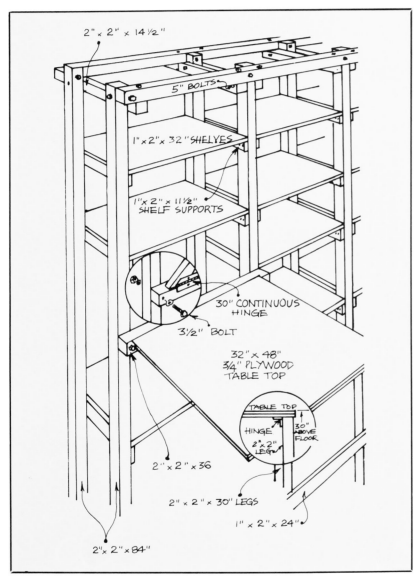

2" x 2" x 14½"

5" BOLTS

1" x 2" x 32" SHELVES

1" x 2" x 11½" SHELF SUPPORTS

30" CONTINUOUS HINGE

3½" BOLT

32" x 48" ¾" PLYWOOD TABLE TOP

TABLE TOP

HINGE

30" ABOVE FLOOR

2" x 2" LEG

2" x 2" x 36

2" x 2" x 30" LEGS

1" x 2" x 24"

2" x 2" x 84"

The Groaning Board

Walls: Painted plywood
paneling
Window: Natural linen shade

Right: This dining area—one end of a long living room—is a cross-fertilization of contemporary and country. A green industrial lamp oversees the solid walnut table. Flanking the table are made-today Windsor chairs and a space-saving banquette, which is actually a reupholstered old trolley car seat. The walnut table, like the banquette, was a secondhand find.

A traditional English butler tray, in front of the window, shuffles a bar around at your beck and call. And the country natural linen window shade is easy to make: Hem the fabric top and bottom and slip in 1″ dowels for weight. Tack up the shade and two pairs of natural linen strips (front and behind).

Opposite: Just because you like the look of turn-of-the-century golden oak doesn't mean you have to hunt out the real thing —even if you can find it. Those solid old pieces have become scarce and costly. The alternative is a new crop of reproductions. Everything in this room, from the Hoosier cabinet to the liqueur decanters, is new. Made today with the look of yesterday, the new-old furniture is surfacing because the design and utility are timeless. And as of old, these pieces are solid oak, well made and good looking, just manufactured with modern technology. This dining setting combines classic design with a very new twist: The old-style office chairs never gathered around a table before but now they offer all-day comfort. The round oak table—an endangered species among antiques today—is brand new. The glass display cabinet with mirrored back both stores and displays dishes and serving pieces. Overseeing the scene is another reproduction—a leaded glass Tiffany-style lamp.

Floors: Rich, bare wood complements golden oak furnishings

Lighting: New Tiffany-style
stained-glass lamp

Photos: Bradley Olman

The Silent Butler

When it exists, the apartment dining room is liable to be small. The solution is to expand your eating options: Here, the two areas in two small spaces were each made to work differently.

The traditional room at right is updated with a white pedestal porch table, an industrial hanging lamp and stripped-down mahogany chairs left natural. The walls are paneled with felt, providing an inexpensive turn on Victorian custom paneling (use a staple gun).

The room at left (part of t kitchen) triples as a unique ing, serving and storage are The make-it-yourself hangi unit was designed to serve.

ded, the cabinet holds dishes, erware, a coffeemaker and like. Unfolded, it becomes a fet or sideboard, a breakfast le or work counter; the choices are limitless. Folding chairs become handy wall sculpture. This attractive box with mirrored tiles on the outside reflects a new way of eating.

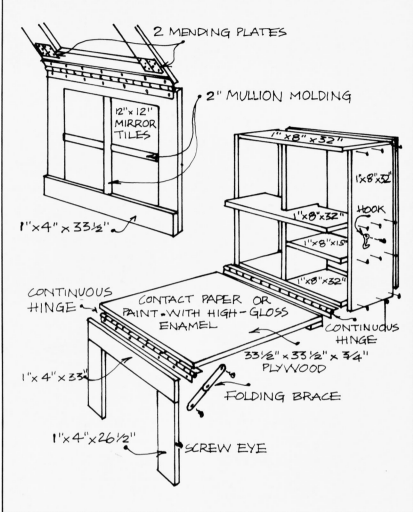

2 MENDING PLATES

2" MULLION MOLDING

12"x 12" MIRROR TILES

1"x 8" x 32"

1"x 8" x 32"

HOOK

1"x 8" x 15"

1"x 8" x 32"

1"x 4" x 33½"

CONTINUOUS HINGE

CONTACT PAPER OR PAINT WITH HIGH-GLOSS ENAMEL

CONTINUOUS HINGE

1"x 4" x 33"

33½" x 33½" x ¾" PLYWOOD

FOLDING BRACE

1"x 4" x 26½"

SCREW EYE

HOW TO DO IT

Drop-Down Table: Ask the lumberyard to precut all wood to your measurements. Build the box first. The shelves and frame are glued and nailed together with 4d finishing nails. Assemble the mirrored front and folding legs. The mullion molding (also available at a lumberyard) is 2" wide, ¼" thick and frames the mirror tiles.

Photos: Bradley Olman

Kitchen-Side Dining

Below: This dining/working/cooking area handles a big load with style even though the space is small. Ignore the tired advice of paint-it-white-to-look-larger. Instead, go for one bold stroke. High-gloss burgundy paint on the walls sets off the area dramatically—and makes that informal dining area just a bit more formal.

Wood, glass, plastic, metal and fabric coexist comfortably here. The light Russian plywood chairs and the plywood and white vinyl table keep the space visually uncluttered.

The window shade is quickly made. Buy simple spring-loaded shade hardware, staple fabric across the top; hem the sides; slip a lattice strip through a small hem at the bottom, or finish with a plastic strip.

The outsized mirror with its easily made cabinet molding frame reflects the kitchen area and the Victorian light fixture.

Right: Another big look for a small space, also adjacent to the kitchen. The turn-of-the-cen-

...ry telegraph table/bench adds ...yle and a sense of humor to an ...dinary area. It rests on an ...nerican Indian print rug that ...ays up the kitchen's American ...dian artifacts. And the slots ...ce reserved for telegrams ...w store napkins and utensils.

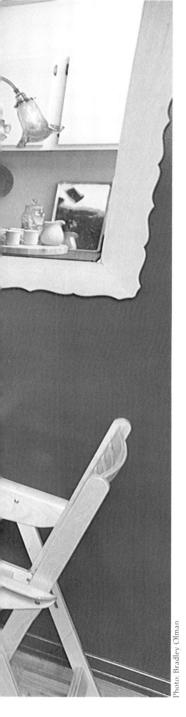

Photo: Bradley Olman

Photo: John Katz

Midnight at the Oasis

Storage: Wicker shelving
Lighting: On-the-floor spots
Walls: Paint two-tone and lus[

This haven is on the fifth floor of a big-city walk-up and used to be rather shabby. The dramatic transformation owes more to imagination (and maybe Sydney Greenstreet) than to money.

The table, chairs and wall shelf are vintage forties rattan, found in antique shops that specialize in thirties and forties pieces (but similar new ones are available).

Real, yet not alive, the palm trees are dried leaves—permanently carefree. Small spots carefully placed in the trees are shot up through the leaves for spectacular, spiky shadows.

Dark walls (and ceiling) keep the atmosphere intimate and lush (and also hide wall irregularities).Old bamboo dining chairs sit atop a sisal rug.

Cutting the Rug

...y collection needs a focus
...d this hoard of thirties finds
...nited by an easily made
...a rug: carpet remnants
...ned in a typically period pat-
...n and glued to a burlap back-
... . Colors are taken from the
...nature cream and green
...ve.

...Other invaluables are dis-
...yed on a flamingo-colored
...lf unit, easily cut from ply-
...od. The pitchers, some
...ning from the insides of old
...rigerators, are thirties sculp-
...e.

...he cafe table is a happy mar-
...ge of a restaurant table ped-
...al with a round plywood top,
...ssily creamed. The once-
...ice chairs look funky enough
...e good again, painted that
...ny thirties green.

Photo: Tom Katz

KITCHENS THAT COOK

The new kitchen is the kitchen extended, retaliating against rigid architectural boundaries by conquering space in unexpected places. The old kitchen was a place where one lone person (usually of the female persuasion) prepared food behind closed doors. But as cooking has become the new participatory sport, the kitchen has become the new playing field, spilling out into the dining area for extra work/play space. Our kitchens are now replete with tools lifted from commercial sources and they are stocked with ingredients from every ethnic cuisine of the world. There is even a new kind of kitchen clutter, which is a revolt against the antiseptic. It is clutter that is a sign of life.

More and more, kitchens are becoming adjunct living rooms, places in which to gather, to participate, to share secrets, to play. The old cliché about the kitchen being the "hub of the home" is more appropriate now than ever.

And the recipes are changing too. The old one used to be: Mix one stove with one refrigerator. Add running water. Apartment kitchens were mere after-thoughts of modern planning, and living in one meant little more than moving in, putting down clean shelf paper and taking pot luck. The galley kitchen—no storage, no window-was as tight as a ship, infinitely less imaginative, rivaled in size and utility only by the broom closet. That has all changed. Granted, the apartment kitchen has its own special problems, but it also has its own unique solutions.

You do not need to break through walls, buy a lot of new appliances or install expensive custom cabinets in order to

ke your kitchen work.
In the last decade or so, basic chen principles have been re-fined because of new values, w demands in home living, w technology and materials. longer is the kitchen a room hide in or shield with louver ors and stand-up screens. ck then, meals seemed to ppen as if by magic. Today, ere has been a definite shift in isibility. From: 1. Yes, Vir-nia, there is a kitchen. 2. In t, why not come in and see w it is done. 3. Listen, Vir-nia—as long as you are stand-there, would you mind peel-ing that onion? 4. And, come to think of it, why not invite the rest of the guests in, too, so everyone can help.

And so the kitchen is now a room to behold and belong in, a room not just for one, but for guests and friends. With that change of attitude has come new kitchen/living ideas:

1. Use your eyes and trust your instincts. Break rules. Who says that the refrigerator, stove and sink must be placed in the perennial triangle pattern?

2. Get organized. You want to use every bit of space you can.

3. Do not be stymied by styles. Your kitchen can reflect your taste. *Personalize.*

As our choices have become more sophisticated, more inter-national kitchen activity has, ironically, gotten back to the basics. We have, once again, discovered the pleasures of making pasta and pastries, of making wine, and turning our kitchens into greenhouses—greenhomes—of herbs, even without the window box.

The new kitchen is a space in which to explore and experi-ment, a place in which to try and taste, create and relax, a room to share and savor.

The Extended Kitchen

This "kitchen" is not really all kitchen. It breaks boundaries and eats its way into the living/dining space. Title this one "The Kitchen That Ate the Plain-White Box."

What makes the transition are quarry tiles that float one room into another, extending the space by using pots, pans, storage, a table and other traditional "kitchen" collections.

The eating/work area has bentwood chairs coupled with a Formica Parsons table, a stylish alternative to the old-time regulation matching dining set. The table's deliberate lines are a sharp rebellion against its mahogany ancestors, yet there is dignity in the proportion of this version that expands and contracts with leaves.

In 1857 Michael Thonet fashioned the bentwood chair of wood steamed and molded into curves. Le Corbusier designed the first of the updated armchairs in the twenties. Lightweight enough for any movable feast, these chairs are affordable, accessible and adaptable.

Overhead, factory lights are a democratic alternative to the chandelier.

The wall storage system (below) was once found only in expensive European-engineered and often custom-made furniture. Like all good radical ideas, the wall system has filtered down through extremist layers into the mass market, losing a bit of its machined quality, a lot of its priciness, but none of its workability.

The Extended Kitchen

Work space is everywhere. Any workroom requires order, easy access and storage space. And every surface is eligible. This kitchen gets its organization from stainless steel grids, hooks, bins, boxes and baskets —all now standard in any kitchen that works. We've learned a few lessons from restaurant kitchens, like hanging pots from ceilings and making the walls work without (or in spite of) standard kitchen cabinets.

Good-looking, durable and easy-to-care-for molded plastic is a new kitchen material. The stacking plastic drawer units function in any room, but in the kitchen they are the handy depository for all those easy-to-use, but hard-to-store conveniences—hand-held appliances, aluminum foil, plastic wrap, pot holders. The stacking drawer units also support sturdy butcher-block counter space.

A flexible metal lamp—long ago borrowed from the architect's office—offers high-powered illumination over this kitchen work space.

A rolling cart—made from heavy-duty stainless steel wire and covered with a slab of butcher block—is a floating worktable that doubles as storage space when stationary. Industrial-looking cooking ware, professional in inspiration, is now widely available from the country's best and biggest housewares manufacturers.

Out and Out Storage

...se and improve every inch of
...e narrow apartment galley
...ith space-conscious ideas and
...ood-looking, efficient equip-
...ent.

Try these:

Closet pole ceiling. Lengths
...f unfinished closet pole (from
...e lumberyard) are attached to
...e wall with pole sockets.
...crew large cup hooks into
...les wherever needed (better
...an S hooks that look great
...ut fall off).

New lighting. A major source
...verhead; small fluorescents
...nder the cupboards.

New floor. Old-fashioned ce-
...mic hexagonal tiles look great
...gain, but now can be found in
...expensive easy-to-grout
...heets.

Open cupboards with painted
...dges—doors off.

Paint only one wall for
...ontrast.

A rolling cart (in the foyer/
...antry) expands storage and
...ork space. Carts abound with
...ins, shelves, drawers.

Cover countertops with
...ardware or dime-store cutting
...oards. They are the same
...ngth as a standard counter is
...eep (24").

Store and display utensils on
...th strips studded with small
...up hooks.

Search out wooden or wire
...acks for everything that moves.

More closet pole pieces glued
...n for cupboard and drawer
...ulls, which replace the old
...glies. Chisel and sand off some
...oundness so they sit firmly.

A knife rack (below) fits in
...he gap between the wall and
...ounter.

Photos: Bradley Olman

Home Cooking

An industriously industrial-looking kitchen need not be a cold, uninviting place but it should be a highly functional room where anyone can find a space to work or at least a place to sit and watch. Here the layout and the equipment combine to make the room both comfortable for watching and efficient for working.

Most of the old cupboards and doors were removed and replaced by a commercially inspired butcher block-top cart (next page), floor-to-ceiling painted pegboard, plastic drawer units and pine shelving —much cheaper than custom cabinets and unique. The result is three flexible work areas with open and closed storage above and below, unified by clean looks, factory lights and a single color.

When it comes to pegboards, all manner of brackets, hooks and supports are now available at hardware stores and lumberyards.

In the work area (below), two narrow pieces of pine shelving placed side by side cost less than a single wide board. Protect them with two coats of satin polyurethane, and set the shelving across stacked plastic drawers.

The shelves over the refrigerator are supported on metal wall brackets screwed into the wall studs. Glass and white dishes add to the airy effect.

Walls: Painted pegboard

Storage: Shelves on pegboard brackets

Lighting: Holophane fixtures

Floor: Black and white vinyl tile

Photos: Bradley Olman

Home Cooking

Above: Yet another extended kitchen creates even more un-expected work space (this one stretches right out into the living room, outside a narrow galley kitchen). Pots and pans hang from a suspended chicken coop; more storage fits on a shelving unit placed in front of the window. Mexican chairs replace regulation wood or metal ones. *Right:* Restaurant/ industrial design has definitely come home. Functional commercial wire shelving fits right into kitchen spaces—and big wheels roll the wagon right to the center of the cooking scene.

The Erector Set

here is more than one way to
tend a kitchen into another
om. Sometimes you can even
 it on wheels.

Strong and square, a sturdy
ilding block with a solid
undation, this erector-set
it was built in just a few
urs. It is representative of
e new philosophy of extend-
g kitchens: Storage and work
eas need not remain shut
ay in the kitchen. Put them
ywhere you need them.

Inexpensively assembled, this
it will expand your kitchen
ea into the dining room or
ing room.

The system is made from
otted angle irons, available in
dustrial supply or machinery
ores and usually used for in-
strial shelving. Mesh chicken
ire and hooks hang up pans
d utensils, and a butcher
ock surface is substantial
ough for chopping and slicing.

HOW TO DO IT

Erector Set: The dimensions of
this unit can be adjusted to fit
any space. This one is 6' high,
28" wide, 30" deep. Use galvanized sheet metal and painted
angle irons. Cut and bolt together the angle irons with $5/16$"
x $3/4$" bolts.

Materials:

   4 slotted angle irons, 6'
   8 slotted angle irons, 30"
   8 slotted angle irons, 28"
   40 nuts and bolts, $5/16$" x $3/4$"
   4 locking casters (3") with
corner brackets; nuts, bolts,
washers
   2 pieces 1" x 2" wire mesh, cut
to fit top and back
   Cut to fit inside frame (about
28" x 30"):
   2 pieces ½"-thick plywood
   2 pieces 16-gauge galvanized
sheet metal
   1 piece butcher block (or
Formica-covered plywood)

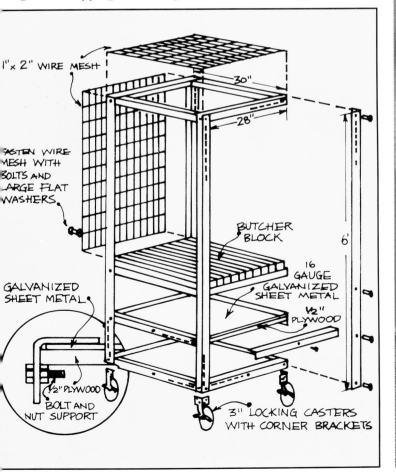

The New Pantry

Ceiling: Glued thin wood strip
Storage: Natural pine cabinets
Windows: Salvaged stained-glass panels

There is more to today's functional kitchen than good design. Layouts and appliances may be modern but the feel—and many components—can be old. This kitchen's warmth radiates from genuinely old accessories, old-look stained glass and plenty of natural wood.

The open display of packaged goods changes with every shopping trip, adding a new dimension to functional art. The cupboards and stained glass are both homemade as is the wood-covered ceiling, which is built from a kit of 3″-wide mahogany strips, thin enough to cut with a pair of scissors.

The combination of open display with the rustic warmth of pine brings a special quality to any kitchen. How-to: To build the cupboards, decide what you would like to store/display; then sketch your plan on the wall. Starting from the bottom, use small angle irons to fasten the shelves to the wall and screw the vertical dividers to the shelves.

The Old Pantry

you are living with an old
chen and the appliances
ork, you do not have to mod-
nize it. Let it live back in time,
en it once was young. Flea
arkets, estate sales, auctions,
rift shops, salvage yards—
ese are the new five-and-
nes for the new antique
chens. What's more, many
chen wares haven't changed
nce Betty Crocker wore
aids. You still can find the old
pendable shapes and mate-
ls new in department stores
d cookware shops. There is
thing depressing about this
pression-era kitchen.

The old-time stove sets the
yle. Most storage is contained
the vintage freestanding
oosier cabinet. And all the
lors here are the perfect pre-
ription for the Depression
ues.

low: An old medicine cabinet
orks well for spices. The mix
old and new packaging and
s adds color and zest.

Photos: Erik Arnesen

Mother Knew Best

A kitchen to remember. Too often relic kitchen appliances are the booby prize that comes with old-world charm: stained sinks, ovens that must be lit by hand, refrigerators that look as if they have been waiting a decade or two for the iceman. Gut, modernize and renovate? Not at all. If the stove and refrigerator work, and if the water runs hot and cold, the rest of the room need not be snazzy modern. It can be preserved. What you add can complement the design that has existed for years.

Everything (except the appliances) in this room is new, all commercially available today. Inexpensive and designed for function, these pieces were not acquired for nostalgia value but because they are timeless. They are still around because they are still good.

But the room does not stop there. It takes obvious, everyday items—the match and laundry starch boxes, for example—and turns them into design statements.

Color can also unify. The main color in this room is blue, just as it would have been forty years before. Blue was billed as the "kitchen color" then, and it still lives on in vintage spatterware dishes, utensils, old-time fabrics, tiles, and cobalt blue canisters.

Country charm and staunch utilitarianism are provided by cast-iron pots and pans, a classic mixer, general-store canisters, porcelain cabinet pulls—even the chocolate chip cookies. All have made a well-deserved comeback. The dish drainer—often hidden in so many kitchens—looks right at home here.

Storage by the Inch

Every inch of space is used in this skinny kitchen—and the result is efficient and charming with hardly any claustrophobic clutter. Notice how the window doubles as storage space. It is all cleverly done with wood lath strips, nailed horizontally to two floor-to-ceiling 1 x 2s, which are held in place by furniture levelers (available at hardware stores), making the unit easy to adjust and remove. Cup hooks hold the kitchen stock—everything from colanders to calendars.

The store-bought shelf units against the wall use canvas strap supporters that soften the look of the wood.

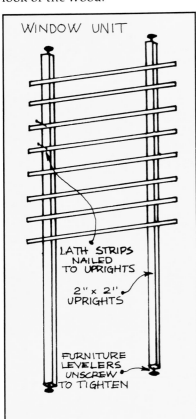

WINDOW UNIT

LATH STRIPS
NAILED
TO UPRIGHTS

2" x 2"
UPRIGHTS

FURNITURE
LEVELERS
UNSCREW
TO TIGHTEN

High-Level Storage

...ose pots and pans and wine-
...sses swinging from the raf-
...s are a grand example of
...m following function. The
...in white box apartment
...chen has been swiftly trans-
...med into a literal showplace
...verything in the place
...ows. And not by accident.
...All the wood pieces were
...cifically engineered to
...ommodate these hanging
...res. Small shelves are care-
...ly measured to be the perfect
...e for spices. The same holds
...e for the racks holding the
...neglasses.

...The interior architecture of
...e space emerged not only
...rough the wood construction
...t also through the gentle
...es of all the objects—curved
...plets against straight wood,
...I slender spice jars alongside
...und, fat crocks, dark enam-
...d pots below pale wicker
...skets. The result: Scandina-
...n in texture, oriental in feel,
...th every inch functional.

...t was all simply constructed.
... that is needed is to adapt the
...nensions to the design of
...ur room. Pine shelving re-
...ced the ordinary kitchen
...pinets. (They were removed
...d stored.) Meat hooks, avail-
...e at gourmet shops, hold
...dly shaped tools such as the
...inese skimmer at left.
...Yucca and spider plants offset
...e crisp look of the pine. Even
...imple wooden tray is of
...erest when hung on the wall.

Photo: Armen Kachaturian

Shelf Life

Photo: Bradley Olman

This entire storage unit—the counter, backsplash, adjustable shelving—adds life to dead space. Not only is this an efficient storage system but it also adds interest to a dull view.

The shelving is easily built from clear pine boards, either painted white or left natural with two coats of polyurethane for protection. For the backsplash and countertop, plywood can be covered with waterproof paper. The informal country provincial paper used here has an adhesive backing for easy application and removal.

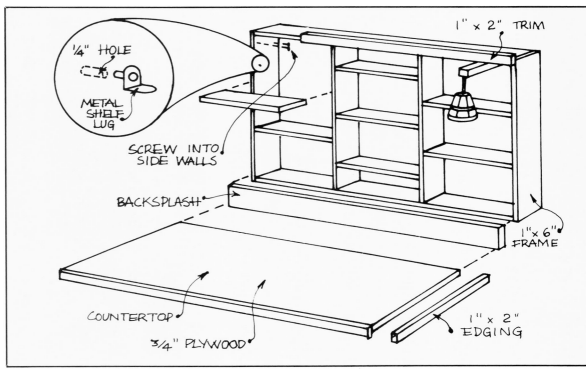

1/4" HOLE

METAL SHELF LUG

SCREW INTO SIDE WALLS

BACKSPLASH

1" x 2" TRIM

1" x 6" FRAME

COUNTERTOP

3/4" PLYWOOD

1" x 2" EDGING

The New-View Kitchen

Window: Wood uprights and glass shelves

imary colors make the differ-
ce in this kitchen—coupled
th practicality and a few
rdworking ideas that let you
ork less. It is easy to convert a
pical apartment kitchen into
space worth looking at.
This room proves once again
at decoration is no longer
fined as something that does
ot function. Basic kitchen
anning philosophy—such as
eping equipment near the
ea where it will be used—has
en adhered to but with new
vists. Equipment has been
pt handy by hanging it on
mple wood strips at working
vel near the counter area.
ld-style cabinet doors were
moved. Now everything is
t in the open—dishes, pots,
rs, cans, staples and spices.
ext, the countertops were
vered in a cheerful self-adhe-
ve vinyl.
A window is usually precious
an apartment kitchen; here it
doubly valuable as storage
o. Lath strips hold glass
helves and colored glasses that
ght up with the sun.

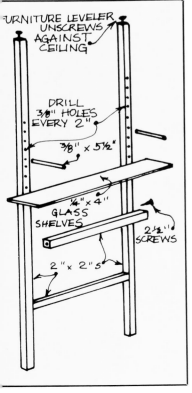

FURNITURE LEVELER
UNSCREWS
AGAINST
CEILING

DRILL
3/8" HOLES
EVERY 2"

3/8" x 5½"

¼" x 4"
GLASS
SHELVES

2½"
SCREWS

2" x 2" S

FAT PAK

Photo: John Katz

HOW TO DO IT

Window Unit: After measuring,
screw the 2 x 2 uprights and
crosspieces together, put the
frame up, using furniture levelers for fitting the height.
Then drill holes in the frame for
the dowel shelf supports, using
a ⅜" bit. Secure frame to window molding using 3" screws.

KITCHENS THAT COOK   153

Short Takes

Design: Stephen Habiague

Left: Don't get locked into label. Just because bamboo shades ar sold to be hung on windows doesn't mean they can not be used elsewhere. Here they hav replaced paint-encrusted cabinet doors. The inexpensive matchstick blinds are available at most oriental import stores. A scissors or sharp knife will cut them to exact size. Fruit baskets and large wicker trays quickly hung under the cabinets, keep the natural look going. The dish drainer also hang on the wall, adding yet another texture and more work space. Another disguise: A hanging vine veils an unexciting windo view.

Photo: David Jordan

Above: You can completely revitalize dingy and dirty cabinets in about the same time it would take to wash them off—and with the same tool. A sponge dipped into blue paint (or any other color, semigloss or gloss), then dabbed onto the cabinets results in a spatterware look.

Left: The lighting strip mountec over the sink adds the extra light you always need over any counter space. The multiple outlet strips are available at lighting supply stores; light bulbs screwed into plug-in adapters bring drama to even the most basic salad preparatio

he Galley Gallery

other times kitchens were corated only with insurance endars on the walls and a agnetic pot holder or two ngling from the refrigerator. oday kitchen accouterments e much more artful. These o kitchens are galleries—gal- y galleries, to be sure—with a p Art mixture of the fun and e functional.

Left: Country comes to the apartment kitchen with a warm combination of antique butcher block, old wooden bowls, pine, copper and pottery, giving the whole a look of organized chaos. The high shelving unifies the space and stores good-looking but seldom-used objects. The wall displays the art of the everyday: cooking utensils, pots, pans, posters, papers. Over the sink and refrigerator are larger shelves and cabinets for food and dishes.

Right: This kitchen-as-show-room uses open shelving to display culinary sculpture. Favorite posters and prints hung from floor to ceiling—as well as an American flag, in a wave to nostalgia—carry the gallery motif right to the top. An off-beat storage design: scarves and hats tossed on an antique chair hung on the wall. This room proves again that anything— from stuffed animals to old chairs—can become art when the frame is your frame of mind.

ALI MacGRAW: Personal Style at Home

When Ali MacGraw first laid eyes on her new home—an apartment in a residential hotel —she immediately fell in love with the space and light (not to mention the room service). But she hated the furnishings. "Where I live is *so* important," she said. "I really know what the environment should look like." And, coming from a background of modeling and photo styling, she knew her tastes down to the last light cord.

"I love natural canvas coverings, real treasures on the walls, a few antiques, old pine." And, looking around, you can see that is exactly what she has. In moved plump, rolled-arm sectional units (secured together as two facing sofas). Next came sturdy, neutral industrial carpet. Tortoise bamboo shades gave the windows a custom look.

The coffee table—home for collectibles and candles—was made with wooden dowels holding up a ½"-glass slab.

And no bright lights in this apartment (enough of those on the set). Instead, some strategic lamps for reading and spots for drama under trees. An ungainly mirror over the fireplace got some curvaceous molding, with mitered corners and satin polyurethane. Next—and last— went an ugly black fireplace, spruced up with terra-cotta tiles.

HOW TO DO IT
Retiling a Fireplace: Measure the area needing tiles, both around the opening and on the hearth.

Buy enough 4" unglazed terra-cotta tiles to cover, allowing for some breakage.

Use a ceramic tile cutting blade or a carborundum saber saw blade to cut edge tiles to size when necessary.

Fasten tiles with epoxy tile kit.

Apply two coats of satin polyurethane to prevent staining.

Grout with gray latex grout.

Coat one or two more times with polyurethane.

Photos: Thomas Hooper

Above: "Sparer is better," says MacGraw, who fell in love with this old pine hutch and had it shipped from California. The lower doors were converted so the shelves could house a music center; originally all three opened separately. Hinging two doors together made for easy access to the compact receiver/tape deck. On the side, take note of the speaker wrapped in burlap. Staples (no sewing) made the disguise easy, with no sound distortion.

Right: An oriental kimono makes a fine piece of art—on off the wall. For hanging, choose a piece of bamboo (fro a lumberyard) with a 2" diam- eter that is 6" or longer than arm spread of the garment. Carefully drill a hole at each end (back side) of the bamboo large enough for a nail or scr head. Sink a plug and screw o simply a nail (depending on th type of wall you have); slip th kimono onto the bamboo and hang.

Above: This view reflects upon two projects that made Ali Mac-Graw's life brighter. A window seat, a favorite place to curl up for some quiet time, and a custom-made mirror. To make a mirror: Have glass cut to size. Use blue mastic to glue it to masonite. Use mirror plates to fasten to frame in back. Put screw eyes in frame and wire up. The frame is simply mitered pieces of curvy molding, glued at the corners. Secure the mold-ing with tape while glue is drying. Fill corners with plastic wood; sand lightly and apply clear polyurethane.

Photos: Thomas Hooper

Left: An old favorite quilt hangs over a pine hutch from metal paper clamps and nails.

Below and Opposite: Any kitchen that is no wider than a leg's length needs a lot of help. Mac-Graw wanted a clean white and butcher block space; simple white dishes, utilitarian pans, a few pretty baskets, a minimum of appliances—simple accesso-ries that would serve any func-tion. (Looks are as important her as function—and some-times more so.)

A small amount of renova-tion came first—new counter, sink and stove top; cabinet doors removed; new hardware below; a simple bamboo shade and a quick and easy grid system made of dowels with hooks to hold things up.

SLEEPING PLACES

Traditionally, the bedroom's been a space reserved for retiring, a place where we escaped from it all, a room for dressing and undressing (and a few things in between), but mainly it was the victim of a stern Victorian closed-door policy.

We have come a long way since white sheets and bedroom furnishings could only be bought in sets—ensembles—those suites of beds, along with an elaborate headboard, matching dressers (a tall one for the man, a short, fat one for the woman) and two matching night tables for a pair of ever-so-matching lamps. In 1952 those bedroom ensembles hit their peak (or nadir, some would say) when a furniture manufacturer sold one million "I Love Lucy" bedroom sets (just like the one on the show) in just ninety days.

Bedrooms are finally beginning to wake up. These Rip Van Winkles of apartment life have finally learned to do other things besides sleep. Now, for variety of reasons from limited space to a new sense of place, bedrooms have become the alternate living rooms.

Now that the lights are on and the door is open we have changed our notions about comfort and utility. As you will see, there are many ideas that can solve the problem bedroom Multifunction pieces solve sto

problems: Beds now behave
sofas, desks become dress-
, bolsters hold yesterday's
tonight's linens. It is often
re handy to hang up jewelry
hooks out in the open, which
kes for functional art. You
see how you can even hang
r clothes on the wall. (If
y look good on you, think
at they will do for your
ls.)

he old prescriptions for
per Bedroom Decorating
Etiquette have finally and mer-
cifully run out. Now anything
goes: chrome carts, wicker baskets, tall trees, wave-quilted
movers' pads, lamps that formerly felt at home only in the
office. Our bedrooms have
blossomed into growing gar-
dens, galleries of art and sufficient storage both in and out
of the closet. And bed linens—
printed and patterned in every
hue, all with enough character
to reflect ours, no matter
whose initials are on them.

Bedrooms are no longer just
bedrooms. They are offices and
eating areas and anything else.
Because more than any other
room in the apartment, the
bedroom gives you permission
to kick off your shoes and make
yourself at home. Finally, the
bedroom has learned something
from itself: to relax. And if you
use your imagination while you
are awake, your bedroom can
make for pleasant dreams.

The Complete Retreat

This bedroom looks luxurious —and that is exactly the point. Yet it is also an office, a study and a second living room.

White-on-white gives this room its fresh look—particularly because of the comforter, draperies and shiny white metal lamps.

More easy mixing: rattan end tables, a clean-lined four-poster of natural elm and a velvet recliner. The bonnet-topped secretary is an eighteenth-century English reproduction.

At the window is a soft, unfussy version of the Austrian shade, with a Mylar reflector to let in double sunlight and give a boost to the low ceiling.

HOW TO DO IT:

Curtain: Each window takes a piece of fabric 6" wider than the window and 2½ times as long. Hem the bottom and sides by machine. Sew on three strips of Austrian shirr tape (a double-thick twill tape encasing a drawstring). Finish the top, allowing a 1½" channel for the curtain rod and 2" for the self-ruffle. To shirr the curtain, pull the cords together, tie them and tuck inside folds.

HOW TO DO IT

Reflector: Make a frame of 1 x 2s and fasten with L brackets. Pull the Mylar taut around the frame. Staple in place. Rest frame on windowsill and nail top corners to ceiling.

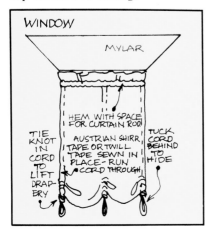

Tenting Tonight

Right: Typical apartment problems—veiny walls, shriveled shag and peeling window frames—can be inexpensively and quickly solved with some obvious solutions: sheets, simple rugs and thinking twice about things you never considered.

First the walls: Without any of the fuss of paint or spackling, hanging up patterned sheets will instantly alter the atmosphere with one showy stroke. First a strip of wood lath was tacked where the wall meets the ceiling. The sheets were stapled to the lath, making loose pleats. (Double flat sheets are exactly 8' long—the same height as most rooms so no cutting or hemming is necessary.) Overlap the sheets where they join and make sure they meet over a window so you can tie back the "curtains."

The comforter is made from the same sheets (matching comforters can often be purchased) and the bolster covers are made from yet another sheet. With what is left over, make a dust ruffle that can be attached to the bottom box spring with Velcro fastening strips (so the ruffle can be easily removed for cleaning).

Two rattan headboards make a sitting place out of the bed.

Unexpected charm from unexpected places: a child's chair works as a night table; a wicker wine rack on the windowsill holds plants and magazines; sisal matting on the floor covers up unsightly shag, without losing softness underfoot.

Below: The wardrobe is little more than two metal utility cabinets with four panels of lattice screen doors. To put it together: Hinge two panels of lattice screen together and attach to each side of the cases (you might have to put two shelving units together). Cut legs of the screens (be sure to adjust bottom shelf to fit flush with bottom of screen). To hide the sides, ¼" tempered hardboard panels are bolted to the 1 x 2 frame with finish washers and stove bolts. If the screen is a tad narrow, screw 1 x 2s where the doors end. Finish off with wooden pulls, magnetic door catches and clear plastic storage boxes.

The Second Living Room

This 24-hour room does it all: It is an office, an eating room, a greenhouse, a living room and —oh, yes—a bedroom. Inch by inch, every bit of space is used night and day, thereby destroying old myths that bedrooms exist for sleeping only.

The all-day bed is covered in hardworking Haitian cotton. The headboard, framed by plastic plumbing piping, is an easy do-it-yourself project. With good lighting and storage close at hand, the bed/sofa also serves as a work space.

That typing table—also suitable for bedside dining—is a chrome-based hospital bed tray that wheels away with a light push. Those in and out boxes on the bed are photo developing trays; they are also used as plant trays on the window shelf.

The modular storage units below the window are varied and roomy enough to store anything. Wire baskets at right hold those oddities that have the awkward habit of winding up in the wrong place.

The green window solution is a working herb garden, complete with hanging grow lights that supplement the sun. Industrial metal shelving supports the plants.

Above the bed, over the sleek chrome yellow wall lamps, three-of-a-kind posters, framed with Swiss clips and glass, add a graceful touch.

HOW TO DO IT

Bed: This padded headboard is framed with 3" PVC (plastic) pipe from a building supply store. Use two elbow and two T joints; saw straight lengths to fit the width and height you want the headboard to be. Then glue the pieces together with PVC glue, wipe clean the writing found on PVC pipes with PVC cleaner, spray paint the color of your choice or leave white with enamel semigloss paint and stand it between the bed and a wall. Cut a piece of ¾" plywood ¼" smaller all around than the headboard space. Staple or glue on a covering sheet of ½" foam rubber, then stretch fabric over the plywood and foam and staple it to the back. Attach the padded square to the pipe with L brackets.

Cover the bed's feet with the same PVC pipe and hide ugly legs or a Hollywood frame. A final touch: Wrap the box spring with the headboard fabric and use a few more yards for a spread.

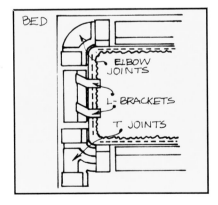

A Touch of Brass

Right: Investing in just a few well-chosen furnishings and some paint can transform any room. This once ordinary bedroom became a hybrid of country French and homespun Greek with a few easy pieces.

Brass beds are usually square-framed and heavy. This half-moon variation is softer and, with its graceful, gleaming focus, is all the wall decoration necessary.

Blue is often a cold color but here, mixed with country-print linens and pine, it becomes friendly. The quilt—in a traditional Greek pattern—contrasts well with the pillows, which have been covered in stitched-together dishcloths. The intensely blue walls are unbroken except for a whimsical collection of wall hangings.

More and more antique reproductions are available, as solidly made as the originals, handsome and worth the price. The Shaker reproduction washstand beside the bed can be ordered by mail. The Victorian fern stand as side table was made from a kit.

Below: The natural pine standing mirror and Shaker chest (both new reproductions) are well accented by another newly produced, old-time designed pine spool chest complete with colorful threads.

Walls: Midnight blue paint
Lighting: Reproduction brass lamps
Storage: Shaker cabinets

Photos: Thomas Hooper

George Washington Slept Here

A city-slick high rise can feel like a country inn. It is a matter of reinterpreting a style without reproducing a stamped-out carbon copy.

The canopy gracing the new four-poster looks old—but it is really a lace tablecloth stretched over the poles. Country green and white wallpaper matches the lace-edged fabric that covers the inexpensive bedside lamps on either side of the bed. The rocker was bought unfinished, then painted white and given dime-store decals for instant heritage.

Prefab 4 x 8 sheets nailed to the wall quickly offer farmhouse paneling. The chair-rail molding for the wainscoting is made of 1 x 4 boards, wide enough to be used for extra shelf space.

Near the window (drapery-less but framed in handsome painted molding) hangs a porch swing. (Make sure it is firmly fixed into the ceiling joists.) The pillows involve more cutting than sewing (a doily sandwich of fabric circles and batting, stitched inside the edge of a large lace circle). Overhead, flowering plants bloom in market baskets lined with foil.

Photo: Thomas Hooper

A Turn on Tradition

A crossbreed of new and old— old ideals mixed with new ideas —is what makes a room more reinterpretation than reproduction.

Although everything here looks old, it is all new—either store bought or homemade. This room is kept clean looking by furnishing with restraint.

The most traditional fabric of all—linen—is seen everywhere but the twist is that they are all linen dish towels.

A trip to a building supplier will get you a bed. Buy turned spindles and then assemble them into a stately bed frame.

All wood pieces are stripped to their natural essence. The reproduction ash armoire and bedside commode are classic eighteenth-century French Provincial—the simple folk carving is the key to their beauty. Unfinished window shutters keep the light in as well as out.

HOW TO DO IT
Bed: To make the upright bedposts, use turned spindles. They are anchored at the top with closet poles and at the bottom with boards.

HOW TO DO IT
Linen Quilt: You will need: Dish towels. For a double bed quilt (finished size 80" x 88"), use 12 24" x 33" towels.

A sheet to use as a backing. Or buy twice as many dish towels and make it reversible.

Polyester fiberfill quilt batting. (Comes in sheet-size dimensions—buy as many as you want for fatness. Nine were used here.)

Colored yarn for tufting. To make the quilt: Sew the dish towels together in a giant patchwork. Then seam the patchwork to the sheet backing (cut to the same size) right sides together, around three sides.

Pile the layers of polyester

batting on top of the big wrong-side-out cover and loosely hand-stitch batting to the three seam allowances and along the top edge of the open side (do not sew towels and sheet together). Turn right side out, and hand sew the opening shut.

For tufts, cut yarn in 8" lengths and, using a wide-eyed needle, sew from the top, through the batting and sheet backing, and back up and out. Knot and tie bows. Tuft either in a random pattern or spaced geometrically.

To make pillowcases: Simply sew two dish towels right sides together, leaving one end open.

HOW TO DO IT
Dust Ruffle: Dish towel fabric or dish towels.

An old sheet large enough to fit the top of your box spring. To make dust ruffle: Use 1½ to 2 times as much fabric as is needed to fit around three sides of your bed. Cut it wide enough

to hang from the top of the box spring to the floor, allowing for a ½" seam at the top and a hem at the bottom. Cut the sheet to fit the top of the box spring, plus ½" seam allowance. Machine-gather the dish towel fabric along the top edge; adjust gathers to fit around the sheet. Sew the ruffle to the sheet, right sides together.

HOW TO DO IT
Dish Towel Shutter Inserts: Buy shutters that have spring-tip rods on the back at the top and bottom to allow fabric to be slipped on (or you can staple or thumbtack the fabric to the backs of the shutters). Measure the length from rod to rod and cut your dish towels to that length, plus 3" for hems. For width, cut the fabric 1½ to 2 times as wide as the opening.

Sew a 1" casing at the top and bottom of the fabric, slip the rods into the casings and fit the rods back on the shutters.

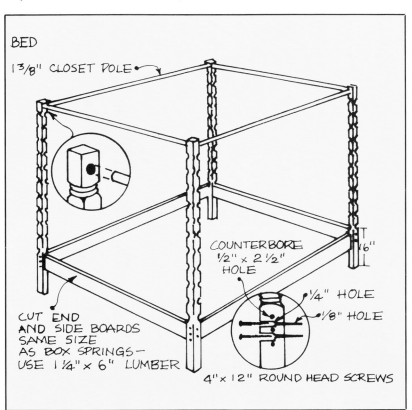

BED

1 3/8" CLOSET POLE

COUNTERBORE ½" x 2½" HOLE

¼" HOLE
1/8" HOLE

6"

CUT END AND SIDE BOARDS SAME SIZE AS BOX SPRINGS— USE 1 ¼" x 6" LUMBER

4" x 12" ROUND HEAD SCREWS

Cloud 9-D

One favorite fabric can take a room sky high. This room—with its clouds and clouds—does just that.

The uniform here is a favorite fantasy fabric-by-the-yard (all from 30 yards of 65"-wide cloth, but bed sheets work well too).

Here are the parts:

Floor-to-ceiling screens look imposing, but weigh next to nothing. Six yards of fabric cover Fome-Cor panels. Stretch the fabric over the screen and glue or tape it to the back. Hinge the Fome-Cor panels with long strips of strong duct tape.

Several ready-made sheer nylon curtains are bunched on rods over the windows to diffuse the light.

The bed's soft ceiling is a quick canopy of fabric hung from closet poles.

Quick covers for the box spring and mattress lend comfort and continuity to rest of the room. Measure enough fabric to cover the mattress top and sides, plus a little extra all around. (Save fabric on the box cover by using muslin for the part that does not show.) Sew elastic around the entire lower edge—rounding the corners—to gather it like a big shower cap. Keep a fitted sheet underneath the bedspread cover for sleeping. Or buy fitted sheets for the mattress and box spring.

Fluffy fake fur (by the yard) is an elegant throw. A Flokati on the floor adds clouds underfoot too.

The squashy hassock uses more of the same fabric (filled with bags of polyester fiberfill).

Bamboo packing baskets make natural, low-lined bedside tables.

A double-jointed deck chair moves around easily and folds out of the way.

The black-and-white update on the old apothecary lamp has strong, straight lines that also contrast with the heavenly effect.

HOW TO DO IT

Canopy: Measure the wall and ceiling area to be covered. (4½ yards were enough here). Hem ½" all around and then mark and sew hem casings for the poles at each end and for the one in the middle of the fabric (depending on the measurements). Drill holes in the ceiling and holes in both top and bottom of the pole ends (see drawing). To attach to a plasterboard ceiling, use Molly bolts. Screw in the bolt to expand the flanges. Unscrew, put bolt through pole and screw back in. For concrete ceilings, use a carbide-tipped drill and lead anchors.

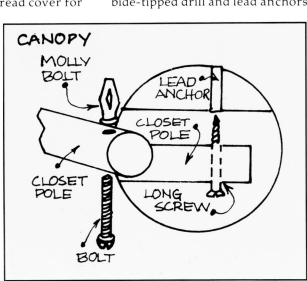

CANOPY
MOLLY BOLT
LEAD ANCHOR
CLOSET POLE
CLOSET POLE
LONG SCREW
BOLT

Photo: Bradley Olman

Low-Slung Sleepers

This bedroom doesn't seem to have been designed so much as art directed—a typically small and predictable bedroom transformed into a working beauty—not through expensive fabrics and furniture—but through a few new ways of turning boring into bold.

The first thing to go was the old metal frame mattress/box spring combination. In its place is a frame built from three painted hollow-core closet doors (and a 1 x 4 crosspiece on the headboard side that doesn't show). Instead of a headboard, the wall is painted the same color as the box—a space saver that lets the dramatically bold black flow right up the wall. (It also nicely frames the Jim Dine poster.) The bedspread is really well-priced prequilted fabric used for ski jackets. The fabric was stitched at the quilting lines, making the seams invisible. Like the bedspread, the room is tucked in, wrapped up —neat and uncluttered.

Inexpensive plastic cubes, secured with Molly bolts, float on the wall, providing bedside storage that doesn't waste floor space. A wooden cube holds not a piece of sculpture but a cactus, showing it off in the best possible light.

A bright red plastic chair highlights the black, as does the cupid poster, which receives an extra large frame to give it breathing space.

HOW TO DO IT
Bed Box: Build the frame from three 15"-wide hollow-core doors and a 1 x 4 crosspiece. Paint with semigloss enamel; set mattress inside on the floor.

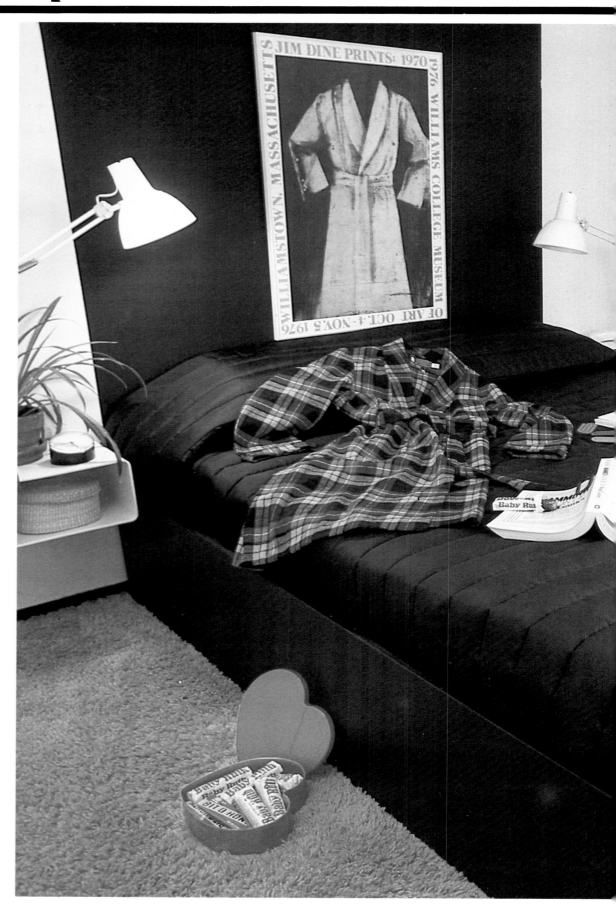

Walls: Painted wall becomes headboard

Walls: Paint one wall a bright color and paint on a supergraphic

Below: Streamline a bedroom by sculpting the space to fit your needs. Instead of jamming the furnishings against the wall, let it free-float in the middle.

This bed—set on a wooden frame—sits in the center of the room. Teamed up with a headboard/desk, it becomes a functional island. Make the desk quickly from two plastic file cabinets with a butcher-block board stretched across the top.

One brightly colored wall becomes the frame for a do-it-yourself supergraphic. Stretch presized canvas on canvas stretchers or buy it already stretched at art supply stores. Mark off a geometric design of your liking with tape, paint in between the tape with acrylics (two coats) and let it dry well before removing the tape.

Cocoon

Scaled-down furnishings do not necessarily make a smallish room seem any bigger. If you take the opposite tack, like the one spectacular bed here, the small room will open up to accommodate the design, particularly if that piece is as dramatic as this contemporary four-poster bed. After setting the stage with one eye-catcher, think carefully about the room's graphic design.

This bedroom works with squares. To balance the strong-lined, stately bed, a few smaller engineered pieces fill in the square.

Start with a desk—cleverly put together from a hanging shelf with a stack of roll-out plastic drawers tucked below. It is a smart way to stretch space while getting around an awkwardly placed heating unit. A mirror visually widens a narrow space while the frame echoes the four-poster lines. Nearby, the hanging globe fixture and gooseneck pharmacist's lamp provide curves for contrast, and pick up the shape of the horn poster.

HOW TO DO IT

Hanging Desk: Have a lumberyard cut a ¾" piece of plywood 18" x 36". Cover exposed edge with ¾" molding tape and paint. Screw two L brackets to the wall 28" up from the floor. Screw hooks or eyebolts to the outer corners of the desk and to the ceiling. Screw desk to wall brackets and run wires from ceiling bolts to desk. To secure, wrap wire around bolt.

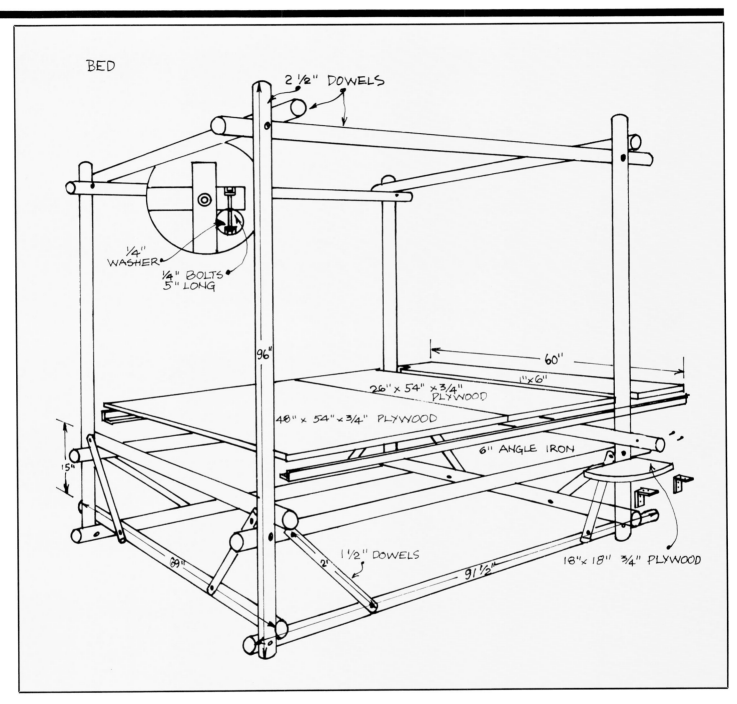

BED

2 1/2" DOWELS

1/4" WASHER

1/4" BOLTS 5" LONG

96"

60"

26" x 54" x 3/4" PLYWOOD

48" x 54" x 3/4" PLYWOOD

1" x 6"

6" ANGLE IRON

15"

1 1/2" DOWELS

69"

2'

91 1/2"

18" x 18" 3/4" PLYWOOD

HOW TO DO IT

Four-Poster Bed: Built from sturdy 2½"-diameter pine dowels, this grid-system bed is really three horizontal frames held together by four uprights. The bottom two frames are braced by short dowels. When bolting it together, it will help to have a friend around to hold the uprights steady.

To make it easier, have the lumberyard cut all dowels to length (see measurements in drawing). Use 5" stove bolts (¼" in diameter) to bolt together each of the three rectangular frames and to attach them to the uprights. Drill holes as shown and countersink the bolts. (Be sure to line up the holes carefully.)

Secure the short dowels (1½" diameter) with 4" stove bolts (¼" in diameter). Screw in 6' sections of angle iron for sup-port on the long sides of the bed. The bed board is made of two pieces of plywood, one cut to 26" x 54", the other to 48" x 54". The foundation dowels at the side of the bed will extend several inches past the head. To fill this space (and keep pillows from slipping), build a shelf from a 60" 1 x 6 board. Cut it to fit around the dowels and lay flat. For the canopy, hem and wrap mosquito netting.

The Bedroom Garden

Weed out any seeds of doubt you may have about indoor farming. You can make any room a garden with little work, little expense and a little bit of time—and the result will be full blooming. Here's how:

Put down layers of heavy-duty sheet plastic, ½" thick, cut-to-fit plywood. Next, add a layer of self-stick tile for the greenroom's floor, and a brick "lip" around the edges. Empty cans—full of color and design impact—make inexpensive pots, hanging planters and plant stands. Stacked up concrete blocks support the plywood shelves—no nailing necessary. Use metal trays from restaurant supply stores for sleek plant saucers.

A ladder—hung horizontally from the ceiling—becomes a trellis. Use four toggle-type ceiling hooks to hang it up. Drill ceiling holes with a ½" spade bit in an electric drill. Make screw hook holes in the ladder with a ⅛" bit. Hang the ladder with thick chains, bought from a hardware store.

Plant patterns repeat throughout the room. Both the print on the wall and the quilt on the bed reflect the bloom of the room.

Shades of Night

A bed can become an environment with a trio of winged screens that prop open by day, slip down at night. Contemporary terra-cotta blocks make the old brick-and-board shelf trick work for bedside service. These are actually foundation tiles and pine 1 x 2s. Of course, this no-nail unit can be changed to fit any space. Besides the stereo system and hard-wearing movers' pads used as rugs, there are other unexpected bedroom furnishings. To the right of the bed is a small white refrigerator for bedtime snacks and drinks. Behind the bed, a mirror frame—repainted—is taken from an old dresser.

HOW TO DO IT

Bed: Put together this winged wonder from the bottom up. All the dimensions are for a queen-sized mattress but you can adapt the plan to any mattress by changing the lengths of the 1 x 10s, closet poles and ¾" dowels accordingly. Follow the directions and dimensions shown in the illustration.

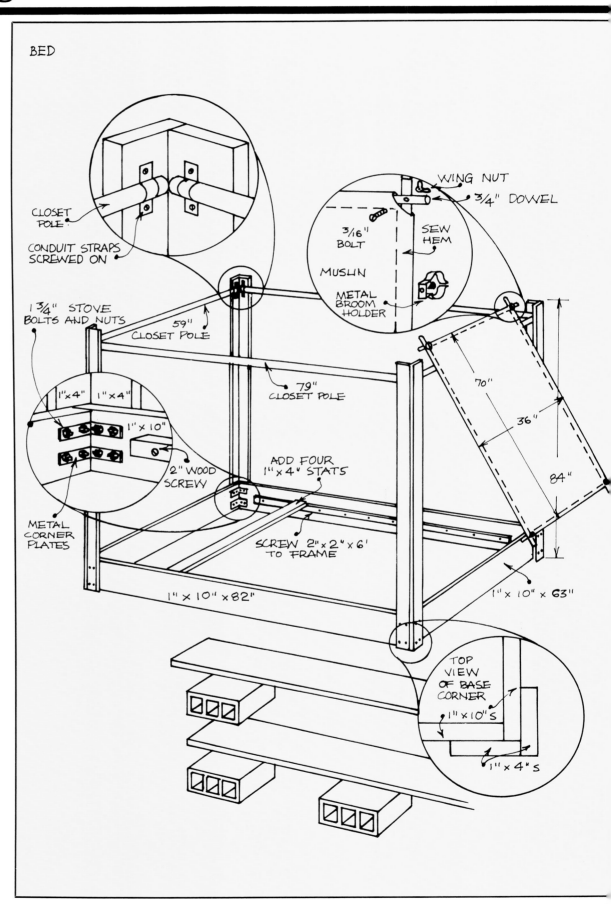

BED

CLOSET POLE

CONDUIT STRAPS SCREWED ON

1 ¾" STOVE BOLTS AND NUTS

59" CLOSET POLE

1"x4" 1"x4"

1"x 10"

2" WOOD SCREW

METAL CORNER PLATES

WING NUT

¾" DOWEL

3/16" BOLT

SEW HEM

MUSLIN

METAL BROOM HOLDER

79" CLOSET POLE

ADD FOUR 1"x4" STATS

SCREW 2"x2"x6' TO FRAME

70"

36"

84"

1"x 10" x 63"

1"x 10"x 82"

TOP VIEW OF BASE CORNER

1"x 10"S

1"x4"S

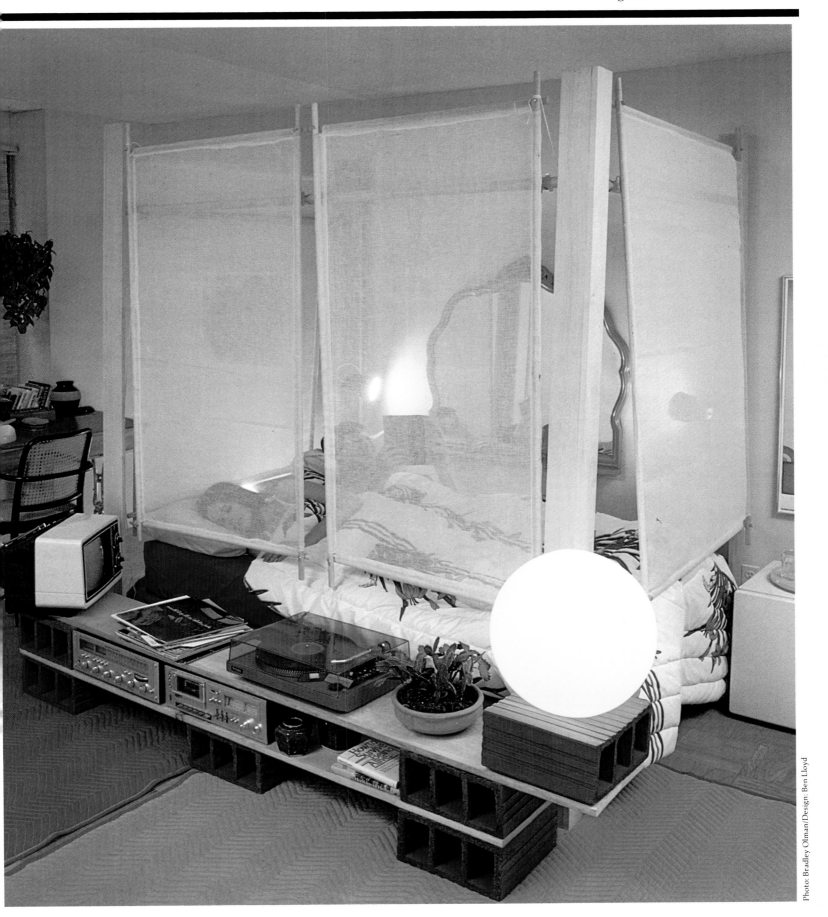

Photo: Bradley Olman/Design: Ben Lloyd

Oldies but Goodies

Style is where you discover it; especially in everyday items waiting to be used in new ways.

It is hard to believe that something right under your nose—the handkerchief—could look so stunning, but look again. This hanky quilt— stitched together from dozens of secondhand printed kerchiefs —splashes on a whole style from disparate parts. The crazy-quilt quality here (all over the room, not just on the bed) has transformed an average space into an intriguing place with warmth and coziness throughout.

HOW TO DO IT
Hanky Quilt:

You Will Need: Hankies (about 54 for a double-bed quilt, finished size 80" x 88"). If you can not find inexpensive old ones at the thrift store, try new brightly patterned dime-store handkerchiefs, washed several times.

A sheet to sew the hankies to and a plain backing sheet (or collect twice as many hankies and make it reversible).

Polyester fiberfill quilt batting (comes in sheet-size dimensions). Use up to nine layers for serviceable warmth.

How to Make It: Lay the hankies on one sheet in any pattern you like and stitch them down by hand or machine. Sew the hanky sheet to the backing sheet, right sides together, around three sides, about ¾" from the edge. Pile the layers of batting on top of your big wrong-side-out case and loosely hand stitch batting to the three seam allowances and along the top edge of the open side. (Do not sew the hanky sheet and the backing sheet closed yet). Turn the quilt right side out and hand sew the opening shut.

Calm and Collected

other myth buried: Antiques not always come in clutters. this invitingly open space the mptation to add just one more ce was resisted. All the vinge pieces are showcased in s setting, yet the result, far om looking museumlike or touchable, is comfortably rm and livable.

Turn-of-the-century brass ds (actually a brass sleeve ound a steel core), once a ggering $11 in the Sears :alog, are now hard to score rgains on. Prices go up with ery twist and turn of detailg in knobs and etched rings the spindles, curves, fourters—the fatter the better. The oak-framed, beveledge mirror is a contemporary the bed and was originally e top of an old dresser. Milk ass chandeliers (easy to rere) lit schoolrooms for deces; find the best prices at ecking and salvage compaes.

Old quilts are also getting icy. Look for good condition, lor, design and intricacy in e pieces and quilting.

The floor is left bare, in keepg with the spare plan.

There is no need to keep tiques segregated into peris. The accessories, like the dside lamp and clock, are thirs and forties specials, found secondhand shops.

Kid Space

Rooms for children once meant endless little duckies and decals; cute was the order of the day. Somewhere between toilet training and puberty, the room went through at least three changes of scenery for the growing-up kid and three times the work and expense for the parent.

No more. There are alternatives today—thanks to new and available products and materials and a changing attitude about children's needs. Now it makes sense for a kid's room to grow up along with the kid.

This room, for example, is designed for the way children really live—not the way we would like them to live. They are messy, and they like playing around. And thus a room with furniture that works the way today's kids play. Here's why:

Kids need room for activities and space for imagination. That is why the bed is elevated and the bed/dresser/desk unit is compact so there is a lot of floor space in the center.

Remember that old apple tree for climbing and building tree houses? Here the bedposts and ladder are an urban tree; the bed, an indoor tree house.

Kids are tough on furniture and so this tube furniture is right for rough-housing, with no sharp edges.

Kids do grow up. Furniture manufacturers keep forgetting that. When the child is too old for the tree house, the top half of the bed comes off to be regular adult height; the chair adjusts for longer legs too.

Open storage is important for children's toys. Another open storage idea shown below: bright, easy-to-make canvas bags grouped on the wall.

Protection is needed for those many kid projects. Roll vinyl onto the floor and everything goes when anything spills.

Photo: Bradley Olman/Design: Jim and Penny Hull

Make Room for Baby

They didn't know it but when they created L-shaped rooms they were solving the room-for-baby problem too. The secret is a sliding door on a closet track that opens and closes on Babydom and makes sure nighttime doesn't become a nightmare.

You will need:

A metal overhead door track (called bypass door hardware in store lingo) with rollers that will fit the track and connect to the top of the door.

A plastic guide for the floor.

Two doors: build a 1 x 2 frame and nail on prefinished sheet paneling or Gatorfoam, or staple on stretched fabric. Grade AA ¾" plywood can also be used.

And more: Leave the baby's floor bare so there is a smooth path for riding toys.

For curtains: Forget pinch pleating and simply sew a piece of hemmed fabric to rings on a curtain rod. Then when the curtains come down, you can recycle the fabric.

For crib sheets or a crib cover: Sew elastic around a piece of fabric, shower-cap style. To figure the fabric size, measure the dimensions of the mattress and add 3" all around so it will tuck under.

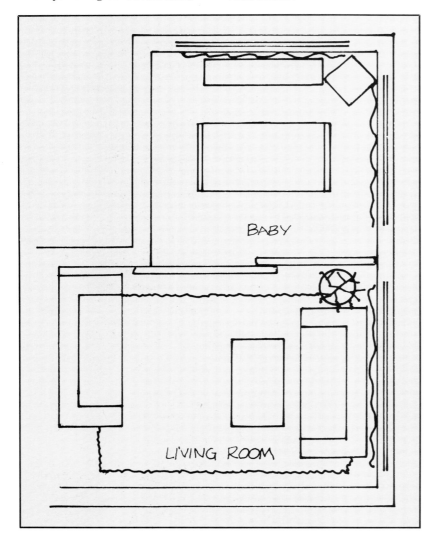

The Room That Grows Up

Babies. The very word conjures decisions, risks, adjustments and anxieties. The least worry should be where to put the crib.

If you overhaul a room every time a kid shoots up a few inches, you will be in the garage sale business full time. Instead, set up a space that is flexible enough to grow with your child. The key: Furniture that doesn't have its purpose stamped on it like so many pink and blue clowns. Make room for a baby with a nursery that will transform.

A baby doesn't need an entire room so the nursery can share space with your office and/or guest bedroom:

Freestanding open shelving (painted metal shelves against the right wall) separate the of-fice from the nursery. One side is for baby, the other for you. Brightly colored plastic storage bins organize where neatness counts.

Flexible, plastic drawers stack up four times with hollow-core doors on each top to make two table areas: One makes a chang-ing table; the other a desk.

Painted insulation board makes an inexpensive bulletin board.

The sofa sits by day, flips into a double bed for a guest by night.

Stacked, rolling storage bins wheel around to be truly useful.

Pick a not-too-babyish fabric for curtains so they can hang around for a while.

A dhurrie rug muffles noise, adds color, washes well.

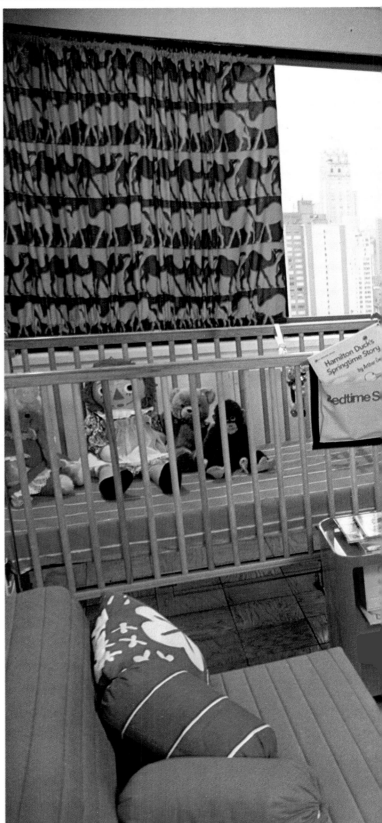

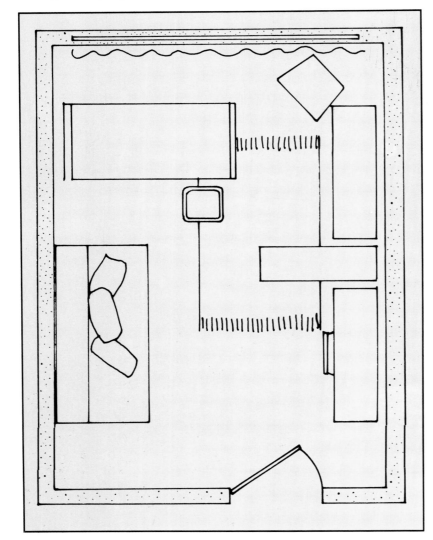

...Six Years Later

And now, the nursery/office/ guest room has grown up. Here is how to pull off the transformation: Move out the crib and replace it with a double-decker bed, claim the rocker for your own and then start moving things around:

The shelving unit moves against the wall to leave more room for play. The colored plastic bins are as workable as ever for stowing toys.

The hollow-core doors and stacking drawer units turn the tables to become a huge, low-level play surface with plenty of space for clothes. Take the hol-low-core doors from the desk and changing table and place them side by side over a shorter stack of drawers (three deep this time—use the extra units in other rooms).

The daybed/sofa still has room for sleep-over guests.

The bulletin board takes its place a little lower, within kid-reach.

The roll-around storage bins —plus pillows—slide into a new role as kid-sized seats.

The dhurrie rug and curtains keep up the handsome work.

A blackboard easel encour-ages the budding artist.

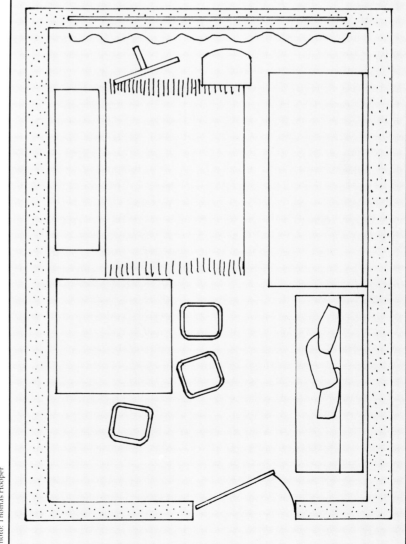

JILL CLAYBURGH: The Back Room Retreat

Old-style movie stars might devote endless rooms and dollars to furnishing their self-esteem. Not Jill Clayburgh. She is too busy. Which is exactly why she wanted to turn her tiny, onetime maid's room-turned-catchall (below) into an efficient work space. And so it did get the movie-star treatment when she cried "Help! I need a place that is all my own—a womb. But what can you do with this?"

The answer is at right: a warm, restful hideaway. First, the peeling plaster and dark corners were camouflaged with a pale, provincial print fabric stapled to the wall.

Plush wall-to-wall carpeting, romantic lighting (such as the Victorian reading lamp over the settee), neutral wood shutters at the window and warm beige paint on the woodwork and ceiling softened the room's hard edges.

Replacing the old bathroom door with natural wood shutters made a match for the window and solved another problem: the opened, bifold door does not block the room.

The nineteenth-century polished iron Directoire bed (taking its graceful curves from the Napoleonic era) supports an overabundance of small patterned pillows.

This cozy office/retreat/guest room has plenty of space-conscious ideas that you do not have to be a movie star to love. And now Jill Clayburgh is: An Unharried Woman.

BATHROOMS

Pity the poor bathroom. From the top of its porcelain to the bottom of its tiles, the bathroom has been most neglected. Not because we do not use it. But exactly because we do. We use it and do not look at it. Frankly, the bathroom is a hard room to love.

But the apartment bath has come out of its water closet. As one of our major spaces it cannot afford to be forgotten.

On the following pages you will see some examples of sink Cinderella stories, ugly duckling tubs that became swank swans—and not just by adding a Jacuzzi or gold-leaf faucets. The key is to personalize your bathroom. If it is modern and you prefer old, take a trip to the salvage center and, for a few dollars, pick up some old fixtures and have them put in. Installation does not have to cost a lot if your plumbing will adapt. Or if you like sleek and contemporary, and think you are stuck with a rotten relic, mirrors and glossy paint can help make the transformation possible. Put paintings and pictures on the wall and make a gallery. Unusual solutions for the boring bathroom come your way via some surprising sources: industrial supply stores, ceiling suppliers, fabric and antique shops, kitchen departments, lumberyards. Even your own living room. Who says you can not transplant that favorite golden oak chest or chrome and glass table

Also, consider your bathroom's use for much more than mere hygiene. What about storage, dressing, grooming, personal care? Think about all the new products we have to-

that did not exist a decade
: hair dryers, electric tooth
aners, curling irons, hair
wers, moisture wands, elec-
facials, bathtub Jacuzzis,
wer massages—all the in-
use tools of personal care.
All that means that we need
hooks to put them on, new
ces to store all these things.
ally, bathroom storage is no
ger one of the great myster-
of the apartment world. We
hang all our bath wares up,
n or sideways on hooks and
lves and brackets, or hide
m in ingenious storage units.

And do not forget the obvious in bath decor: right in the
bathroom departments of many
stores and specialty shops. Bath
technology has gone far beyond
color coordinated plastic soap
dishes and toothbrush holders.
Now even our sprays and soaps
come in distinctive packaging.
Towels and shower curtains no
longer look like they were
stolen from the Holiday Inn
(even if they were); they are
now designed by the same people who clothe bodies.
Use your own ingenuity to
get exactly what you want

without calling in a demolition
crew. It is not easy to disguise a
toilet bowl; you cannot put slipcovers on a bathtub. But you
can, for example, encase a sink
in wood. You can take advan-
tage of the room's high humidity and, with a few grow lights,
make a greenhouse.
Bathrooms—the most private
public place in the apartment—
can be more than engineered
closets, more than segregated
stations for our comfort. A
bathroom should do more than
run hot and cold.

Old-Time Comfort Station

Somewhere along the line this bathroom had been modernized —made to look contemporary, despite the older fixtures, which have workable charm, and despite the older architectural details such as the wainscoting and medicine cabinet. This place needed "downdating" not updating. You can also install this more-or-less thirties look if you are renovating— good, old sinks, toilets and tubs can be found at salvage yards or demolition sites.

The rest of the room "downdates" just as easily: older wide, wooden Venetian blinds from the twenties, and a new vinyl floor replaces the usual green tile.

The other surprise here is what is on the wall—old framed prints, family photographs, sheet music, magazine advertisements, lighthearted letters. The marble shelf in their midst is right at home. The old shaving mirror was rescued from a secondhand shop. Under the sink is an old wooden footlocker that handles the overflow of towels and toiletries.

All the accessories—the wooden toilet seat, the porcelain faucet handles as well as the soap dish and towel racks— abound at flea markets and thrift shops.

and-Aids

e worst fault of this white-
bathroom was its predict-
ility—the fixtures, medicine
st, lights, flooring and walls
re carbon copies of every
er high-rise bathroom.
ere was some under sink
rage but not enough.
he idea was to warm it up
ckly, to personalize it with a
k and bright look. Now
rything has that built-in
lity, yet you can take it right
ng when you move.
he specifics:
ome things seem very per-
nent until you tinker around
h a screwdriver. You can
ally take down a medicine
st (check for screws inside at
back), then replace it with a
inet of your own choosing.
t is not screwed into studs,
u will need to use Molly bolts
out yours up.) This antique
dicine chest brings the
rmth of wood into an other-
e very clinical room.
nexpensive, industrial
oseneck lamps, or most any
ting replacement, can be
oked right into the same wir-
as the old one.
You can disguise ugly ceramic
s with a coat of epoxy paint
over the tiles in the shower)
 crisp, self-adhesive vinyl
ll covering.
 variety of modular, on-the-
ll storage units stretches the
arly nonexistent counter
ce. This green plastic system
 right into the mounting of
 old holders and can be taken
 for easy cleaning.
Blot out a floor you do not
 with rubber-backed wall-
wall bathroom carpet. Cut it
fit and lay it on top of the
sting flooring.

Photo: Bradley Olman

Hot and Cold Renovation

This room—pre-revival—is typical of the bathrooms you are confronted with in older houses. Barely the bare essentials. Outdated—but still working—fixtures. No storage. Shabby and uncomfortable.

Now look at it. Built-in natural wood cabinets and walls restored to a beauty it never knew before.

Here is how it happened.

The wainscoting and flooring are made with tongue-and-groove fir strips. (Nail one strip into place; the next strip slips into the first, and so on. Four coats of polyurethane seal the wood for even the most humid household.)

Sink pipes are boxed in by paneling. The front swings down, like a bin, for extra storage. Enclosing the tub adds a custom, built-in look.

Vinyl fabric goes on the wall —and stays there—with vinyl fabric paste.

A D-ring shower curtain rod gives you privacy-in-the-round where none existed before.

The window opens onto an airshaft. Opaque Plexiglas keeps the view of you rated G. The window opens down for air.

HOW TO DO IT

Sink Enclosure: For the basic frame you will make a 2 x 2 frame enclosing three sides of the sink. Fasten this frame to the wall with nails (into studs) or with toggle bolts.

The sides of the box are like the tub's sides, alternating 1 x 2s and 1 x 6s spaced apart.

To figure the size of the frame: A 2 x 2 should run across the front of the sink and be lined up flush with the sink corners. Then butt the side pieces against the front 2 x 2 and run them back to the wall. Figure the height of the frame from the floor to just under the lip of the sink. (Caulk between the underside of the sink and the top of the boards.)

To make the drop-down, bin-like door: The top and the bottom boards on the front of the sink are stationary so fasten them as you did the side boards. To have something to attach the catch to, put a horizontal 2 x 2 inside the front. Then build a 1 x 2 frame for the door (as shown) that will fit into the opening, leaving ½" clearance on each side. Use a magnetic catch as shown to close the door. Use butt hinges and add a chain so it will not drop open all the way to the floor.

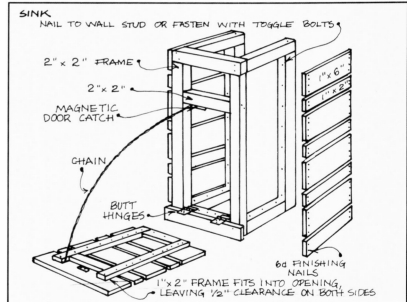

HOW TO DO IT

Bathtub Enclosure: Though complicated looking, if you reduce the box to its simplest elements, it is not so tough. The tub is surrounded by a frame of 2 x 2s on which boards are nailed to give it a finished, saunalike look.

First, you will need 2 x 2 pieces of lumber (fir was used here) the length of the tub, plus a foot or so. Cut the upright 2 x 2s to a height ¾" short of the lip of the tub. (The width, like the length, is up to you.) Then put the frame together with 8d finishing nails.

Nail 2 x 2s inside the top of the frame and just under the lip at each end of the tub. Cover the top with ¾ tongue-and-groove floorboards. Caulk between the lip of the tub and the boards.

For an interesting pattern on the sides: Use the tongue-and-groove boards again. Or alternate 1 x 2s and 1 x 6s, leaving a small space between each one to match the sink enclosure. Or simply nail 1 x 2s, 1 x 4s, 1 x 6s or 1 x 8s onto the frame (no spaces).

Urban Renewal

Under the influence of sleek industrial design, this small, square bathroom triples as a utility room and storage space as well.

Bring the turn-of-the-century look of ceiling tin (it is called sheet steel these days)—down to eye level on the walls—a one-step tile effect without fuss. Three or four careful coats of polyurethane on both sides (before you handle it too much) are essential to keep the metal from rusting. Cut the tin to fit with metal cutting shears; then glue it up with panel adhesive.

Corner the space for storage: Triangular shelves are held up with wooden cleats. Plastic storage baskets stack underneath.

The tub is closed off with a simply constructed divider.

Opposite: You can fit everything into this bathroom, including the kitchen sink—literally. Why cope with a shallow bathroom model when eminently more functional sinks are available? Housed in this easily built, high-gloss white box (and supported by it), the kitchen sink looks right at home.

Over the sink: Lights that really work (you probably last saw them in a basement).

Below the sink: The chrome heater hangs on the wall to maximize floor space.

To the right, this wall-hung ironing board is designed for what you want from it most of the time—folded down out of the way. Take the legs off a small ironing board and hinge it to a 1 x 4 mounted on the wall (use toggle bolts or wood screws into a stud). Support the ironing board with a couple of flap-table hinges.

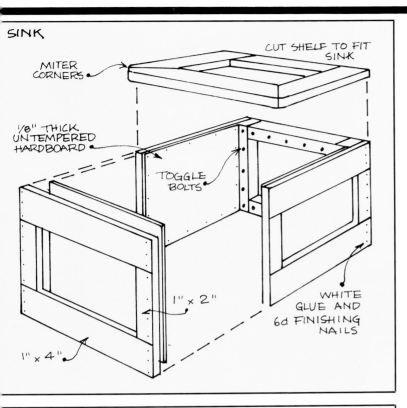

SINK

MITER CORNERS

CUT SHELF TO FIT SINK

⅛" THICK UNTEMPERED HARDBOARD

TOGGLE BOLTS

1" x 2"

WHITE GLUE AND 6d FINISHING NAILS

1" x 4"

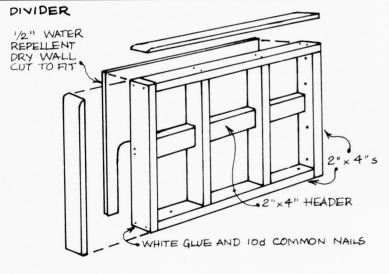

DIVIDER

½" WATER REPELLENT DRY WALL CUT TO FIT

2" x 4"s

2" x 4" HEADER

WHITE GLUE AND 10d COMMON NAILS

HOW TO DO IT

Divider: To build the divider, first make a simple mini-wall— a frame of 2 x 4s with upright 2 x 4s inside. Add 2 x 4 headers in between the uprights. (Align the headers with the lip of the tub.)

Cut a piece of ½"-thick water-repellent dry wall to extend just above the edge of the tub lip. Nail it onto the headers. Nail dry wall on the other side.

Then put this wall at the end of the tub and secure it to both the floor and the wall. Use toggle bolts for the wall and 10d common nails for all but concrete floors. For concrete, drill ½" holes with a carbide bit, fill the holes with wooden pegs, then nail the mini-wall into the plugs.

To finish, nail a board across the open end and top of the wall. Use epoxy paint.

HOW TO DO IT

Sink Enclosure: To build the front and two sides: Each is a frame, consisting of 1 x 2s on the sides and 1 x 4s across the top and bottom. For the back: You will need extra support for the weight of the sink so build a frame of 2 x 2s. Glue and nail the four frames together, using white glue and 6d nails. Then cut the pieces of hardboard to fit the openings inside the front and side frames and attach them with ¾" #16 brads.

Next mount the box on the wall with toggle bolts (or wood screws if you can find studs to screw into). Concentrate the toggles at the top of the frame so they will help support the sink's weight.

Make a shelf frame for the lip of the sink to sit on. (The size depends on how much shelf you want.) If you want rounded corners, cut with a jigsaw, then sand smooth. Fasten the shelf to the box with white glue and finishing nails. Fill the nail holes with wood filler.

Use epoxy paint for water resistance, then drop in the sink and caulk around it.

Short Takes

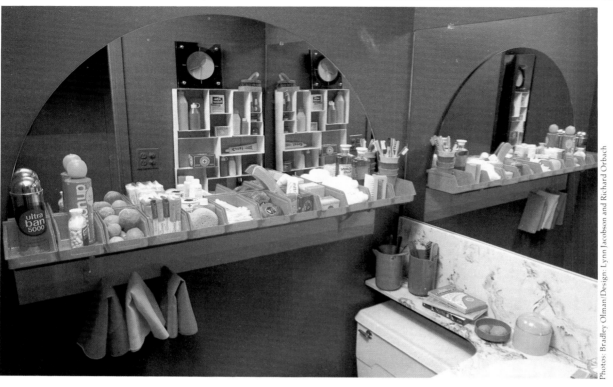

Photos: Bradley Olman/Design: Lynn Jacobson and Richard Orbach

Top Left: This bright bathroom storage solution brings those back-of-the-cabinet items out into the open so you can find them. Individual plastic bins set on a glass shelf keep everything handy. The stripe design under the shelf can be applied with paint but vinyl paper or fabric tape is easier. Dish towel racks, meant for the kitchen, work in the bathroom as well.

Below Left: Even the most ordinary bathroom can have flair along with function. The regulation medicine cabinet was removed here and replaced with a wall-length mirror and a homemade shelf unit. Plus a new ceiling—actually a fake. It is simply a single plywood board, hung on chains, anchored with ceiling hooks and covered with either self-adhesive mirror square tiles or stainless steel tiles.

Left: Put an end to gloomy bathroom lighting and give yourself an attractive display shelf at the same time. Build the shelf from two lengths of 2 x 10s, one for the actual shelf, the other for the vertical back. Cut the vertical back 1½" shorter than the horizontal piece. Nail them together and then nail a short board ¾" thick on each end. Screw a 4' fluorescent fixture to the back of the vertical 2 x 10 and wire it up. Add a line switch for turning the light on and off. Paint the shelf with gloss enamel, stain it or leave it natural. Next lift the whole thing into place and screw it into the wall through the two end boards.

Reflected in the mirror: A long ladder from floor to ceiling in front of the window doubles as combination towel rack/curtains.

Left: When you are stuck with a set of ungracefully aging bathroom fixtures, it pays to do a little homework:

Slick up a chipped basin and tub with epoxy paint. Then add racing stripes with plastic tape.

The mirror is the better half of an old golden oak dresser. Simply unscrew from the bureau base. (Many mirrors are also sold separately.) Drill holes through the frame into the wall and secure with Molly bolts or expansion anchors.

Below: Most bathrooms suffer from high overhead—storage space is needed but no one ever thinks to look up. Here you can see what a few sticks of wood can do for the plain white-box bathroom. Use all 1 x 2s for the ceiling grid. Use narrow boards for the shelves. If you glue and screw the wood pieces together and use some ingenuity about wedging it all in, you can get by with very few holes in the walls, easily patched when you move.

ONE-ROOM LIVING

Living in one room used to mean a way—and fact—of life for students and those who could not afford more. These days many people are living in one room because they want to, not because they have to. Some people who move into small two or three room apartments now take down the walls and make the place work like one large room.

But even in one small room, an efficiency had better be efficient. Because your living room is also your bedroom . . . is also your dining room, guest room and work space. More than any other kind of apartment, one-room living really must work.

New products coupled with new ways of thinking about our space have changed one-room living from the static, monastic image it used to have.

Start by exorcising old furnishing phantoms. The ghosts of parents' home furnishings are as outdated as the plastic slipcovers that encased them. A new rule reigns: Make sure that every piece of furniture does at least two things. A sofa can now become a bed; with wider choices for size and comfort, sofa/sleepers work well every night. Murphy beds—once the laughingstock of 1940s movie —can be updated with colorfu screens and utilitarian closets hide inside. And the standard bed—once unthinkable in suc a limited space—becomes a massive sofa when piled with pillows and pillows and pillow Loft beds—sky-high sleeping– make extra space where you never thought to look for it. There is even a revolving book case on the market with a bed that drops out of the back.

Furniture manufacturers have begun designing clever pieces for small places that ful

that magic word: multifunc-
ion. A table is a desk, an end
ble is a dining table, a bar is a
chen counter, and chairs
ake fast entrances and exits if
ey fold up. One manufacturer
akes an end table that quickly
rns into a dining table
th chairs that store and stack
atly inside.
These are just some of the
ms on the market that prove
at both the furnishings in-
stry and designers have
gun taking the plight of the
e-room dweller seriously.
nally. But that is not enough.
Ultimately the responsibility

falls on you, the tenant, to
influence your space enough to
make attractive utilitarianism
the main attraction. You have
to create the distinct areas in
which you will eat, sleep, relax,
work. That doesn't mean these
areas cannot overlap—lighting,
rugs, colors, fabrics and screens
all help to create "rooms" out of
space.

And storage. That is the biggest problem in any size apartment. But thanks to a new
aesthetic, the tools of our life—
the pots and pans as well as the
pens and papers—can hang out
anywhere. Full view is the new

view. Nothing needs to be dis-
guised anymore. You will see in
this chapter (and in a special
section all about storage) that
there are ways to get whatever
you want wherever you want.
It means bending and stretch-
ing and mending some old
ways. It means being alert
about the new products and
projects that can step up a
room's efficiency. It means
thinking about your life's functions in terms of space and not
rooms. But now—thanks to
technology and a change in our
consciousness—a one-room
apartment can work like four.

The Engineered Apartment

This room is organized into activity areas—bed/sofa, the alley office, and the round butcher block dining table—and each area sprawls into the other when necessary. This apartment is carefully engineered.

Behind the black folding doors (below) is a closet converted to a work area, complete with storage bins, desk, pegboard space and work light.

The white shelving system (right) is a working wall divider. One side is a stereo component/record storage shelf; the other side is a headboard with bedtime reading lamps. The divider sets up another office area as seen on the following pages.

The big round table becomes even larger with a couple of leaves but it is also a worktable suitable for craft projects, paper work and food preparation too. The oversized black coffee table is an easily built plywood box covered with vinyl tile; inside are shelves and drawers for storage.

The simple hanging lamp is easy to connect: Run wire from an outlet up to the ceiling, drop it down through a screw-eye that's fastened into the ceiling. Run the wire through a brass-plated curtain rod so it will not sway.

Photos: Bradley Olman/Design: Philip Tusa Design, Inc.

This sofa is actually a "floating" bed (supported by short, hidden legs) that doubles as a sofa. The office area is the other side of the wall of shelves. A file cabinet and desk-top, flexible reading/working lamp and storage shelves are ready to work. Corkboard covers walls.

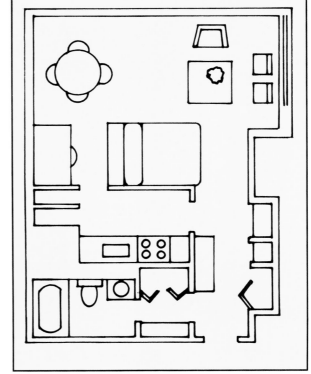

The simple hanging lamp is easy to connect: Run wire from outlet across ceiling, drop down through a screw-eye fastener into the ceiling. Run the wire through brass-plated curtain rod so it will not sway in the breeze.

HOW TO DO IT

Coffee Table: This mysterious black box is both a coffee table and a sophisticated storage system. Build it from plywood (see illustration) with a flip-out front door. Nail wood strips inside for loose shelves that slide out. Cover with self-adhesive floor tile.

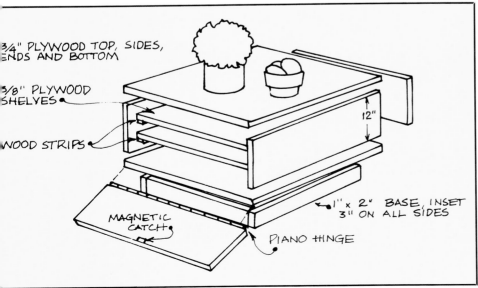

3/4" PLYWOOD TOP, SIDES, ENDS AND BOTTOM

3/8" PLYWOOD SHELVES

WOOD STRIPS

12"

MAGNETIC CATCH

1" x 2" BASE, INSET 3" ON ALL SIDES

PIANO HINGE

Spaceworks

This is one room that works like five: living room, office, dining room, bedroom and guest room. A look around this room will prove that ease and high function are not limited by space. Everything is as convertible as it is comfortable.

The classic canvas director's chairs operate in the conversation area but are also light enough (without seeming lightweight) to be picked up and placed around either (or both) of the two Parsons tables.

The blue Formica table at left is a desk by day. At dusk it converts into a dining table or buffet by simply clearing everything off into waiting wicker baskets and pulling up the chairs. The Parsons table next to the sofa, when relieved of its end-table duties, serves dinner tête-a-tête.

The industrial shelving (sprayed blue) does more than hold books. Just as importantly, it serves as a room divider between the living and sleeping areas. On the other side is a Murphy bed wall (not shown), updated. Nowadays they don't fall down unannounced. The Murphy is housed behind simple white bifold doors so it looks like an innocuous closet when hibernating. Best of all, it takes up no floor space. The wicker sofa can sleep a guest.

Other ideas restate some important concepts about one-room living:

To keep floors clear for footsteps, plants are hung up.

Room dividers are not necessarily vertical. This fuzzy rug defines space between work and seating areas.

Curtains and draperies? Not here. Leave windows bare (even if the view is not the greatest) to make the room seem larger. For privacy, venetian blinds slide down.

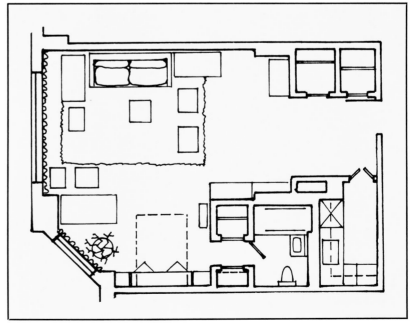

Left: In one-room living orga-
zation is the key word (hence:
ficiencies). This desk (which
so answers to the name of
ning table) is as functional as
s colorful. Laminated in
ight blue Formica, the table
ears well and looks swell. And
cept for the essentials
hone, typewriter, workbas-
ts), nearly everything is out
the way. Yet there is plenty
place for storage at hand.
anging from the wall near the
ndow, sitting atop glass
elves, are places for paper,
ns and other supplies. These
ys art and office supplies are
signed well enough to keep
t in the open if you buy with
eye for looks.

Above: Just because a table is
usually sitting next to a sofa
does not mean it is bolted down.
Move it out when you want to.
This one, for example, can do
well for dinner for one or two—
but liberated from the corner, it
can serve more formal functions. When wedded to its
brother across the room, it
makes a table transplant for
larger dinners.

An easel is in the corner—
and not just for those works in
progress. Here it is a freestanding frame for that favorite finished work.

Baseball bases, stacked and
stored under the Parsons table,
are ready to be pulled out for
shortstop seating.

Not Just Another Pretty Place

For all its high-gloss style, this one-room apartment in the thirties mode works strictly for the twenty-first century. Sleeping, dining and comfort are the true high points of this very efficient efficiency.

This studio apartment may look like a period piece—1920s or 1930s Art Deco—but in fact it is a *suggestion* of that design time. More a state of mind than a state of design, nothing in this room is actually authentic Deco. The mirrors, the geometric pattern on the floor, the shiny satin pillows, the molded plastic tables, the lighting—all recall the thirties but stop short of being a carbon copy.

Too often rooms end up formal and stodgy because some perfectionist has decided to be "true" to a period rather than to his own instincts. The point is not to get locked into exact imitations. Here are the details:

The elegantly quilted sofa becomes the bed for today, complete with built-in end tables.

Contemporary wicker chairs have the lines of our times with the texture of yesterday.

The high-styled coffee table is the rebirth of an idea born in the Deco era. The slick satin pillows can be pulled up for short-order dining.

Behind the sofa: desk and buffet service from one heavy-duty Parsons table.

One good, large painting deserves importance. Then you need no other.

At right, the Italian floor lamp is contemporary but its sharp, well-defined lines recall other eras. The exposed sound system in the corner and carefully selected accessories heighten the sense of machined detail.

Walls: Paint one wall a single striking color; a singular painting does the rest

Floor: Pattern in tile

Lighting: Sleek Italian Plexiglas

Photo: Bradley Olman

Not Just Another Pretty Place

This sleep sofa does more than aid your slumber. Like so many variations on themes evident in today's expanding furniture market, this sofa has adjustable arms that flop down—so it becomes an end table as well as a sleeper. The pillows become a comfortable backrest when the sofa is converted into a bed.

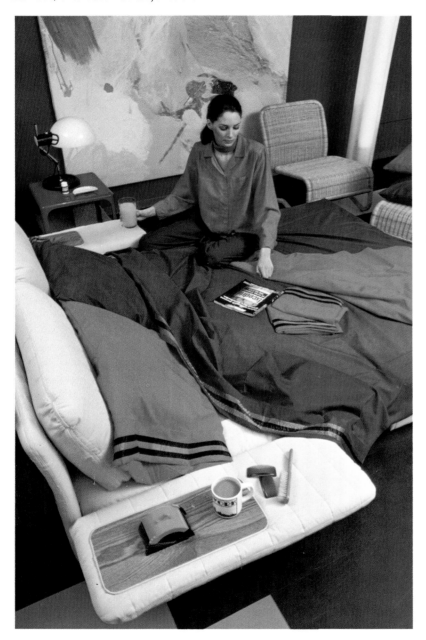

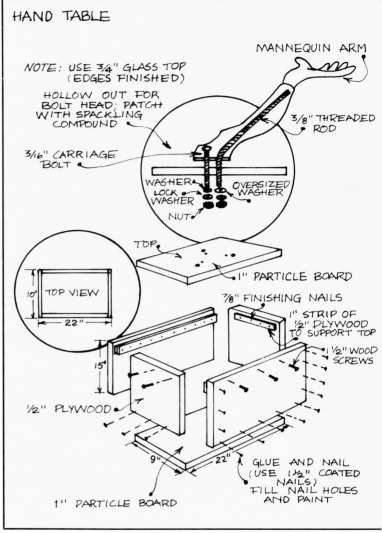

HAND TABLE

NOTE: USE 3/4" GLASS TOP (EDGES FINISHED)

HOLLOW OUT FOR BOLT HEAD; PATCH WITH SPACKLING COMPOUND

MANNEQUIN ARM

3/8" THREADED ROD

3/16" CARRIAGE BOLT

WASHER
LOCK WASHER
OVERSIZED WASHER
NUT

TOP

TOP VIEW
10"
22"

1" PARTICLE BOARD

7/8" FINISHING NAILS

1" STRIP OF 1/2" PLYWOOD TO SUPPORT TOP

1 1/2" WOOD SCREWS

15"

1/2" PLYWOOD

9"   22"

GLUE AND NAIL (USE 1 1/2" COATED NAILS) FILL NAIL HOLES AND PAINT

1" PARTICLE BOARD

This Daliesque sculptured table (at right) fills a corner as well as a need. The mannequin arms literally hold up the glass top, reaching out from a simple plywood box. (For details, see illustration above.) This setting proves that the functional need not lack wit. Clear glass keeps the corner feeling uncrowded as do the readily available chrome and Plexiglas chairs.

On the table, more Deco designs: new teapot, silverware and inexpensive tinware; an old vase and embroidered hand towels from the forties used here as napkins. The old leaded-glass doors are freshly painted and hinged together to form a screen. Apricot-colored acetate gel (from an art store) taped to the back of the glass warms the daylight. At night, a glowing spotlight sits on the floor behind the screen.

For more Deco dimension, one wall has been covered with mirrored tiles, palm trees cut from black self-adhesive paper. The tiles are also self-sticking and easy to install.

The floor shown on the previous page and reflected here the mirror at right is made from an original arrangement of colored tiles that can be adapted to your room. First, plan out your pattern on paper (as shown in the illustration above). Then arrange the tiles on the floor in the same design. The tiles used here are made glossy vinyl.

ALTERNATIVE SPACES

"The sweat ethic." It is what's needed to turn around an ungainly, unexpected space into a place you call home. It is taking old factory space and transforming it into a livable loft by lovingly carving an apartment out of it—a kitchen in that corner, a bedroom over there, the living and dining areas in the middle. In lofts and commercial spaces, once converted, there are no walls to fence you in. It is free-form living in which dictated spaces are out. You can even have a "backyard" in your living room if you want (and without rain). You can extend the kitchen as far as you want. You can build huge walk-in closets. And these alternative spaces are ways of assuring yourself built-in architectural detail: oversized windows, large open spaces, wood floors, high ceilings.

If you moved up to the top

or of an old house and cre-
d rooms out of what used to
an attic—that would be a
ret.

These alternatives are all part
he new urban frontier,
ere pavement pioneers
taking formerly useless
ce and making it livable.

The movement reflects a new commitment to the cities, a revival of the spirit of the settler days.

Lofts, garrets and commercial spaces have become the new big-city living locations that offer greater choices and opportunities for making your living

space to your own specifications. On the following pages we show you a number of spaces that have had their faces lifted. It takes much muscle, some money, as well as rethinking old ideas and supplanting them with new concepts about new spaces.

Lofts

It is hard to believe that the sleek and modern living space at right was carved out of the old building below.

Yet, inside this floor-through former factory—smack in the center of an urban industrial area—is a very uptown-looking place.

More and more people are sculpting their own space within the caverns of old buildings. And with space that is impressive to start with, you can get away with less in furnishings.

The vast open space and high ceilings are reemphasized by low-scale, contemporary pieces. The light palette helps the feeling of space.

Foregoing draperies or curtains is part of the emphasis. A flood of white and natural light helps the room stay spacious and spare.

Use very few pieces—low, modular seating units and a rolling coffee table are comfortably flexible.

Track lighting and built-in spots throw illumination where you want it, while keeping the surfaces clear of lamps.

Careful use of plants softens starkness.

Dark wood floors, especially with light furnishings, look rich enough to get by without a carpet.

The industrial wire stacking unit can be moved at will.

The kitchen, presenting an organized view at the end of the living area, is uncluttered and functional. It was designed with the elegant dining area in mind.

The sleek lines and open counter space make this kitchen seem roomy and inviting. Helping out are a wide butcher block counter and open storage to display kitchenwares. Extending the kitchen is a birch veneer plywood table.

Lofts

You can get the loft look in your own apartment—even if it is on the first floor of a five-story walk-up—by thinking of your space in big strokes. For instance, the room at right has a skylight gracing it and built-in drawers, topped off with pillows for seating. But you can do the same thing by carving out a closet. Move in a chest of drawers, or build a simple plywood box (recess the top if you like), then top it with a 5"-thick foam slab for a mattress.

A giant-size Luxo lamp rules the area—minimally furnished with two director's chairs and freshly painted metal trunk.

Behind the mask of this dark, dated factory building is a surprise: a gracious cheery living space. This live-in loft is large and luxurious—a design dream.

The floor space, for example, is massive enough to accommodate duo-toned patterns (which are accomplished by painting with homemade stencils). Large trees make a pleasurable park atmosphere. The seating units are high Italian contemporary.

In another corner of the room is a work/play area—with space enough for both the office and the baby, thanks to a trellised-in recreation area.

The wonderful windows are best kept bare; the city outside beats draperies every time.

Lofts

Open spaces, large slanted windows, high ceilings, wide-wood floors—just because this room has interesting architectural details does not mean it can get away without adding architecture of the interior kind. But whether it is a loft, garret or commercial space, it still must work hard at many tasks.

This room shows a variety of contemporary options. The storage bed is characterized by an engineered utility that replaces storage futility, with pull-out drawers that make shoving stuff under the bed legitimate. The natural wood bedstead seems to float the mattress. Above the bed, a primitive quilt, of antique origin, is working art, starring as a textured headboard that defines space and defies gravity. And no more matching little end tables, dyed to match the bedroom suite. Instead expect the unexpected: An artist's trolley rolled to bedside holds the essentials. Its clean design and roomy storage keep it moving.

A backyard transplant is the hanging hammock that adds an obvious but often overlooked dimension to indoor relaxation.

From paperwork to Scrabble, a working table must do more than serve meals. This one has a glass slab slapped on top of a wicker foundation—yet another outdoor transplant, from the patio. Bedroom chairs have abounded since Thomas Sheraton invented them in the late eighteenth century—in stained and japanned wood with rush seats. Sheraton might be pleased with this variation: Steel-framed with vinyl seats, designed for all-weather outdoor use, which somehow makes them look sportier indoors as well.

Camille comes home—the chaise up front is a new twist on the grand duchess chaise, but updated in contemporary canvas, quilted for texture. Chaises have finally come into their own as a useful piece of casual furniture, now mass manufactured by some of the country's best.

Loft and garret windows— for all their charm—are often troublesome. Roll-up matchstick blinds are inexpensive and attractive. Plus, they are available in any size so they will fit any sized window.

Window: Matchstick blinds

Floors: High-styled, hard-working sisal

Garrets

It may be hard at first glance to imagine that behind an unprepossessing façade and up steep, rickety steps, tucked high under a slanting roof, is a wonderful, unconventional living space. But it is true.

Garrets are found all over the country. They have all the characteristics that command huge sums when labeled "penthouse" but as attics they are the best bargains on the block. Garret spaces are pioneer penthouses, with charm and individuality already there before you even move in.

A garret doesn't have to be bursting with Old World furnishings. This one has all the clean, white airiness (yet none of the ordinariness) of a contemporary three-room apartment:

If you opt for modern charm, here is the angle:

Slanted ceilings are, of course, cozy and terrific. A garret given. But they do keep wall space to a minimum. The solution is to hang paintings on the ceiling itself—the highest form of the art.

Old-time imperfections in the walls and ceilings can be inexpensively covered by 4 x 8 sheets of paneling found at building supply stores.

The brick-bare chimney recalls the rustic origins—for contrast.

With the ceiling reaching f the floor at the sides of the room, you are best off with furnishings both few and low

Neutral colors for the mod lar quilted sofa, plush chair a hassock are at ease with the

Apartment kitchens have enough space dilemmas without the added problem of missing half a ceiling, but that is exactly the joy (and the curse) of this garret kitchen. You can make it work *for* you by using imagination for some illuminating ideas—like this simple light fixture installed on the angle right into the ceiling.

Some other ways to combat the crunch in this kitchen:

Set everything out on open shelving—these are pine, mounted on ordinary standards and brackets. When staggered, the shelves give ample room for the tall and short of your wares.

Finesse the lack-of-drawers problem by hanging everything hangable. Baskets keep odd-shaped items at your fingertips.

A couple of stools are handy for sharing cooking chores or using at a quick-meal counter.

Photo: Bradley Olman/Design: Richard Burford

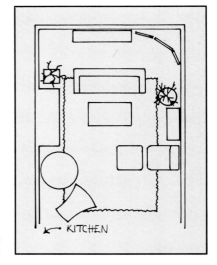

← KITCHEN

igh sweep of space.

The modern canvas chair olds its own beside a wicker ble, found at a flea market.

An oriental carpet defines the ving area and enriches the oom's contemporary pieces.

In an awkward corner at ight, a handsome screen is imply three glass-paned front oors hinged together. You can nd the doors at antique shops.

Photo: Erik Arnesen

Garrets

There are as many different ways to transform a garret into liveable space as there are ways to live in them. The amount of remodeling varies. Some garrets are raw spaces—just exposed beams and rafters. Others need only cosmetic work. More often, though, a garret was left simple to store things. The floor and ceiling may be finished but you will probably find no plumbing, heating or cooling units and few electrical outlets.

This garret illustrates the transformation possible in an attic that once lacked proper insulation, electricity and flooring—but did have lumpy, bumpy walls along with its charm.

The Victorian atmosphere here makes thorough use of the garret's angles in order to keep the spirit of the room intact. Some angles were improved upon: The coffee table is made from an old theatre seat (simply remove the old seat and replace it with a marble top).

Through a curtained en-

ance—which allows privacy without having to build a door in the irregular space—is the bedroom (at right). The redwood wall is a rustic glory. Large pieces of furniture keep it simple: the carved oak bed and bird's-eye maple bureau. The comforter (new sheets sewn together to make a removable quilt cover) and the lace curtains graciously relax. Notice, for example, how the walls are accented by placing the oriental rugs at angles. The rich mix of textures and patterns results in a warm opulent atmosphere.

New wall paneling was the major change. Rough-cut redwood plywood boards were nailed to the original 2 x 8 rafters. Trim moldings and baseboards are lath and the painted portions of the wall are plasterboard (texturized to hide the irregularity of the old structure). Lengths of old oak flooring found at salvage yards were laid right over the old floor, then sanded and finished with two coats of polyurethane.

Commercial Spaces

No dentist's chair or drill can now be found in this room—but those were the main attractions here before this commercial building was renovated. The result is The Next Frontier—office buildings converted into housing. Rooms like this combine the architectural bonuses of older buildings with the advantages of modern interiors.

One grand feature of old buildings—the oversized windows—was emphasized with large, movable panels, pine frames with mosquito netting stretched tight. For energy conservation, the windows were fitted with double-paneled insulated glass.

The relaxed off-kilter furniture arrangement is a pleasant surprise and keeps your eyes roving until you discover other features—high ceilings and boxed beams. An upholstered sofa, fat, squashy pillows and muted, romantic colors soften and contrast the dark wood furnishings and white walls.

HOW TO DO IT

Window Panels: They swivel on a pivot system. The wooden frame is attached to the windowsill, top and bottom, with ½" stair bolts. Each bolt looks like a screw with two threaded ends. The tapered end goes into the frame; the straight end into the sill. So the frame swings freely, the bolts are screwed into T nuts that are a size larger (5/16") than the bolt. Washers separate the frame and the sill to keep things working smoothly.

The installation is similar to putting in a sliding door: The hole that the bolt slips into at top is deeper than the bottom one. The frame top slips in first, leaving room for the bottom to clear the sill.

The frame is made from pine 1 x 5s that are mitered, glued, then connected with ½" #5 corrugated fasteners. Staple mosquito netting to the frame's back. If you want, mask the staples with lattice.

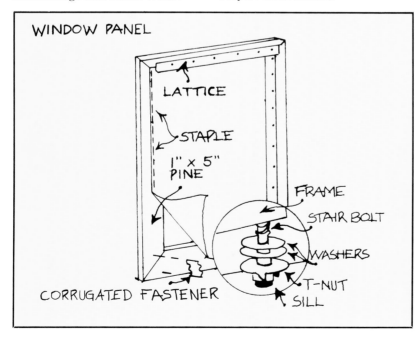

WINDOW PANEL

LATTICE

STAPLE

1" x 5" PINE

CORRUGATED FASTENER

FRAME

STAIR BOLT

WASHERS

T-NUT

SILL

JOHN BELUSHI: The Long-Playing Sound Room

Funnyman John Belushi was sounding off about sound. "You gotta gimme a soundproof room with terrific acoustics—or else," he said in that quiet, understated way of his. Seems his neighbors had been complaining about the level of his loudness. Belushi's *Saturday Night Live*-lihood has meant that —like the rest of us—he likes to play his music (loud) after he comes home from work, which in his case might be 3:00 A.M. His neighbors, unfortunately, didn't follow the same schedule —but woke up to call the police.

Belushi wanted a small, windowless room in his apartment converted into a super-sound sanctuary. The results are on this page—with a new ceiling and new walls that make the room smaller on each side. Sound is trapped by insulation stuffed into walls and rugs on several surfaces. Also building walls off-parallel (see drawing below) improves acoustics. Some specifics:

The furniture: heavy-duty modular, easy to move, easy to lounge on.

The lighting: clip-on theatre spots with barn door shutters.

The accessories: a video tape recorder (housed where a fire once raged), a board-and-nails guitar rack, an electric piano, an angle-iron unit for bar and stereo storage (next page).

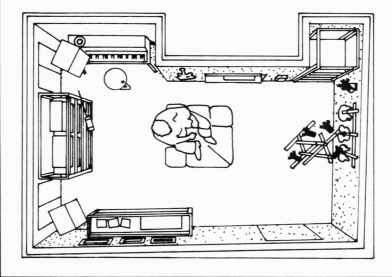

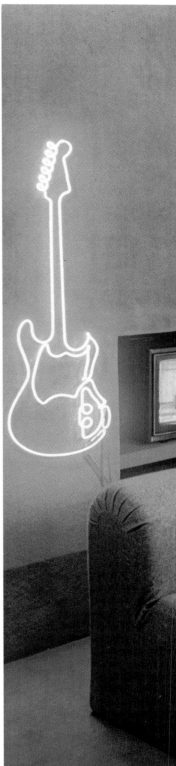

Photos: Thomas Hooper

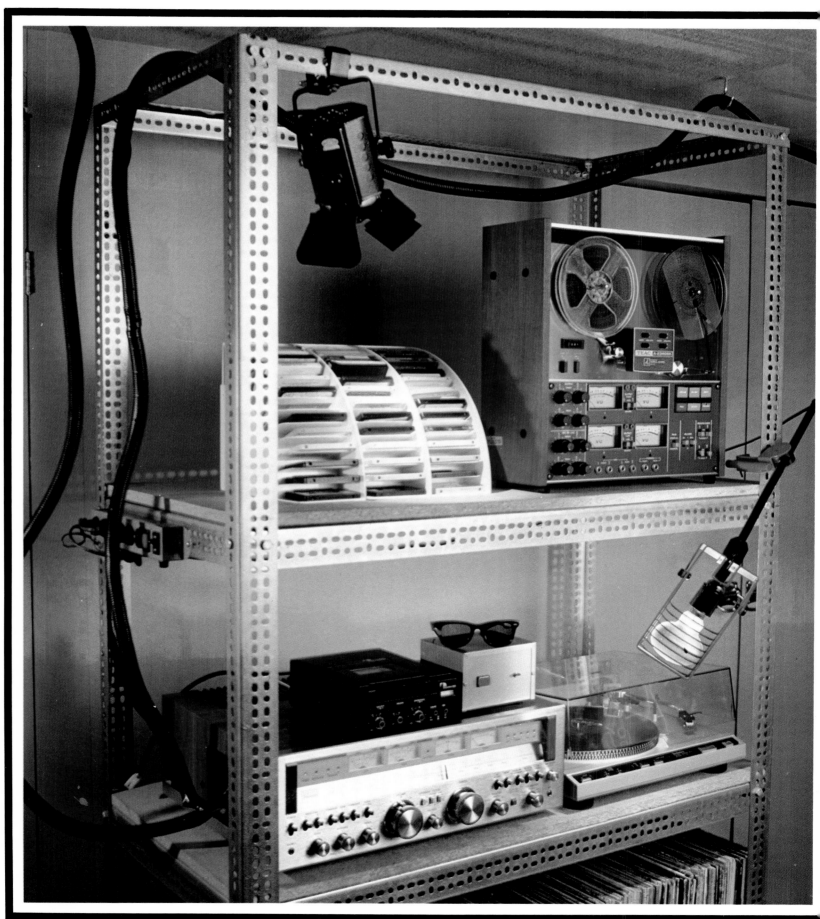

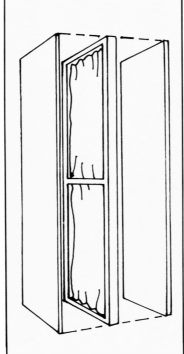

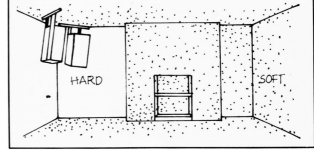

HOW TO DO IT
Record/Equipment Storage Unit:

Materials: 7 10' lengths of slotted angle irons (look in Yellow Pages under "Industrial Equipment and Supplies")

4 3" locking casters with corner brackets (from a hardware store)

3 or 4 pieces particle board for shelves, 12½" x 59½"

64 bolts, 5/16" x ¾"

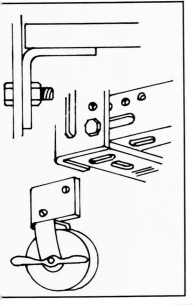

Dimensions for Belushi's record cart can be adjusted to any size (keep width at 13" for albums) and the bar is built on the same principles.

Cut: 4 51" uprights
      8 60" long rails
      8 13" crosspieces

If possible, buy from a supplier who will cut the angle irons. To do it yourself: Put iron in a vice and cut with a hacksaw (wear goggles and gloves for protection from flying cuttings).

Bolt the two upright end frames first (see diagram). Then join the long rails to the inside of the frame, bolting casters to bottom.

HOW TO DO IT
A Soundproof Door:

Materials: 4 8' 2 x 4s (cut to fit doorway)

Note: Reduce door height and width by ½" to allow for addition of weather stripping/ soundproofing and to make the door easier to hang

2 sheets ½" plywood
Fiberglas insulation
Staples, finishing nails, white glue, hinges

Use the existing door for a pattern, allowing for weather stripping and any new carpet on the floor. Assemble 2 x 4s as shown. Glue and nail one plywood side to 2 x 4 frame; stuff and staple insulation tightly; glue and nail other plywood side. Hinge to open into the room, then apply self-stick weather stripping.

HOW TO DO IT
Soundproofing a Room:
To soundproof any room, you must build the second wall at least 4" away from the existing wall. (The more space between the two walls, the less sound will escape the room.) If you think it is needed, a new ceiling can be built under the original.

Sound Principles: Measure carefully and, using 2 x 4s, nail together the new wall of studs, building in crosspieces for support. Leave about 16" between each stud and, on the walls that will be carpeted, place crosspieces at shoulder height— where people may lean against them. The walls are then filled with padding to prevent sound

leakage. Instead of high-priced commercial soundproof padding, we discovered that inexpensive thermal Fiberglas insulation (the same stuff used for roofs and attics) works just as well. Pack in the padding tightly (but not so tightly that it causes the carpet to bulge) and staple in place. Put sheet rock on half the walls. Then using tacks, carpet the other walls, the floor, the ceiling, even the door (see above for how to build the door); short-pile industrial carpet does the trick.

Ups and Downs: To soundproof the floor and ceiling, follow these "sandwich" recipes: new floor: 2 x 4 studs (16" apart, nailed to the old floor), insulation, chipboard, carpet padding, carpet. New ceiling: 2 x 4 studs (16" apart, nailed to ceiling joists), insulation, sheet rock or carpet. Build floor and ceiling before walls and allow for 8" difference that new walls will make in the room's perimeter. Also, if the studs in the old floor and ceiling go north and south, build new ones going east and west.

APT IDEAS

As the name suggests, this section is stocked with adaptable ideas, information and illustrations of the pieces that make up a whole room, the elements that give it personality.

You will see pretty pictures too, but, like so much else in this book, the furnishings in these pictures do not just sit around looking pretty—they *work*. And if you look closely,

the photographs and drawings provide some simple solutions to some complex problems.

Some examples of what you will find:

Long, narrow hallways are often the unwelcome tag-alongs to charming, elderly apartments. What to do with them? Here are innovative ideas for two-toned painting and for art galleries that give

corridors new personalities.

This section will answer the nagging question of how to find the space for an office at home: movable walls, for instance, make two spaces out of one—thanks to the use of lightweight screens. Other ideas show how to carve out work spaces that disappear when necessary.

Plants. You probably already know how to care for and feed

n—but where do you put
n? We do not mean decora-
chic plant placement (a lone
n in a dark hallway for
ctly aesthetic purposes), but
es where plants can grow
glow, from bedroom green-
ses to roll-around planters.
torage is always the big
blem in any size apartment.
se pages offer systems for
sing books and records,
crafts and collectibles, clothes
and sound equipment.

And more—workable prin-
ciples for how to make a lamp
out of just about anything, how
to make a desk or a table, how
to tame the frame, and how to
treat your windows.

All these ideas can work hard
in your home without you having to work too hard or spend
too much. You will not have to
rush out and buy an expensive
new breakfront or shelving system. No. Some of these ideas
are projects, requiring some do-
it-yourself time. Others are
simply fast ideas that make the
difference between an apartment with a half life and one
that lives. And after looking
through this section, we are
sure you will come up with
some apt ideas of your own.

STORAGE: Book Systems

Clean-looking natural pine shelving that stretches clear across one wall not even stopping for the windows can organize an entire room. This shelving system was engineered from five store-bought units, which can be put together easily and can be adjusted for the space you have. Once you have chosen the units and assembled the ready-made shelving system, you can make some custom additions that will fulfill special needs.

At one end of the system, add a desk by resting a hollow-core, unfinished birch door on one shelf. Support it at the other end on a square frame of pine 2 x 2s, screwed into the door/desk top.

The special paperback-size shelves and the dictionary stand are easy, make-it-yourself projects.

Illumination comes from mock industrial track lighting—really inexpensive metal shades from a building supply store.

HOW TO DO IT

Paperback Shelves: Make these shelves longer or shorter to fit your collection's requirements. Use these dimensions as a reference: Have the lumberyard cut two pine 1 x 10s 24" long. Also get four pine 1 x 6s together to form a V. (Glue first for added strength.) Repeat for other two 1 x 6s. Then glue and nail the edge of this V-shaped shelf to one of the 1 x 10 side pieces. Glue and nail to other 1 x 10 at the same angle. Repeat for other shelf, spacing the shelves 10" apart. Set unit in larger bookshelf.

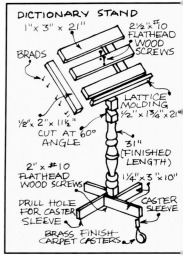

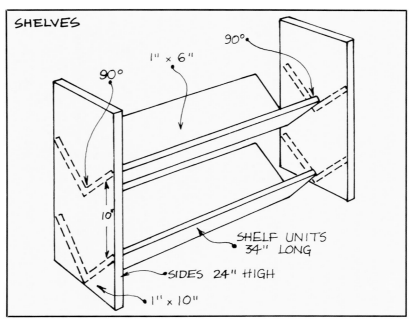

HOW TO DO IT

Dictionary Stand: Drill hole f[or] caster sleeves on the bottom [of] each 1¼ x 3. Glue and screw boards to base of turning. To make the top, nail the ½ x 2s [to] the back of the 1 x 3s with brads. Glue and nail molding [to] edge of tray. Saw off turning [at] 60-degree angle. Drill holes f[or] screws and screw tray to turning. Insert caster sleeves in holes. Force in casters.

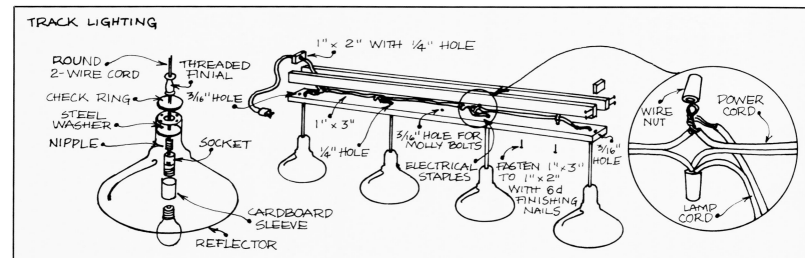

HOW TO DO IT

Track Lighting System: Buy all the electrical parts labeled in the drawing at a lamp or hardware store. In addition, get reflectors (at a builder's supply store), eight wire nuts, 10' of white two-wire-round lamp cord, enough power cord to reach from the light to the nearest wall plug, three Molly bolts and the lengths of 1 x 2s. Nail the 1 x 3 to the 1 x 2s, making a U-shaped trough. Nail in the end pieces and drill a hole for the power cord in one of them. Drill ¼" holes in 1 x 3 for cords. Wire lamps and thread cord through holes. Staple en[d] down; peel back insulation. Attach power cord to wires with nuts and electrician's tap[e]. To hang: Drill three 3/16" holes in the 1 x 3s. Mark and drill ⅜ holes. Insert Molly bolts and hang. (On concrete, use a carb[ide] tipped drill and lead anchors.)

Photos: Bradley Olman

STORAGE: Book Systems

Right: This unfinished floor-to-ceiling shelf system is surprisingly simple and versatile. Build it from four 2 x 4s cut to fit from floor to ceiling. Follow instructions on the diagram at left. Adjust the dimensions to fit your needs.

Once the 2 x 4s are on hand, use a saw and an electric drill with a 1½" spade bit to drill holes and cut slots as shown. From ¾" plywood, cut five shelves 15" x 36" and one shelf 18½" x 36". (The wider shelf toward the bottom is deep enough for a stereo system.) Notch this shelf to fit between the uprights. Use metal L brackets to fasten the uprights to the floor and ceiling. The distance between the uprights depends on the width of your shelves; allow for a 6" overhang on shelf ends.

Below: Build narrow shelves for those skinny paperback books that usually get lost on regulation bookshelves.

Build the shelves just deep enough to hold standard-sized paperbacks—6 to 8 inches. Then cut shorter sections to nail at the end of each shelf for built-on bookends.

These shelves fit standards and wall brackets found in hardware stores.

Photo: Bradley Olman/Design: Lenore Lucy

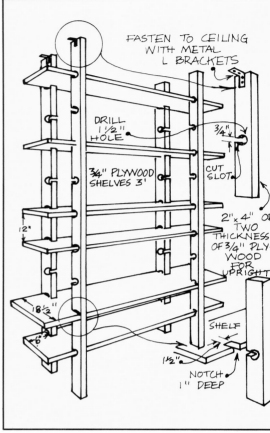

Photo: Fred Lyon

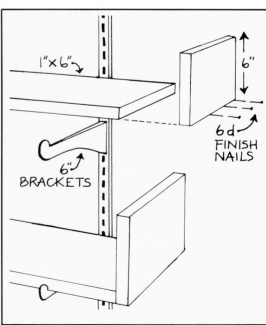

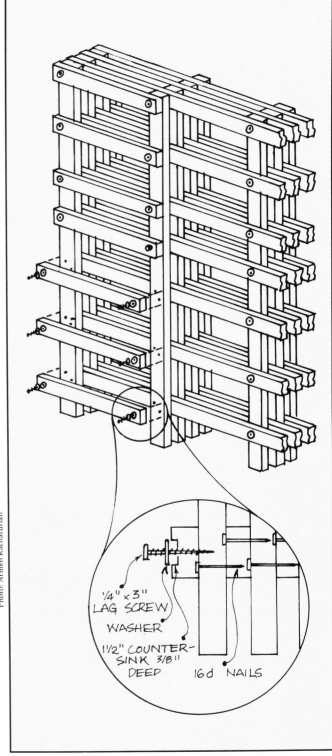

Photo: Armen Kachaturian

This shelving system is as simple as child's play—you can knock it together from a big pile of 2 x 4s.

The dimensions are up to you but if you are going to load the system with books and records, limit the horizontal pieces to a depth of three feet. And sketch your complete system before you truck off to the lumberyard; it is better than finding that you guessed wrong—after you are back home.

Leave the boards natural or stain them (light oak stain was used here). Seal with two coats of polyurethane (sand lightly between coats).

Start building by leaning the uprights in position along the wall. Nail them into the wall studs if you can (use 8d nails). Make sure these initial 2 x 4s are exactly vertical—use a carpenter's level to check. Then nail on the first layer of horizontal shelf pieces; check with the level as you go.

Continue stacking and nailing until the shelves are as deep as you need. For a professional touch, attach the last horizontals with countersunk lag screws.

¼" x 3" LAG SCREW

WASHER

1½" COUNTER-SINK 3/8" DEEP

16 d NAILS

STORAGE: A Sound System

Pull the plugs on your old sound principles and build a music system that solves all stereo storage problems.

HOW TO DO IT

Materials:

2 pine 1 x 1s (cut 26" long)
4 pine 1 x 3s (cut 7' long)
6 pine 1 x 4s (cut 7' long)
4 pine 1 x 3s (cut 18" long)
1 36" x 34½" x ⅛" hardboar⸝ panel

From two 4' x 8' sheets of ¾⸝ knotty pine plywood, cut:
2 doors, 35¾" x 8"
1 door, 35¾" x 13"
2 top braces, 35¾" x 8"
3 shelves, 16½" x 36"
3 shelves, 15" x 36"
1 lower back panel, 36" x 33⸝

6 #10 x 2" screws with trim washers
12 flat washers
12 screw eyes
1 pound #6 finishing nails
8' sash chain
3 door handles
1 roll ¾" birch plywood tape

Build the sides first—alternate three 1 x 4s and two 1 x 3⸝ (the 7' boards) for each side. Then nail an 18", 1 x 3 cleat across the top and bottom of each side piece.

Next, nail on a lower back panel of plywood. Then nail i⸝ the lower four shelves.

Stand the unit up for the re⸝ of the project. Attach the top back brace, nail a 1 x 1 strip to each rear edge of the sides as shown. Then nail the top back panel to these strips.

Install the top brace across the front as shown. Before in⸝ stalling the top shelves, figure⸝ out where you want your equipment and measure the height of each component wit⸝ the dust cover open. Allow an extra inch for headroom, and nail in the shelves.

Then install the doors for th⸝ lower three shelves. Sash chai⸝ and screw eyes hold the open doors flat. Attach the door han⸝ dles and glue edge tape to the plywood edges. Countersink the nails, and fill holes with wood putty before varnishing.

BACK BRACE 8" x 36" x ¾"

FRONT BRACE 8" x 36" x ¾"

½" INSET

1" x 3" x 18" PINE

USE #3 FINISHING NAILS ON SIDE BRACES (NAIL FROM BOTH SIDES FOR STRENGTH)

2¼" INSET

USE #6 FINISHING NAILS FOR SHELVES, BRACES, AND LOWER PLYWOOD BACK

16½" x 36" x ¾"

APPROXIMATELY ½" SPACING BETWEEN ALTERNATING 1" x 4" x 7'—(6) AND 1" x 3" x 7'—(4) PINE STRIPS

1" x 1" x 26" STRIP HOLDS UPPER HARDWOOD BACK

½" INSET ON TOP 3 SHELVES

13" x 35¾" x ¾"

33" x 36" x ¾" LOWER PLYWOOD BACK

15" x 36" x ¾" (3 LOWER SHELVES)

⅛" CLEARANCE

HOW THE HINGE WORKS

2" INSET ON 3 LOWER SHELVES

1/0 SASH CHAIN

SIDE

BIRCH EDGE TAPE ON ALL EXPOSED PLYWOOD EDGES

SCREW EYE—SPREAD SLIGHTLY TO INSERT CHAIN (12)

TRIM WASHER (6)

FLAT WASHERS (12)

DOOR

8" x 35¾" x ¾"

#10 x 2" FLATHEAD WOODSCREW (6)

DOOR DETAIL

3/8"

DOOR EDGE

PREDRILL ⅛" HOLE IN DOOR EDGE FOR HINGE SCREW

DRILL ⅛" HOLE 1" FROM FRONT EDGE

TORAGE: Music Boxes

Photos: Thomas Hooper

u do not have to hide your
mponents away in dark
ces. If they are well designed,
u can treat them like sculp-
re—even putting them on
destals.

OW TO DO IT
easure the length and width
each component and use
ose dimensions for the top
d bottom panels of its
destal. Build them any height
u like.
Have the lumberyard cut ¾"
wood to your specifications.
il the pieces together, leaving
e back of each box open for

extra storage—albums, tapes
and maintenance gear.
Fill any holes or hammer
dents with wood putty and sand
the entire surface smooth
before painting or polyurethan-
ing. You can also cover each
pedestal with vinyl paper
(self-adhesive or glued on with
vinyl wallpaper paste); in this
case, sanding and puttying are
unnecessary.
If you put the pedestals on a
rug or straw mat, you can even
hide the wires under the floor
covering (where you do not
walk) and avoid the typical
stereo system octopus.

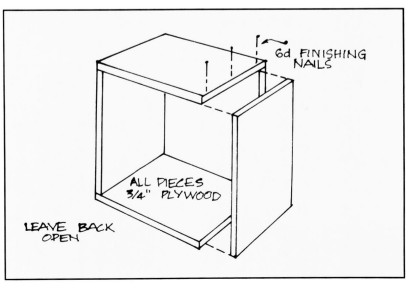

6d FINISHING NAILS

ALL PIECES ¾" PLYWOOD

LEAVE BACK OPEN

STORAGE: Packing Cases

Right: Take the trunk table trick one step further—a piece of ¼″ plate glass resting on top makes for see-through storage as well as offering a dandy display case. Cover the inside with paper or fabric.

Find old trunks at a Salvation Army store or antique shops. Get one that is in good condition since broken hinges and big dents are hard and costly to repair. Refinish the old wood, shine up the brass and metalwork and the unit is made.

Below Right: Let old suitcases travel out of the closet and be-come a coffee table. Find the cases or trunks in thrift shops. Most clean up with soap and water. A coat of paste wax protects the finish. Or glue on a fabric covering (canvas or corduroy look good).

Below: These boxes seem to adhere to the wall by defying gravity but they are resting quite prosaically on shelf standards and brackets. The boxes were from department and discount stores—refurbished with spray paint (wallpaper or fabric work well too). The letters are art supply stick-ons.

Photo: Bradley Olman

WORKSPACE: A Clean Well-Lighted Place

kinds of spaces in all kinds of [roo]ms can be converted into [effi]cient work areas.

[Righ]t: A standard drawing table [wit]h a comfortable swivel chair [sta]nds in a corner. Moved near [a w]indow, it gives you a room-[wit]hin-a-room with a view. [Wal]ls become bulletin boards [wh]en work stuff is tacked up. [U]se bright colors to ward off [the] feeling that you are work-[ing] in a closet. Stack files and [boo]ks on existing shelves, even [add] a few more, and put in [filin]g cabinets to fit the floor [spa]ce. Move in a small desk or [dra]wing board for the work [sur]face.

[Belo]w Left: Double take—even [ord]inary, everyday items can be [put] to use in the home office. [He]re a couple of bricks organize [des]k-top clutter.

[Belo]w Center: You can add a new [roo]m without knocking down [or b]uilding walls. Simply turn a [wal]k-in closet into much-[nee]ded office space.

[Belo]w Right: A tacking strip is a [sim]ple way to unclutter your [des]k while keeping oft-used [sup]plies within reach. [M]ake one by nailing wood [stri]p to the wall. Then pin or [tac]k up your papers, work tools, [pic]tures or whatnot.

Photo: Thomas Hooper

Photo: Dick Swift

Photo: Bradley Olman

Photo: Fred Lyon

WORKSPACE: Homework

Left: This basic, inexpensive se-
ving cart serves you work in
bed—over easy. It is a high-
function station that fits in a
where. Here are the elements

The compact white office f
unit also comes in a variety o
colors and fits on top of the
color-coordinated cart.

On the left handle hangs a
wicker magazine rack (tape o
wire it on). A tiered wicker ra
(top shelf on the right) orga-
nizes loose papers.

A slip-on wire basket hang
below the top shelf and becomes a movable medicine ca
net. On the middle shelf, clea
fishing tackle boxes hold sma
items. The tray holders and a
office file divider on the lowe
shelf hold books. On the very
bottom, large wheels let you
move the caddy around—and
out of the way.

Opposite: One end of a room is
enough for a U-shaped workspace. The key: consolidation

Assorted pieces became thi
slick office-at-home. The des
in the middle uses a kitchen
wall as its base (for extra stor
age). Cut a 30"-wide hollow-
core door to fit the length of
cabinet unit's top. Fasten the
door to the top with screws.
Paint, Formica or Con-Tact
paper will finish off the piece

Against the wall, workspac
and more storage space is pro
vided by a set of drawers topp
with another hollow-core doc
(supported on the desk at one
end) and a store-bought book
case stacked on top. To complete the U shape, slide in a
drawing table and some plast
storage drawers. A rolling fil
cabinet slides out of the way.

Baskets of supplies, magazines and books, as well as
working tools—typewriters,
sewing machine—all have a
place here. Lighting is handily
supplied by a hanging fluores
cent tube and a clamp-on lam

WORKSPACE: Corner Offices

The office on the sly: a wall area turned into workspace.

Below: This hallway becomes an efficient work area with the artful addition of two clean-lined filing cabinets and a wooden slab slapped on top. The eye-level hanging plastic bins, a versatile clamp-on desk lamp and simple wicker baskets are functionally pretty.

Right: A bedroom Parsons night table can double for daytime duty when a set of sturdy plastic drawers is wheeled underneath. Once again, a useful clamp-on desk lamp can be extended over any desk-top area.

Below Right: A drop-down leaf exposes not only an efficient work spot but ample storage space.

Photos: Bradley Olman

WORKSPACE: Eating at Your Desk

e table can quickly change
ctions from dining to work
ou plan a bit beforehand.
he room at right illustrates
t how this is done. The table
tches roles and becomes
rkspace with the simple ad-
on of the tools of the trade.
rything can be stored away
wooden trunk next to the
kcase.

he sawhorse table (below)
bles as both innovative
rkspace and dining place. Its
ign is obviously simple, it is
y to forget about. But when
need an inexpensive table,
t, there is nothing better

than a hollow-core door on two
hardware store brackets and
2 x 4s. The kimono becomes
clothing art with the addition of
a dowel slid through the arms
and supported on two nails.

HOW TO DO IT
Sawhorse Table: Four metal
sawhorse brackets make this
table easy to put together. Slip
two 2 x 4 legs into each bracket,
then clamp 2 x 4 crosspieces—
cut to the width of the hollow-
core door tabletop—between
the two brackets. If you want
permanence, nail the 2 x 4s in
place.

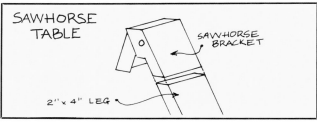

Photo: Thomas Hooper

Photos: Bradley Olman

APT IDEAS **253**

WORKSPACE: Closets with a Cause

If you are willing to sacrifice closet space, you can get yourself a whole extra room for working—with little work.

Below is the apartment shop, so economically planned and put together that there is plenty of room to do all your carpentering in one small space. A simple sawing system replaces sawhorses: Two 1 x 4s rest between the wood plank workbench and a dowel-studded 2 x 4 on the back wall. Holes (drilled into the ends of the 1 x 4s) slip over the dowels to position the boards.

The closet case at right is a neat transformation for that Fibber McGee storage space. A bunch of boards, some self-adhesive cork and a Formica counter turn it into a trim and tidy office.

Inexpensive, colorful plastic bins and accessories hold all kinds of office supplies and rest on shelves supported by L brackets, or the bins can also stack on top of one another. A roll-under-the-desk chair can be kept out of sight and out of the way. Bonus: You can close the door on your work.

MOVABLE WALLS: Divided It Stands

variation on the screen theme
he freestanding door wall—a
y to fabricate an office by
ng some prefab materials.
e five doors define an office
a without the hassle of
or construction. And it all
ly breaks down (so you
n't have to) when you move.
uild this portable office
n five hollow-core doors
ght from a lumberyard or
der's supply store. There
several ways to fasten the
els together. The easiest
thod is to hinge the end
els to the back panels. Fas-
the three back panels
ether with metal mending
es and screws. Make the
k top from another nar-
er door or a piece of ¾"
wood. If you use plywood,
on a wood strip along the
nt to make the top look
ker and to add rigidity. Fas-
the top to the panels with
tal L brackets and screws.
nother way: Join the panels
ether with loose-pin hinges.
t way you can simply pull
the pins and the system
s apart in seconds (especially
venient for nomad types).
Other variations on this same
me: Cover screens with fab-
change the configuration (a
hape—below—works well);
Fome-Cor panels or ply-
d instead of hollow-core
rs.

Photos: Bill Maris

MOVABLE WALLS: Staged Screens

Left: If your door opens straight into the room, you can build an instant entryway with movable walls.

Make the screen panels from ¾" x 6" birch veneer plywood boards, 7' long. Connect them with ¾" double-action hinges. Edge with birch wood tape, then sand the panels and leave the screen unfinished—bare is beautiful—or paint or cover with self-adhesive paper.

Right: Shoji screens—hinged together and freestanding—make a whole garden where there was once only a barren white wall. Shojis are available by mail order or from import stores.

Sticks and stones are the building blocks for this scene stealer. With the backlighting through the screens and a well-placed mirror, the effect is dramatic. Putting it together isn't.

The weathered branches and the plywood base they stand on come as a unit from a display store. If you have access to fallen timber, it is easy to hold scavenged branches erect with Christmas tree stands. Or brace them with pieces of lumber, notched to fit the trunks and nailed to a plywood base.

Camouflage the base with boulders—papier-mâché or real limestone—and white rocks (from a garden supply store).

Photos: Fred Lyon

256

Photo: Thomas Hooper

MOVABLE WALLS: Primal Screens

Left: Pop up—and then prop up—an instant wall and park it anywhere. Build the wall any height or width—but make sure it is not too big to carry out when you move. There are two ways.

HOW TO DO IT

Instant Wall #1: Nail together a framework from 1 x 2s (or use artists' canvas stretcher strips for walls up to 72" tall), then cover the frame with fabric. Hold the new wall upright with L-shaped brackets attached to an existing wall.

Instant Wall #2: Sandwich a lightweight panel (Gatorfoam, Fome-Cor, styrofoam or thick cardboard) between two pieces of furniture, or hang it from ceiling hooks. Paint the new walls or use adhesive paper or thin wood strips.

Right: When a room lacks architectural personality, make an instant "bay window" with etched glass panes—actually three new French doors will give you a whole new view. The windows' "etched" glass is just a good-looking illusion.

HOW TO DO IT

Window/Screen: The glass panes are really doors stencil-painted to make them look etched. Three spotlights on the floor behind the window provide warm glow-light.

Tape a stencil to each of the panes of three French doors. Paint over the stencils with white gloss enamel paint. It runs easily so keep the brush as dry as possible. Hold the brush perpendicular, then use an up-and-down dabbing motion to paint, keeping the area of the stencil you are working on as close to the glass as possible with your free hand. A blow dryer can speed up the drying. Join the doors together with butt hinges.

Photos: Armen Kachaturian

Photo: Thomas Hooper

WINDOWS: Screening Rooms

A common problem—what to do with big windows on one end of a boxlike room—meets an uncommon solution: screens that add architectural dimension plus color. The screens shown here are both easy to move and easy to make.

These screens are substantial and heavy duty, made by hinging together hollow-core closet doors painted with enamel.

The 16" x 7' doors are easy to find and to work with but for less than half the investment in materials (and a bit more work), cut six panels from an 8' sheet of ¾" plywood.

The window treatment in the room is a trick borrowed from camp. It is mosquito netting—inexpensive and billowy. Unfinished wood rings hanging from a closet pole hold up the curtai. Just hem the netting, sew on the rings and position the pole with L-shaped brackets.

Photos: Thomas Hooper

he design here is made from e decorated parts of paper ns, soaked off their sticks and lued in place.

The valance is a piece of ghtweight Fome-Cor (from an t supply store) finished to atch the screens. Then it is tuck to the window frame with double-faced tape.

Soak the fans in warm water to remove the sticks, then glue them to the screens with a mixture of two parts white glue and one part water applied with a soft brush. Use a dry cloth to smooth out wrinkles and remove excess glue.

HINGE PANELS
WITH DUCT TAPE

STRETCH FABRIC
AROUND BOARD

CUT PANELS
FROM 1/2" THICK
GATORFOAM WITH
A SABER SAW
OR MAT KNIFE

FASTEN WITH
DUCT TAPE

WINDOWS: Sheer Fabrication

Cover up a nonview (and still let the sun shine in) with sheer fabric pulled over artists' canvas stretchers. (For outsized windows, make the frames from 1 x 2s screwed together.) Staple the prettiest sheer fabric you can find to the artists' stretchers and hang the screen with screw eyes and L hooks. An extra piece of wood wedged between the sill and the frame keeps the air flowing in when you want it.

Skylights aren't the privilege of loft dwellers only. By cheating a little you can have one or several.

No cutting through the roof is required: The light source is several fluorescent fixtures hidden behind a window frame you build with 1 x 2s, aluminum strips and translucent plastic panels.

They do not require high ceilings either since you can adapt the dimensions to suit the scale of any room.

Note: For skylights more than about 4' across, build two or more frames.

HOW TO DO IT

No-Sky Skylight: To determine the size and angle of the skylight, first draw a pencil line for the frame's top and bottom edges on the ceiling and the wall. Measure the angle that these two pencil marks create. To make the frame, glue and nail together 1 x 2 clear pine strips. Then screw 2" x ⅛" aluminum strips to the front edges of the frame. Illuminate the frame with General Electric Brite Stiks, which should be wired in series. Add as many as you need. Next nail 2 x 4 strips flat onto the ceiling and wall edges to form support for the frame. Lift the frame into position and attach to the sidewalls and to the 2 x 4 strips with nails. Slip in the plastic panels. These will need to be cut professionally beforehand.

Photo: John Gregory

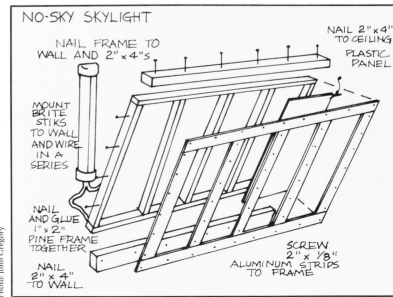

NO-SKY SKYLIGHT

NAIL FRAME TO WALL AND 2"x4"s

NAIL 2"x4" TO CEILING

PLASTIC PANEL

MOUNT BRITE STIKS TO WALL AND WIRE IN A SERIES

NAIL AND GLUE 1" x 2" PINE FRAME TOGETHER

NAIL 2" x 4" TO WALL

SCREW 2" x ⅛" ALUMINUM STRIPS TO FRAME

WINDOWS: Corrugated Shade

ho says a window shade must
p around a top roller to
ork? This handsome window
vering is made from corru-
ted cardboard.

The shade here fits inside the
ndow frame but you can
ake one any size you like to
ver up an awkward window
uation.

OW TO DO IT

t the corrugated strip for the
ade at least a couple of feet
nger than the height of the
ndow. (You can buy corru-
ted packing material—called
rro-flex—in 6′ wide rolls that
e 250′ long.) Staple it to a
ngth of 1 x 2 wood strip and
rew in a couple of screw eyes.
ld the blind up in place to see
here to put the screw hooks in
e wall.

When you string up the cord,
art with two lengths at least
ur times as long as the blind—
u can always cut off any
cess later. Tie cords to each
rew hook behind the blind,
n the cord down, underneath
d up over the front. Then run
through the metal rings tied
the screw hooks and over to
e wall cleat as in the illus-
ation.

The bed canopy is made of
e same corrugated material,
oked into the ceiling.

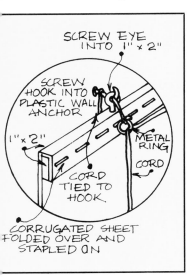

SCREW EYE
INTO 1″ X 2″

SCREW
HOOK INTO
PLASTIC WALL
ANCHOR

1″ X 2″

METAL
RING

CORD

CORD
TIED TO
HOOK

CORRUGATED SHEET
FOLDED OVER AND
STAPLED ON

Photo: Bradley Olman/Design: Ben Lloyd

Opposite: For privacy at night and light in the morning, this canvas window shade adjusts from top or bottom and can be manipulated with the pull of a ring. The design was borrowed from the sail of a Chinese junk. All four corners adjust independently, and vertical straps keep the shade from flapping in the breeze. Canvas is attached to bamboo poles for support.

Below: Traditional window treatments tended to draperies that went from floor to ceiling, blocking out all view as they plodded their way across the window. New treatments never forget the window's light, providing options in function and materials. This window exercises both of those options. It's a wood-slat drapery that is slung over the whole window opening.

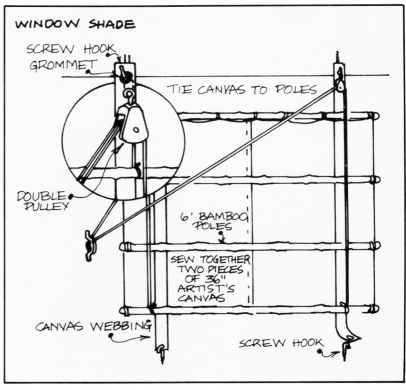

HOW TO DO IT
Canvas/bamboo window shade:
Cover—and uncover—two windows in one bold stroke with yet another alternative to conventional curtains: a bamboo-canvas pulley system, with a design borrowed from the sail of a Chinese junk. The illustration gives the basic how-to instructions. You can get bamboo poles (cut to the window's width) at an import store. Canvas works best and comes by the yard from a fabric store—or you can use any stiff or heavy fabric you like. All four corners of the shade adjust independently, for up and down options, and vertical straps keep the shade from flapping in the breeze.

Design: Ben Lloyd

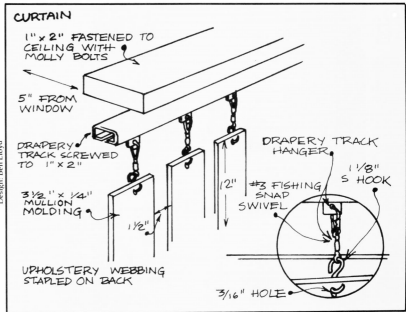

HOW TO DO IT
Wooden Curtain:
This wooden slat drapery will work with any window because you just sling it over the whole window area; it does not need a million little measurements.

The drawing at right tells all. Lay the slats out on the floor, carefully spaced, then staple the upholstery tape to them. For fishing swivels, look in a sporting goods store (they come in black, brass or chrome).

TABLES: PVC Chic

This table lets you keep an eye on your favorite poster. Plastic piping and fine art may not seem like the most harmonious coupling but the result is high visibility when you put them together right.

HOW TO DO IT
Cut the PVC (polyvinyl chloride) pipe with a fine-toothed saw. Put all the pieces together, plumber style: Clean the ends with acetone and stick them together with pipe cement.

After painting with spray enamel, add tape stripes along the top edge (either art drafting tape or auto pinstriping tape).

Top with Plexiglas.

The illustration shows sizes used for this table.

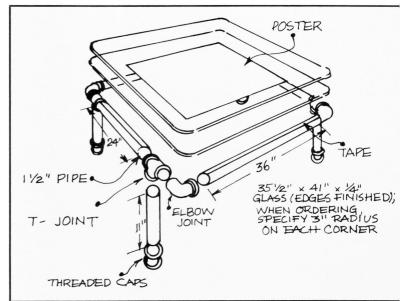

POSTER

1½" PIPE

T-JOINT

24"

11"

ELBOW JOINT

36"

TAPE

35½" × 41" × ¼" GLASS (EDGES FINISHED); WHEN ORDERING SPECIFY 3" RADIUS ON EACH CORNER

THREADED CAPS

TABLES: Slat of Hand

Photo: Thomas Hooper/Design: Chet Ross

Cover a plain plywood box (rough edges and all) with thin cedar strips for a coffee table that floats on top of a lighted base.

HOW TO DO IT

Go to the lumberyard for ⅛″ cedar strips—one package of random-length strips covers about 32 square feet. Cut the strips with a utility knife or scissors. Although manufacturers recommend contact cement, white glue also works.

To apply the strips: Spread glue or cement or both on a section of the box and the back of a strip with a 4″ rubber roller. Wait a few seconds until the glue gets tacky and stick the strip in place. When the pattern is complete, protect the surface with a light oil finish.

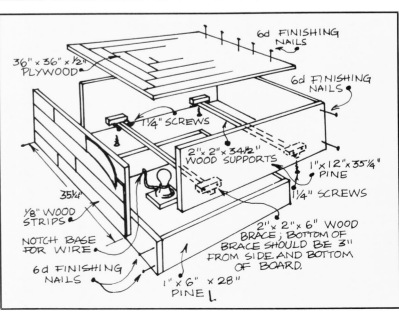

36″ x 36″ x ½″ PLYWOOD

6d FINISHING NAILS

6d FINISHING NAILS

1¼″ SCREWS

2″ x 2″ x 34½″ WOOD SUPPORTS

1″ x 12″ x 35¼″ PINE

1¼″ SCREWS

35¼″

⅛″ WOOD STRIPS

NOTCH BASE FOR WIRE

2″ x 2″ x 6″ WOOD BRACE; BOTTOM OF BRACE SHOULD BE 3″ FROM SIDE AND BOTTOM OF BOARD.

6d FINISHING NAILS

1″ x 6″ x 28″ PINE

TABLES: Freewheeling Function

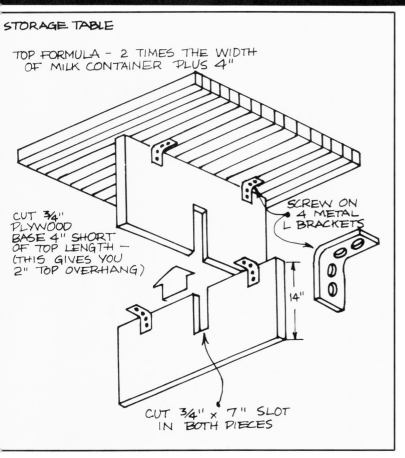

STORAGE TABLE

TOP FORMULA - 2 TIMES THE WIDTH OF MILK CONTAINER PLUS 4"

CUT 3/4" PLYWOOD BASE 4" SHORT OF TOP LENGTH — (THIS GIVES YOU 2" TOP OVERHANG)

SCREW ON 4 METAL L BRACKETS

14"

CUT 3/4" x 7" SLOT IN BOTH PIECES

There is a law somewhere that says the utility of a room increases geometrically by the number of working surfaces.

Left: The butcher block on the coffee table is natural looking and eminently serviceable. Underneath, plastic milk cartons with casters for rolling storage.

Right: Table tree, a table with a ficus growing right through it, rescues wasted space.

HOW TO DO IT

Coffee/Storage Table: This table can be a low buffet or a full dining table. Stash four plastic milk cartons on casters underneath the butcher block, for serving-cart-style meals.

The table is a butcher block top that sits on a big X base, made from two pieces of 3/4" plywood. Cut slots in the middle of the base pieces with a saber saw. Glue wood edging tape to the plywood edges and paint the base pieces. Screw on the top as shown in diagram.

HOW TO DO IT

The Tree House: To draw the half circles for the top two pieces, use a yardstick with a nail in one end and a hole for a pencil point 24" from the nail. Cut out with a saber saw. Glue wood tape to exposed edges of plywood pieces. Assemble, as shown in diagram at right, then paint or stain.

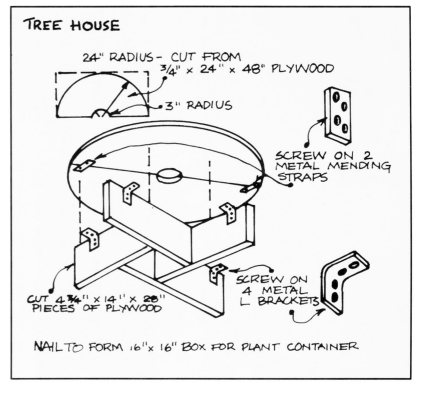

TREE HOUSE

24" RADIUS - CUT FROM 3/4" x 24" x 48" PLYWOOD

3" RADIUS

SCREW ON 2 METAL MENDING STRAPS

CUT 4 3/4" x 14" x 28" PIECES OF PLYWOOD

SCREW ON 4 METAL L BRACKETS

NAIL TO FORM 16" x 16" BOX FOR PLANT CONTAINER

TABLES: Back to Base X

Right: Four wood frame storm windows can also turn the tables. Find them at salvage yards. Get four storm windows of the same size and design, or try six narrower ones for a hexagonal base. Hinge together.

The tabletop is a piece of ¾" plywood, and the window base and tabletop were painted to match. Screw four small wood blocks into the underside of the tabletop (fitted to the base's inner corners) so the top will not slide.

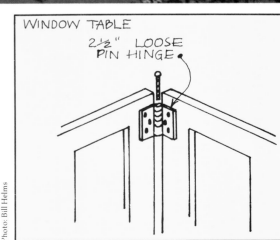

WINDOW TABLE

2½" LOOSE PIN HINGE

Photo: Bill Helms

Left: A hollow-core door opens the way to a coffee table—with a few easy steps.

HOW TO DO IT

Coffee Table: Saw a hollow-core door in half. Carefully cut slots as shown and slip the pieces together to form an X shape. Top with a slab of ¼" plate glass.

Buy a 1'3" x 6'8" hollow-core closet door. Get two 7" lengths of blind stop molding to finish the hollow-core ends. Cut the door in half. Take each half and pencil in a 7½" x 1⅜" slot on center. Cut out the slot with a saber saw. Plug the cut ends with wood molding, using white glue. Use 2" veneer tape on exposed edges (smear contact cement on wood and tape, wait 15 minutes, then apply).

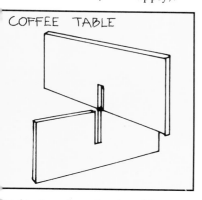

COFFEE TABLE

Right: Another classic table design that will not cost the price of an antique: Build your own museum piece with modern materials and stain or paint it dark for a traditional look (or leave it natural).

HOW TO DO IT

X Table: Screw the wood frames together as shown in the drawing. Put the assembled sections on top of each other with the 2 x 6 uprights spaced 30" apart. Then pencil mark the half lap joints (where the notches go). Cut these with a saw and chisel and assemble as shown. Furniture levelers will correct any small errors in measurements and will make the table steady.

Photo: Armen Kachaturian

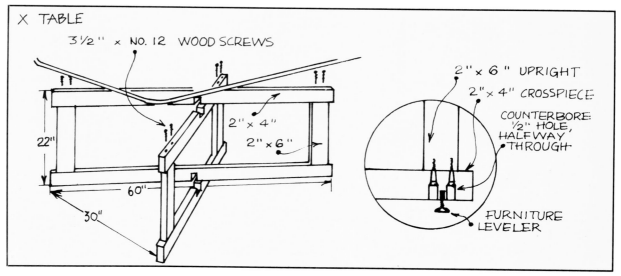

X TABLE

3½" x NO. 12 WOOD SCREWS

2" x 6" UPRIGHT
2" x 4" CROSSPIECE
COUNTERBORE: ½" HOLE, HALFWAY THROUGH

2" x 4"
2" x 6"

22"
60"
30"

FURNITURE LEVELER

TABLES: Grand Illusions

Industrial chic goes tongue-in-cheek with this dustbin pedestal table. The sturdy Italian chairs, high-end Milanlike lamp and squares of different grades of sandpaper stapled on the wall all complete the picture.

HOW TO DO IT
Dustbin Table: Add wood 2 x 4 blocks to L brackets to make the tabletop high enough for eating. Put a concrete block in the can for stability. The table surface is a sheet of galvanized steel from a sheet metal shop, glued with contact cement to the plywood. Finish the tabletop with pine half-round edging strips.

Opposite: The bright, heavily lacquered coffee table has an inset electric hibachi in the middle (removable and replaceable by jade plants).

HOW TO DO IT
Lacquered Table:
   Materials:
   1 4' x 8' sheet of birch plywood
   8 4' lengths of ¾" quarter round
   2 50⅝" long 1" x 2" pine strips
   12 3" L brackets
   #4d and #6d finishing nails

This table comes out of one well-managed 4' x 8' sheet of birch plywood.
   Build the top first by screwing the 1" x 2" strips to the underside edge of the plywood. Nail on the edge molding and cut the center hole with a saber saw (optional) to fit a hibachi or planter.
   Nail the base sides together, add the shelf cleats and the shelf. Attach the base to the top with L brackets, and you are ready to finish. Fill cracks and gaps with putty. Sand thoroughly and paint with enamel, then add a final coat of polyurethane for luster and durability.

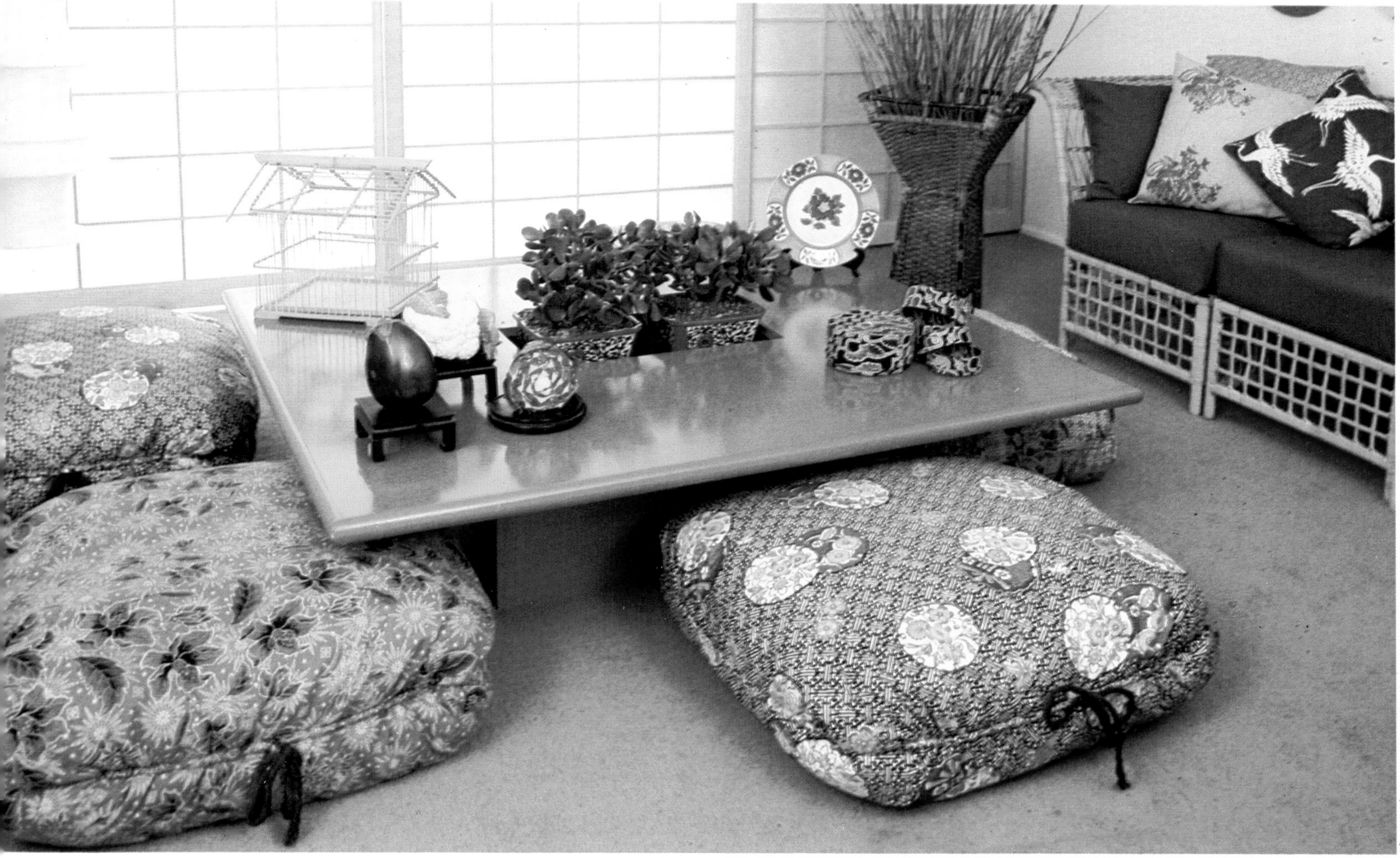

Photo: Thomas Hooper/Design: Camille Lehman

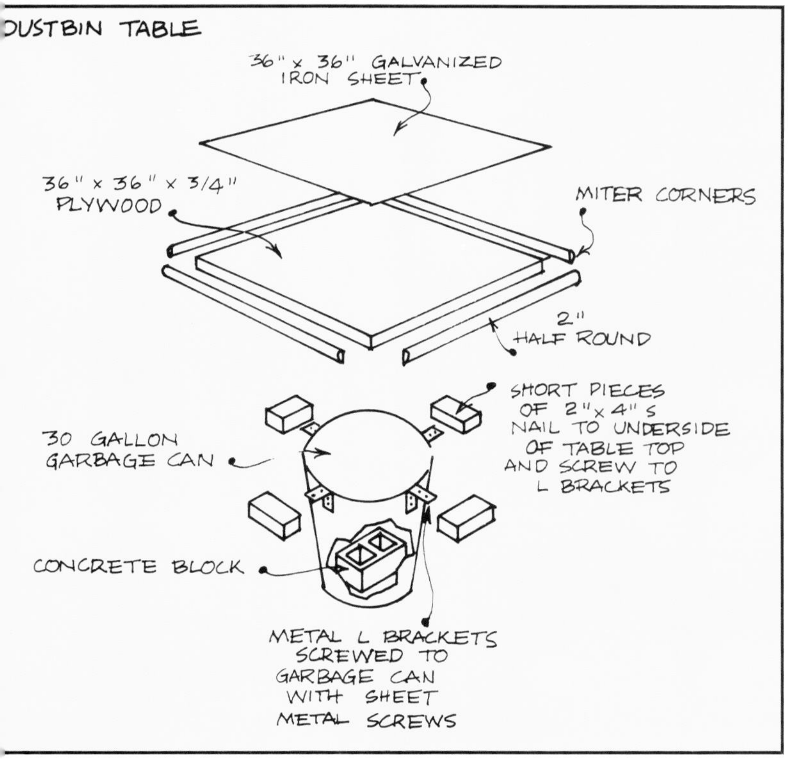

DUSTBIN TABLE
36" x 36" GALVANIZED IRON SHEET
36" x 36" x 3/4" PLYWOOD
MITER CORNERS
2" HALF ROUND
SHORT PIECES OF 2"x 4"s NAIL TO UNDERSIDE OF TABLE TOP AND SCREW TO L BRACKETS
30 GALLON GARBAGE CAN
CONCRETE BLOCK
METAL L BRACKETS SCREWED TO GARBAGE CAN WITH SHEET METAL SCREWS

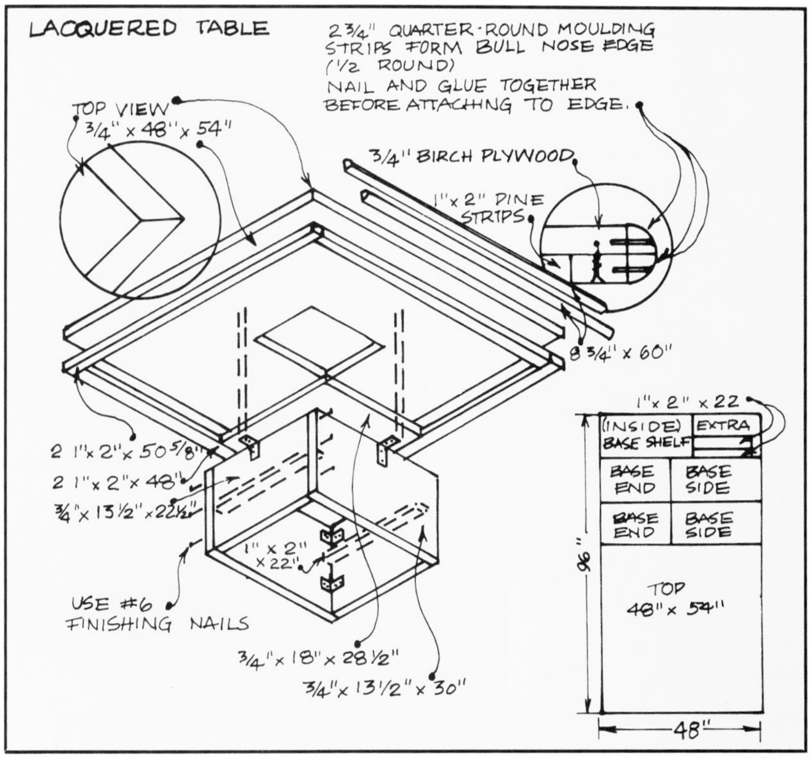

LACQUERED TABLE
2 3/4" QUARTER-ROUND MOULDING STRIPS FORM BULL NOSE EDGE (1/2 ROUND)
NAIL AND GLUE TOGETHER BEFORE ATTACHING TO EDGE.
TOP VIEW
3/4" x 48" x 54"
3/4" BIRCH PLYWOOD
1"x 2" PINE STRIPS
8 3/4" x 60"
2 1"x 2"x 50 5/8"
2 1"x 2"x 48"
3/4"x 13 1/2"x 22 1/2"
1" x 2" x 22"
USE #6 FINISHING NAILS
3/4"x 18" x 28 1/2"
3/4"x 13 1/2" x 30"
1"x 2" x 22
(INSIDE) BASE SHELF
EXTRA
BASE END
BASE SIDE
BASE END
BASE SIDE
TOP 48"x 54"
96"
48"

FRAMING: Square Roots

Time was when framing meant spending dozens of dollars on a work of art worth considerably more than that. It meant packing up the work and taking it to a professional, who'd give you the mitered edges, the shining glass and the sealed back.

But now, posters are an essential part of the art of today—and it does seem silly to spend $75 on a frame for a $15 poster. More than that, we now hang photographs, treasured objects, collectibles and articles of clothing. That professional with the mitered experience can't help. So, once again, more options: How to tame the frame.

Right: Improve your outlook on life with this lace and plexiglas version of the old pressed-flowers-in-the-diary trick.

The poster behind the sofa only looks framed. Cut to size a ¼"-thick piece of Fome-Cor, heavy cardboard or hardboard with a mat knife or saber saw. Then mount the poster with spray adhesive.

HOW TO DO IT

Plexiglas frame: Sandwich old handiwork between two 1/8"-thick sheets of Plexiglas. Keep the pieces together with clear Plexiglas screws in the corners (see illustration below). You will need a special Plexiglas bit to drill the holes. To hang, use monofilament fishing line or a very fine chain.

Left: Framing does not need to mean mitered corners and matting. This 1904 sheet music cover is positioned on blue construction paper, then sandwiched between ⅛"-thick glass and ⅛"-thick Masonite. Swiss clips (from art stores) hold the whole thing together. The illustration below shows how the clips work.

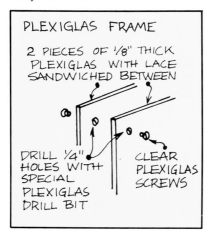

PLEXIGLAS FRAME

2 PIECES OF ⅛" THICK PLEXIGLAS WITH LACE SANDWICHED BETWEEN

DRILL ¼" HOLES WITH SPECIAL PLEXIGLAS DRILL BIT

CLEAR PLEXIGLAS SCREWS

⅛" HOLE

SWISS CLIP

Above: You can frame a mirror just like a poster. Here's how:

Have the lumberyard cut 1 x 3s to length. Assemble and join with white glue and 1½" mending plates. Place mirror behind frame and allow 1¼" overlap all around to fit mirror. Screw in 4" mending plates at the corners (see illustration).

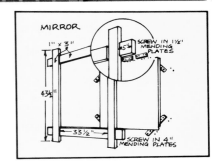

...ove: You do not need eight ...tle frames for eight small ...osters—one window frame ...n open up your point of view. ...Hit the junkyards for an old ...indow or door with lots of ...nes. Look for odd shapes, ...cely aged wood or weathered ...int. Cut out the posters from ...poster book and tape one ...ehind each pane. Use screw ...es and wire to hang it.

Right: A two-dimensional poster comes to life when floated a few inches from the wall.

HOW TO DO IT
Floating graphic: Hang the graphic from screw hooks in the ceiling and transparent monofilament fishing line (10 pounds test or heavier). Attach to the frame with two more screw hooks.

LAMPS: Make One Out of Anything

The unexpected—a wicker tray, a rattan mannequin, an ice sculpture—can become charming when light comes from imaginative sources. You really *can* make a lamp out of just about anything. The projects on these pages show you specific principles that can be applied to your own taste and ideas. For example, any ceramic figure can become a lamp. And anything that covers a bare bulb can become a lampshade. Electrical supply stores provide any and all parts and hardware—and also offer useful advice. Do scout everything else—from a five-and-dime to display houses —for offbeat light sources.

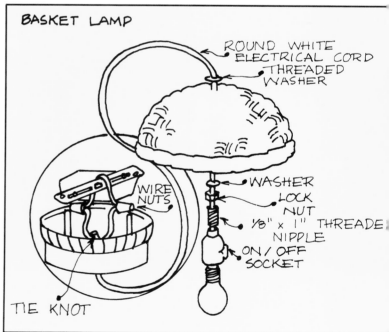

HOW TO DO IT

Lantern Lamp: A few lengths of 2 x 2s and cord transform a plain paper lantern into a standing fixture.

Cut the 2 x 2s to length as shown in the illustration. Notch crosspieces with a saw and chisel. Drill two holes in the top board and corner brace for cord.

Assembling: Screw the 2 x 2s together. Glue on bracing triangles, top and bottom.

Wire it up as shown.

HOW TO DO IT

Basket Lamp: A big basket can hold lots of light. If the weave is loose enough, you won't need to cut a hole for the cord. Wire it as shown in the illustration above. Or hang it from an eyebolt held into the ceiling with a Molly bolt anchor. Run the cord to the corner of the room, down to the baseboard and along to the nearest outlet. Add a plug and line switch. This method also works with a stainless steel bowl, a colander and other similarly shaped objects

Photo: Thomas Hooper

Photo: Thomas Hooper

WINE LAMP

9" HARP

"BRASS
PIPE

THREADED
WASHER

½"
BRASS
DISK

7½" DIA
BALL
OF JUTE

⅛"
THREADED
PIPE

9"
WOODEN
BASE

BOTTOM
BASE
VIEW

CUT GROOVE
FOR CORD

COUNTERBORE 1"
HOLE TO ALLOW
FOR WASHER AND NUT

HOW TO DO IT

Twine Lamp: Any large-scale spool—of wire, wool or twine—can become a lamp. This big ball of jute macramé cord came from a craft store. You will also need a wooden plaque for a base. Stack and screw together the pieces on a length of threaded pipe (see illustration at left). To make the base sit flat, use an electric drill with a 1" spade bit to counterbore a depression in the bottom of the wood plaque, then continue with a ⅜" bit to drill a hole on through. This way the nut and washer at the bottom of the rod nestle right into the base. The groove for the wire is easy to cut with a wood chisel or even a sharp knife.

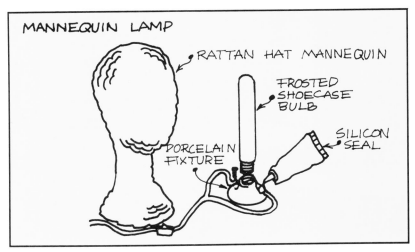

MANNEQUIN LAMP

RATTAN HAT MANNEQUIN

FROSTED
SHOECASE
BULB

PORCELAIN
FIXTURE

SILICON
SEAL

HOW TO DO IT

Mannequin Lamp: Any hollow form, open at the bottom, closed at top, can be lighted this way: Wire a porcelain ceiling socket, screw in a long, skinny showcase bulb and, in this case, plop a straw hat over the works. Hat stands are available at display stores. Cover the bare wires on the socket with silicon rubber sealer.

LAMPS: Make One Out of Anything

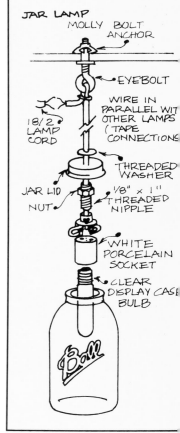

JAR LAMP

MOLLY BOLT ANCHOR
EYEBOLT
WIRE IN PARALLEL WIT OTHER LAMPS (TAPE CONNECTIONS
18/2 LAMP CORD
THREADED WASHER
JAR LID NUT
1/8" x 1" THREADED NIPPLE
WHITE PORCELAIN SOCKET
CLEAR DISPLAY CASE BULB
Ball

Photo: Thomas Hooper

HOW TO DO IT

Jar Lamp: Here is a variation the kerosene lamp, using an old-fashioned canning jar. D a 3/8" hole in the jar lid for the pipe nipple.

String all the parts togethe as above, on round white ele trical cord, and attach the tw wires to the terminal screws the socket. Screw in the bulb screw on the jar and hang.

HOW TO DO IT

Swan Lamp: This plastic ice mold is yet another example how just about anything can become a lamp. You can buy hollow swan like this (or a mermaid or many other mol at a restaurant supply store. Wire it up as shown.

Photo: Bill Helms

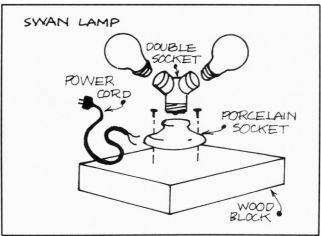

SWAN LAMP

DOUBLE SOCKET
POWER CORD
PORCELAIN SOCKET
WOOD BLOCK

Photo: Thomas Hooper

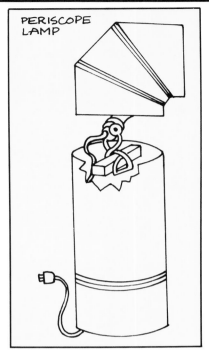

PERISCOPE LAMP

Photo: Bradley Olman

HOW TO DO IT

Periscope Lamp: No nuts, bolts, or skill are needed to make this lamp. It is made of stovepipe sections with a clamp-on light inside—an easy way to make sculptural lighting for little money.

Since builders' supply yards

stock several sizes of stovepipe, you can make the lamps almost any scale. Before assembling, wedge a wooden crosspiece (the same length as the diameter of the pipe) into the pipe to hold the clamp-on light in the curve of the hood. Paint the inside of the hood to reflect more light.

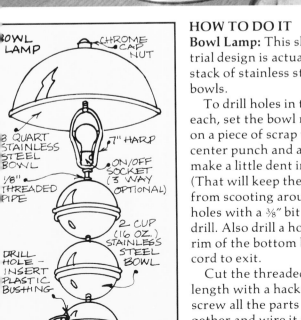

BOWL LAMP

CHROME CAP NUT

8 QUART STAINLESS STEEL BOWL

7" HARP

1/8" THREADED PIPE

ON/OFF SOCKET (3 WAY OPTIONAL)

2 CUP (16 OZ.) STAINLESS STEEL BOWL

DRILL HOLE — INSERT PLASTIC BUSHING

WASHER LOCK NUT

HOW TO DO IT

Bowl Lamp: This sleek industrial design is actually a clever stack of stainless steel mixing bowls.

To drill holes in the bottom of each, set the bowl right side up on a piece of scrap wood. Use a center punch and a hammer to make a little dent in the bottom. (That will keep the drill point from scooting around.) Drill the holes with a 3/8" bit in an electric drill. Also drill a hole near the rim of the bottom bowl for the cord to exit.

Cut the threaded rod to length with a hacksaw, then screw all the parts tightly together and wire it up.

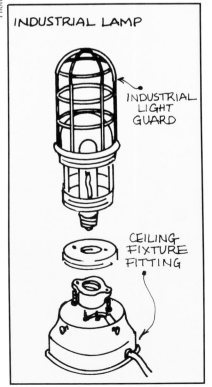

INDUSTRIAL LAMP

INDUSTRIAL LIGHT GUARD

CEILING FIXTURE FITTING

Photo: Thomas Hooper

HOW TO DO IT

Industrial Lamp: This lantern-like lamp practically makes itself. Its shell is an industrial light guard from a hardware store. For the base, match the guard to a porcelain ceiling fixture from a lamp shop. Wire as shown. A long showcase bulb fits inside the glass dome.

HALLWAYS: Cures for Tunnel Vision

If you have always taken a narrow view of hallways, take off the blinders: Think of them not as mere corridors to pass through but as extensions of other rooms. With space so scarce, spotlighting and adorning a hall is just one more chance to make a mark on your surroundings.

Have a private showing in your hallway. Ferret out gorgeous old frames and showcase antique portraits. Or, for up-to-date, but old-time-looking portraits, have sepia prints made.

Whether the collection is permanent or the show moves to another hall, you can have a versatile gallery by hanging portraits from picture rail molding. It will serve two purposes: The walls are left nail-free and the gallery takes on a Victorian air. The picture rail is attached near the ceiling and has a lip to hang hooks from.

For more turn-of-the-century design, try wainscoting one or more walls with sheet steel panels (formerly tin and used for ceilings). Paint or give them two coats of polyurethane so there is no chance of rust.

me was, if you wanted fabric
n the walls, it took hours of
moothing out tiny bubbles of
ue or tacking it to clumsy
ames. Now there is a simple
lution, called Fabri-Trak, that
ses the work and protects the
bric (available at wallpaper
ores).

Frame a wall with long plastic
rips that have "jaws" at the
p to hide raw edges and an
hesive strip to hold the fabric
ght. The fabric is stuck to the
hesive edge, then stuffed into
e "jaws," using a special tool
at looks like a fork without
es.

The hall works as a gallery
ere too. One grand romantic
ster opens up the narrow
ace and makes the biggest
pression—much more readily
an many smaller ones would
. The made-yesterday (but of
meless design) clock deserves
e throne position at the hall-
ay's end.

PLANTS: Indoor Bloomers

You do not need a backyard to enjoy a bed of flowering wonders. They can add living color to any room that has the right light. The following plants can be identified on the chart below:

1. Stephanotis Floribunda: Needs full to medium sun; keep soil fairly moist.

2. Clivia Miniata: Needs medium sun to partial shade; keep fairly moist.

3. Paphiopedilum Macrathon (Lady Slipper Orchid): Requires medium sun to partial shade; evenly moist soil.

4. Anthurium: Needs medium sun; keep evenly moist; keep leaves clean.

5 and 6. Agave: Needs full to medium sun; keep soil dry to fairly moist.

7. Cymbidium (Orchid): Needs medium sun; soil fairly to evenly moist; blooms fall to spring.

8 and 9. Opuntia: Needs full sun; dry soil.

10. Carnegiea Gigantea: Needs full sun; dry soil.

11. Echinocactus (Golden Barrel Cactus): Needs full sun; dry soil; cooler winter.

12 and 13. Sinningia Gloxinia: Needs medium sun; fairly moist soil.

14. Gardenia: Needs full to medium sun; fairly moist soil.

15. Strelitzia Reginae (Bird-of-Paradise): Needs full to medium sun; evenly to fairly moist soil.

PLANTS: Balcony Garden

re is the city version of that ecial truck-garden patch tra- ionally tucked in close to the mhouse. In town, you can- t dig your toes into the soil t you can certainly harvest ur crops, indoors or out, nerever there is space.
Here are a few things to ow about growing vegetables d herbs:

Vegetables: Start tomatoes, ppers, cucumbers and onions om plants (not seeds) when- er you can. For tomatoes, the all varieties are best because ey will not sprawl. Yield in 45 55 days. Most varieties of een bell peppers yield in out 60 days. Radishes grow om seeds in about 29 days.

Herbs: Buy plants, if possible, d start harvesting as soon as u bring them home. Pick the leaves from most herbs to ep new growth coming. Keep eet basil leaves pinched back the plant will get tall and aggly. Snip the tops off ves for mild onion flavor. l grows tall and wide so leave om. Keep oregano trimmed ck. Parsley is a short, thick nt; pick the outer sprigs and ve the middle ones to grow.

OW TO DO IT

anters: A container can be actically anything so long as it lds dirt, has drainage holes or s a bottom layer of gravel. Or eamline things by making y of these quick-build boxes. Each box is made from ugh-sawn cedar 1 x 8s. The rners are butted together, en nailed with 8d galvanized sing nails. Decide your di- ensions, cut the boards with a w and assemble.

Photo: Thomas Hooper

PLANTS: Garden Spots

Peppers, tomatoes, onions, radishes, peas—all in the bedroom. Growing. With a sunny **window**, you can grow vegetables in your apartment, and in just a few weeks you will have something fresh to nibble.

Build vegetable beds from 1" x 12" boards and a hollow-core door (see illustration). Build the boxes first; top with a door. Then screw the side uprights to the boxes; nail the top crosspiece to the side pieces. Attach the middle upright with L brackets to the top and door. Add adjustable shelving.

Temperature and Humidity: Ideally, 70 to 75 degrees by day and 60 to 65 at night. Heat wave? Peas and lettuce may fade but the rest will take up to 90 degrees for a few days. A direct draft from an air conditioner could be fatal.

Pollination: With no bees around, you have to take over or there will not be any fruit. You can shake the tomatoes, peppers and peas while they are in bloom, or pollinate them by using a small brush to transfer the yellow dust from flower to flower.

Watering: Vegetables need a lot of water. Clear plastic pie dishes let you see if excess water is draining out. With no breezes to help, keep water off leaves and stems by using a long-snouted can. Water in the morning so sun will not burn them and roots will not soak overnight.

Yield: You get more quality than quantity. Onions, radishes and leafy vegetables will fill their containers. Peppers and peas will not be bumper crops but they are delicious.

Feeding: Liquid fertilizer suits indoor containers. In the lightweight phony soil that is best for pots, tomatoes and peppers need a shot while they are flowering. But use half the

dose recommended on the package. If the seed pack or nursery mention "slightly acidic soil," get aluminum sulfate and follow package directions when you mix the soil.

Light: Vegetables must have four to six hours of full sun for leaf and root crops—eight is better for yielding the fruit. You may need to add grow lights. To supplement weak sun, figure 16 hours a day of lamp light. The light should be rigged so it is 15 inches above the soil and you have enough lamps to average 15 to 20 watts per square foot of growing area.

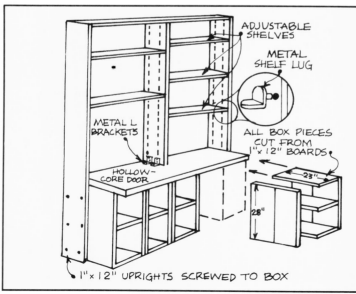

ADJUSTABLE SHELVES

METAL SHELF LUG

METAL L BRACKETS

ALL BOX PIECES CUT FROM 1" x 12" BOARDS

HOLLOW-CORE DOOR

23"

28"

1" x 12" UPRIGHTS SCREWED TO BOX

PLANTS: Garden Variety Planters

Photo: Thomas Hooper

Photo: Jessie Walker/Design: James Blackowicz

ve: This freestanding plant
y doubles as a window treat-
nt and room divider.

)W TO DO IT

or Planter: Build the tray
me with four lengths of 1 x 4
gh sawn cedar boards.
ten the corners with nails
I glue. Use ¼" plywood for
bottom. Nail in the ply-
od, then seal cracks with
od putty.

Vaterproof it with a couple
oats of polyurethane. Let
h coat dry thoroughly and
d lightly between coats. Line
tray with plastic sheets.

ve right: With this easily built
od unit you get lots of space
hanging plants, a big gravel
lf for nonhanging greenery
l a full-scale window treat-
nt—all in one.

HOW TO DO IT

Window Planter: Build the
frame from good grade fir 2 x
4s, screwed together. Drill part
way through the 2 x 4 with a
drill bit slightly larger than the
screwhead. Then continue all
the way through with a bit the
size of the screw shank. Finally,
drill a pilot hole in the adjoining
piece with a bit slightly smaller
than the screw threads. Once
the whole framework is assembled, fill all holes that show
with wooden plugs. Buy special
plugs with a knob on the end, or
use short lengths of dowel rod,
glued in. Nail on the plywood
bottom.

   Waterproof the tray. Attach
the legs and overhead beam to
the tray. Drill screw holes and
use wooden plugs as described
above. Fill the tray with gravel
and load in the plants.

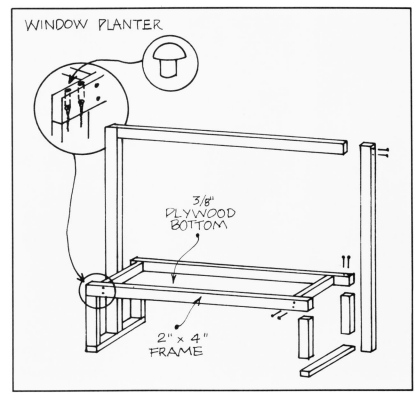

WINDOW PLANTER

3/8" PLYWOOD BOTTOM

2" x 4" FRAME

PLANTS: The Upstairs Greenhouse

Add a built-in jungle to your backyard or balcony with an easy-to-install greenhouse that will keep your place looking lush and green for many months of the year.

You can build it one panel at a time (it takes no more than a long weekend). Since the greenhouse is not attached to the balcony or yard, you will not be making any structural changes.

The greenhouse temperature is controlled by opening and closing the glass doors or windows of your apartment. You can add some optional special equipment—a fan to circulate the air, a double layer of plastic to stretch the seasons, a thermometer, humidifier/vaporizer —but none of these is a must.

To cut down on summer heat: Take out the removable vents on the sides for a little air circulation and cover the top with cheesecloth. In the fall even the most sensitive plants —tropical and seedlings—remain healthy until the greenhouse temperature gets down to 50 degrees.

When you are ready to move your plants into their new home, keep your sun-loving plants on the outer edges and your sun-shy varieties shielded on the inside. Exposures to the south, east or west give best growth.

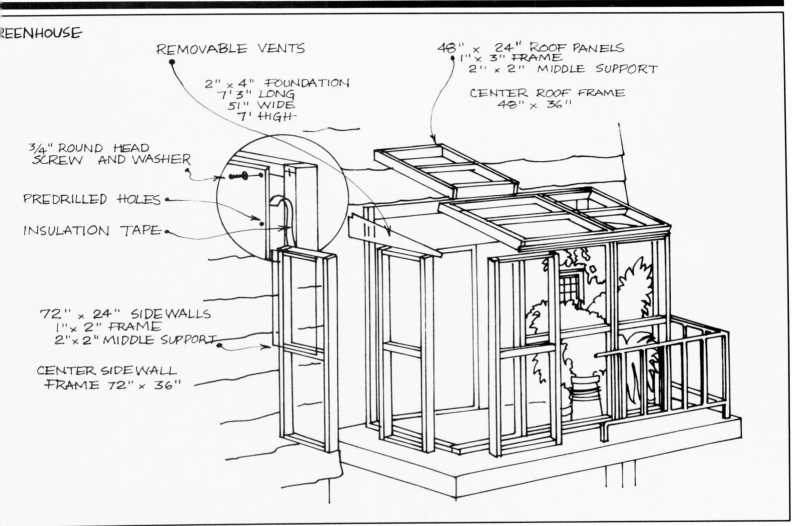

REMOVABLE VENTS

2" x 4" FOUNDATION
7' 3" LONG
51" WIDE
7' HIGH

48" x 24" ROOF PANELS
1" x 3" FRAME
2" x 2" MIDDLE SUPPORT

CENTER ROOF FRAME
48" x 36"

3/4" ROUND HEAD
SCREW AND WASHER

PREDRILLED HOLES

INSULATION TAPE

72" x 24" SIDEWALLS
1" x 2" FRAME
2" x 2" MIDDLE SUPPORT

CENTER SIDEWALL
FRAME 72" x 36"

HOW TO DO IT

Greenhouse: Build ten basic panels, then screw them all together on your balcony. Although the panels that form the sides and roof of the greenhouse are several different sizes, the construction of each one is basically the same. For the sidewalls, nail together a frame of 1 x 2 strips with a 2 x 2 strip in the middle for extra support. The roof frames are made from 1 x 3s.

When you get a frame put together, fasten on precut pieces of storm window plastic. (Make the frames to match the sizes the plastic comes in.) Predrill holes all around the edges of the plastic sheets. Stick

sponge tape insulation to the edges of the panels, set beads of latex bathtub caulking on the tape for a good seal and then screw the plastic panels in place. If you want more insulation, use two plastic sheets for each panel, one screwed to the inside, the other to the outside of the frame.

When all the panels are finished, lay a 2 x 4 box foundation on the balcony floor; use shims where necessary to make it level. Add two 2 x 4 uprights against the side of the building, plus a crosspiece at the top. Fasten with metal angle brackets and screws. Fill gaps between uprights and building with foam insulation.

Now fasten the side panels in place on the 2 x 4 base. Screw the frames to the base and to each other. Or, if you decide to put plastic on both sides of the frames, fasten the panels with strips of wood screwed to the inside edges.

Screw one end of the roof panels to the 2 x 4 crosspiece; fasten the other end to the side panels with metal L brackets or strips of wood. Staple aluminum screening over the triangular openings at the ends of the greenhouse. Then cut triangular plastic panels to fit inside these openings. Fasten them in with wing nuts for easy removal when you want more ventilation on sunny days.

APT INFORMATION

Putting together an apartment often means a lot more than buying and arranging furniture. In fact, putting together an apartment frequently means taking it apart first—fixing, stapling, drilling, hammering and dozens of other tasks. Sure, you can tip the building guy $15 to hang that lamp from the ceiling—but save your money: The following pages show you how to do it yourself and help to fill in the blanks about filling in the cracks of plasterboard, concrete and plywood ceilings. There's a special section that explains all about track lighting —how to choose it and how to install it yourself. And if you like your lighting sources a little lower than the ceiling, we also show you how to figure out the makings of a lamp.

In addition, there's a special self-protection manual all about your rights as a tenant. You may be surprised to learn how many you do have—and exercising them is not nearly as rigorous as most legal calisthenics. The key here is Protect Yourself, and we show you how to do just that—before, during and after your lease runs out.

Because living in an apartment is not just finding the right one (which this section also describes) or moving into one (ditto)—but also knowing what to do when something goes wrong.

Self Help: You as the Expert

A few decades ago, Doing-It-Yourself meant off-duty executives puttering around in their garages over the weekend in sprawling suburban homes, while their wives put in time at the potter's wheel at the local community college. It's all different now. After the back-to-nature and liberation movements of the sixties and the self-fulfillment and self-reliant movements of the seventies, we've been instilled with a new consciousness that, indeed, we can take pride in our own creations—whether they be a picture frame or a seating system.

This section tells you how to do many of the things that need to be done—yourself. You can be the expert when it comes to making a lamp or a coffee table or a desk—or even when you hang a lamp and then need to camouflage the hole you made in the ceiling.

The Handy Under-the-Sink Toolbox

THE BASIC KIT

1. Hammer: A 13-ounce curved-claw hammer is the handiest size. Buy a good one (not the $1.39 specials). Steel shanks are the strongest and Fiberglas the most flexible for good hammering action.

2. Screwdrivers: A set of three or four screwdrivers should meet most of your needs. Find a set with varying sizes, plus a small Phillips (often called cross-tip).

3. Pliers: Ordinary slip joint pliers work fine for most jobs, although parrot nose pliers open wider, squeeze harder and are especially good for plumbing work.

4. Adjustable wrench: Get a 6" wrench and a 9", for extra big jobs.

5. Mat knife: A handle for replaceable razor blades. You always have a sharp knife—great for opening packages.

6. Push drill: Start holes for screws and plastic anchors with this handy little tool; often handier to use than an electric drill. Bits store in the handle.

7. Cordless electric screwdriver: This works like a push drill and also drives screws. Keep it plugged in and charged up, then detach it when you need it.

8. Putty knife: Use it to fill holes in the wall with spackling compound and for scraping paint. Knives come in various widths and degrees of flexibility, but one medium-width, fairly stiff blade does most jobs.

9. Ice pick or **Awl:** Useful for various poking and chipping chores.

10. Combination square: Use to measure and mark exact right angles. Especially useful when cutting boards and assembling pieces for your projects. Also measures 45-degree angles, and the metal rule slips out to make a straight edge. Some even have little spirit levels in them.

11. Block plane: Use this to smooth the edges of wood pieces after sawing and to plane off mistakes in fitting.

12. Staple gun: If you plan to put up ceiling tile, reupholster furniture, or fasten fabric to a frame, this will come in handy. Keep a supply of ¼" and ½" staples.

13. Portable electric drill: For most people the quarter-inch drill is handiest. (Quarter-inch refers to the largest size drill-bit shank it will hold.) There are many different types of drills with many different options on the market but here are the important ones: Variable speed—so you can use the drill as an electric screwdriver and have better control when drilling holes; a reversing switch—so you can unscrew screws; and double insulation (a plastic or part plastic tool casing)—so it is almost impossible to get a shock.

Also, buy a good set of high-speed drill bits and a couple of screwdriver bits—flat blade and Phillips. Spade bits let you drill large diameter holes. Beyond that, there are all kinds of attachments to make your drill do everything from sanding to pumping water.

14. Portable electric saber saw (also called portable jigsaw): This saw is an inexpensive little workhorse that will do a number of different jobs well. Although designed to cut curves in relatively thin material, it will chew its way, with reasonable accuracy, through most materials that you are likely to use. It is a smaller version of the big circular saw carpenters use but it is a lot less noisy, more portable, and less expensive.

You can cut straight lines by clamping a straight stick to the wood, to guide the saw base, then use a block plane to smooth up the cut edge. You can also get special blades for plastic, metal, and other special materials. Two features to look for: double insulation and variable speed.

A SHOPPING TIP

When you buy any tool, choose one of good quality, one that will last a long time. Since a hand tool acts as an extension of your arm or hand, pick it up, hold it in your hand, and get the feel of it before you buy. This will tell you more about the quality and craftsmanship of the tool than anything else, and whether you will feel comfortable working with it.

IN THE BOTTOM OF THE BOX

Other items you will want in the under-the-sink toolbox: chalk, pencils, white glue, cup hooks, spackling compound, wood putty, a small G clamp and bar clamp, nails, screws, and drill bits. Anything else for more major projects can be rented from a tool shop.

A WORD ABOUT WOOD

All measurements for standard plywood are given as 1 x however, in reality, the actual size is ¾" x 1¾" because wood shrinks at first. If you are using hardwood on any project, take note that the size will be different from the 1 x 2 plywood.

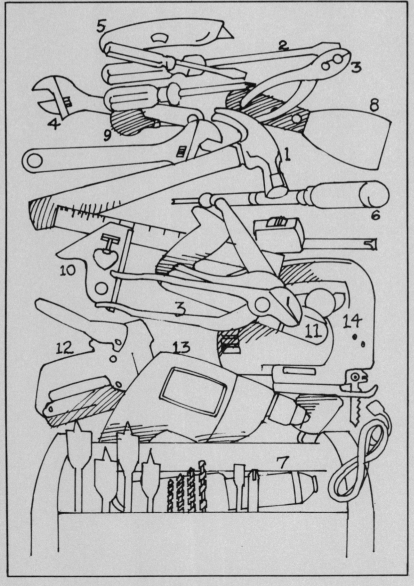

How to Hang Anything from the Ceiling

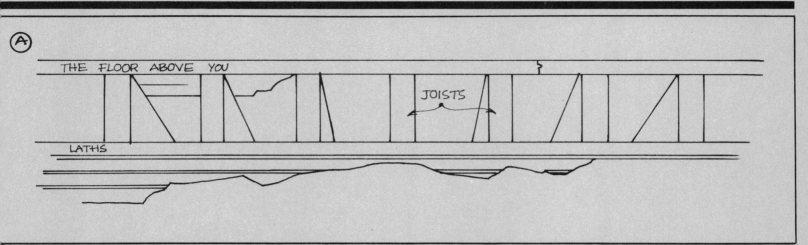

Ⓐ THE FLOOR ABOVE YOU
JOISTS
LATHS

...ce you get your bolts and
...ls together, you can hang
...thing—up to 200 pounds—
...ust a few minutes. What you
...g and how you hang it
...ends on the kind of ceiling
...u have. Here are step-by-step
...tructions for whatever is
...r your head:

...TH AND PLASTER
...ILINGS

...ound mostly in older build-
...s, this type is probably the
...iest to deal with. The only
...cky part is locating the
...oden joists when you want
...hang something heavy.

...Hanging heavy things: If
...u are going to put up some-
...ng that takes a lot of weight
...hammock, for example), hang
...rom screw hooks in the
...sts, which are wooden beams
...ced 16" to 24" apart that
...n the length or width of your
...ling. First you must find
...em.

...How to do it: You will need an
...ctric drill, a screw eye or a
...ew hook, and a coat hanger.
...e easiest way to find a joist is
...drill a hole straight up. If you
...e lucky, you will hit one on
...e first try. If not, drill
...ough the same hole again
...ntwise. Then straighten out
...e coat hanger and poke it
...rough the hole. If you hit
...mething solid, it is a joist.
...easure how far away it is by
...eping your thumb on the
...nger, then lightly mark the

appropriate spot on the ceiling.
If you do not hit anything
solid on your first try, it means
the joists run in another direction. Drill slantwise again—in
the same hole as before—but 90
degrees left or right. You
should definitely hit a joist with
another poke of the hanger.

Then drill a hole slightly
smaller than the shank diameter of your screw eye or screw
hook. Twist it in tight.

Hanging light things: You
can hang plants (not trees) from
the laths, which are little boards
that run across the joists to

support the plaster ceiling.

How to do it: You will need an
electric drill with a spade bit and
a toggle hook or Molly bolt. The
only reason you might use a
joist to hang something light in
your lath and plaster ceiling is
because you want it in a specific
spot. So first, drill a tiny hole
with a regular bit exactly where
you want to hang it. If you hit a
joist, just twist in a screw eye or
screw hook and you are done.

If you do not hit a joist,
switch to a toggle hook or
Molly bolt. Drill a hole just big
enough for the closed toggles to

fit through. (Instructions are
usually on the toggle packages
that come in a complete set.)
Then push the toggles and bolt
into the ceiling, making sure
enough of the bolt sticks out to
screw the swag hook on.
Screwing the hook tight will
lock the assembly in place.

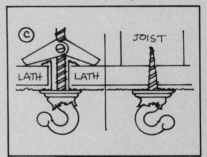

Ⓒ JOIST
LATH LATH

If you use a Molly bolt, drill a
hole the same diameter as the
bolt and insert it into the ceiling. As you tighten it, a split-
sleeve will expand against the
inside of the ceiling and hold it
tight. Unscrew the bolt and the
Molly will stay put.

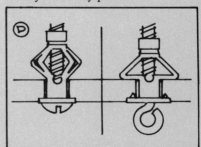

Ⓓ

Hanging very light things: If
you are hanging something that
weighs under 25 pounds, just
twist a little screw eye or screw
hook right into one of those
laths.

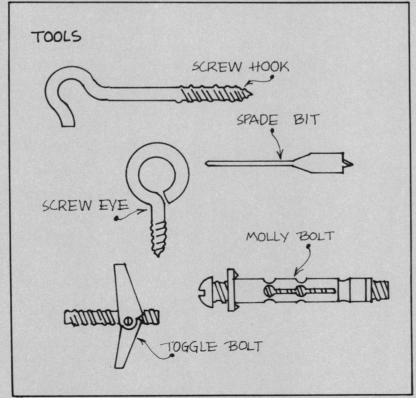

TOOLS

SCREW HOOK

SPADE BIT

SCREW EYE

MOLLY BOLT

TOGGLE BOLT

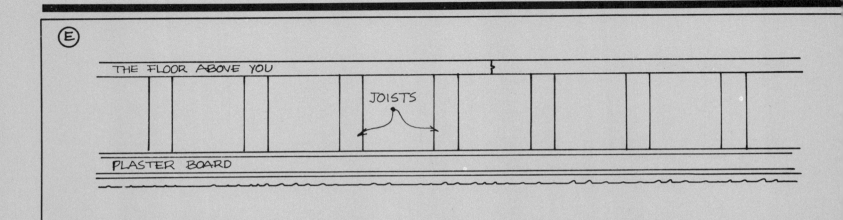

The floor above you

JOISTS

Plaster board

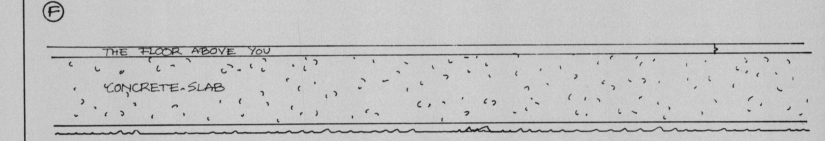

The floor above you

Concrete slab

PLASTERBOARD CEILINGS

You will find these mostly in new low rises. For hanging purposes, plasterboard ceilings are almost the same as lath and plaster—minus the laths.

As before, hang heavy things from the joists. Lightweight items (under 50 pounds) can be hung from the plasterboard with a toggle hook. Follow the same instructions as for a lath and plaster ceiling.

CONCRETE CEILINGS

You will find concrete ceilings mostly in modern high rises. It is tough to drill a hole in concrete, but a carbide bit and an electric drill will do wonders. You will also need to get an "anchor" and a screw eye or screw hook. An anchor is made of soft material (lead, fiber, or nylon) that is threaded up the middle to receive the screw eye or screw hook.

How to do it: Be sure your carbide bit is the same diameter

as the anchor, then drill a hole straight up—exactly where you want to hang something.

Insert the anchor into the hole. Make sure it is a tight fit. As you twist the screw eye or

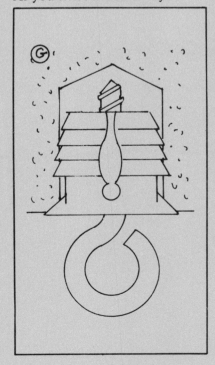

screw hook into the anchor, the soft material will actually expand into the concrete and hold the screw tight.

Important: The friction of the anchor against the concrete is all that is keeping things off the floor. Make sure the anchor fits tightly. If you are going to hang lots of things, you might want to put up a plywood ceiling (see below). Instructions are the same but use anchors instead of toggle bolts.

HOW TO MAKE A PLYWOOD CEILING

Measure the area you will use to hang things. Pick up a piece of ½" plywood from the lumberyard—cut to fit your measurements—and attach it with a toggle bolt in each corner. Paint it to match the ceiling.

Then, with screw eyes or screw hooks, you can hang anything. When you move, just pull the whole thing down and fill the four holes.

PATCHING UP

In most cases patching up simply means filling in the ho with spackling compound.

But if you use an anchor, p of it will still be visible after y remove the eyebolt. A few ta with a hammer will knock the offending anchor up into the ceiling so you can smooth ove the surface.

If you have a textured ceili try dabbing the soft, wet spackling compound with a damp sponge to approximate the texture.

HOW MUCH WILL IT HOL

In most cases the ceiling wi fall before the hanging hardware will. Here is how much sturdy ceiling will hold:

Plasterboard: Up to 50 pound anything heavier, find a joist

Lath and Plaster: 75 to 100 pounds; anything heavier, st looking for a joist.

Concrete: Up to 200 pounds lead anchor.

All About Track Lighting

track system does it all. Affixed to the ceiling, it leaves floor space free, and it can also help change the look and mood of rooms with a mere flick of a switch. Track systems offer multicolored bulbs and filters, and are completely adjustable, moving as you move your furniture and objects within a room. Plus, track lighting can do a lot to visually alter the dimensions of space. Bathing the wall of a small room with light will make the space seem bigger. Large spaces on the other hand become more intimate with overhead spots complementing other lighting. Track fixtures, of course, can also help direct proper work light to desks, workshops, game tables, and kitchen counters without cluttering up work surfaces with table lamps.

Track lighting is easy to install, though you might need an electrician if you want the wiring recessed or if you put in more than one circuit with dimmer controls. To set up a system, the greatest effort goes into the preshopping decision. Before you buy ask yourself the following questions:

Where will the light be required?

What is the scale and size of the space?

Is the room or arrangement of the room apt to change, altering the lighting requirements?

Where will the track be mounted?

Will it plug into a wall outlet or be wired into a recessed power box in the ceiling?

Do the fixtures have proper tension or a locking device so they remain in position when aimed toward a particular area?

Does the mounting device on top of the fixture fit the track you are considering?

HOW TO CHOOSE A TRACK

There are two types of track: 1) a continuous open-channel track or 2) a track with outlets prespaced along a closed channel. Continuous channel track offers the most flexibility. Fixtures can be set in anywhere along its length and can be readily changed if the function or room arrangement changes.

Where lighting requirements are not apt to change, and flexibility is not the prime concern, you might choose closed channel tracks, which are protected from grease and steam. They can be painted along the bottom edge for a neater, finished look. Fixtures "stab" into outlets along the length of the track.

Both types of tracks are sold in various lengths and finishes. Most track sections are prewired and polarized to assure a safe, properly grounded electrical connection. They plug together as easily as model train tracks and, with flexible corner connectors, can be hooked together at any angle.

CHOOSING A POWER SOURCE FOR YOUR TRACK

There are two ways to supply power to a track system:

1. Connect the track to a recessed power box in the ceiling, which conceals the wiring. (A licensed electrician is needed for this job.)

2. Plug the track into a standard wall outlet with a cord-and-plug accessory. To minimize the cord, run it along the ceiling-wall line, down the corner of the room and along the baseboard to the outlet.

A word about circuits: The average 15- or 20-amp circuit in a normal room can safely supply about 1,200 watts of power. Add up the wattage of each bulb on your track to be sure you do not exceed your limit and blow a fuse.

A single circuit track system is sufficient for most apartments. However, more exciting effects are possible with a multicircuit system. You might have colored lights on one circuit, white light on another, all on the same track. In this case an electrician divides an ordinary electrical circuit into two, three, even four separate circuits, and replaces a wall switch with several switches or dimmers. Instead of the regular single-circuit track, you install a multicircuit track, which is deeper, and must be connected to a power box in the ceiling.

MOUNTING A TRACK

The easiest way to mount a track is directly on the ceiling by simply using the precut holes in the top of the track. Insert appropriate wood screws or toggle bolts through the holes. To attach a track to a concrete ceiling, drill holes with a special masonry bit, insert a

lead or plastic anchor, then use a sheet-metal screw ½" longer than the plug to secure the track to the surface. (See How to Hang Anything from the Ceiling.)

To light objects on a wall or to wash a wall with light, the track should be mounted 2 to 3' from the wall when ceilings are 7½ to 9' high. Move the track one foot further from the wall for every two additional feet of ceiling height. If the track is mounted too close to the wall, any object hanging on the wall will be shadowed. If the track is too far from the wall, the light source may be reflected and cause glare.

CHOOSING THE TRACK FIXTURES

Cylinders, squares, and spheres are the most common fixture shapes. They are often used to provide work or accent lighting. Shovel-cut cylinders are especially made to wash a wall with light.

A WORD ABOUT LOW-VOLTAGE LIGHTING

Low-wattage bulbs and fixtures are more expensive than standard equipment but their cost is offset by their long life and savings in electricity. They use half the power of standard bulbs, and can be attached to any track. Low-voltage lighting is whiter, crisper, gives off less heat, and is more brilliant than standard lighting. When a low-voltage fixture is capped with a tinted filter, it improves the quality of colored light.

Anatomy of a Lamp

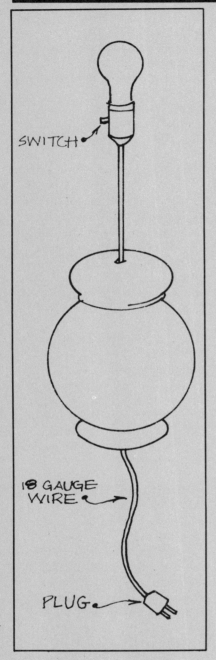

SWITCH

18 GAUGE WIRE

PLUG

Which wire: The wire you need for most lamps is 18-gauge, two-wire rubber, or plastic-covered lamp cord (called 18/2).

To connect wire: Split the insulation at the end of the wire with a knife, and cut off about ¾" of insulation from each wire. (Drawing A.)

Then unscrew the terminal screws on the plug or socket, and wrap one of the exposed wire ends around each of the screws. Retighten the screws and reassemble the socket or plug. (Drawing B.)

To splice lengths of wire: Twist the two pairs together as shown, and wrap with electrician's tape so one pair cannot touch the other and cause a short. (Drawing C.)

Line switch: A line switch installed at a convenient point on the lamp cord is especially effective with lamps that have no other on/off switch. Instructions come on the switch kits (from any lamp or hardware store) and they are assembled like this. (Drawing D.)

A safety note: To keep the wire from pulling off the terminal screws of a socket or plug (and to avoid shock), separate the two lamp cord wires and tie a knot like this. (Drawing E.)

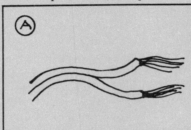

A

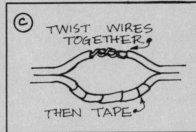

C

TWIST WIRES TOGETHER

THEN TAPE

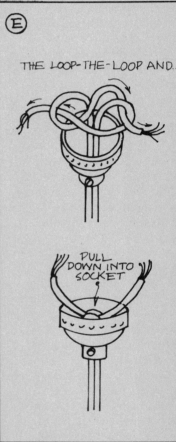

E

THE LOOP-THE-LOOP AND..

PULL DOWN INTO SOCKET

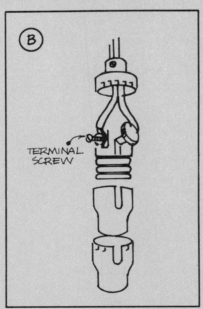

B

TERMINAL SCREW

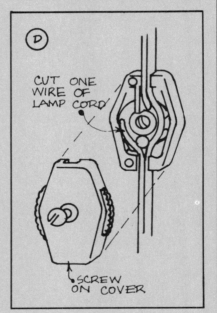

D

CUT ONE WIRE OF LAMP CORD

SCREW ON COVER

What You Should Know as a Tenant

When you own your own home, if you have an argument with the landlord, you are fighting with yourself. When you rent an apartment, you are usually arguing with an anonymous voice on the other end of the line, or writing monthly checks to a phantom address. But what happens when that post office box does not fix the lock on the outer door? What if you get no heat, and you want to know how to give your landlord heat about it? What happens if you need to sue your landlord? Do you know the difference between arbitration and negotiation? And what about finding a new apartment? How can you make sure you are getting a good one? And after you have secured an apartment, how can you make it secure? All this is explored on the following pages, which offer some basic tenets about tenancy.

Finding the Right Apartment

With some places you will want to sign a lease after your first walk-through. But even when the apartment has that can't-live-without oak floor or enormous bay window, you still need to pay attention to some of the everyday things: the way the place is laid out, what kind of neighborhood it is in, how the fixtures work. Here is a step-by-step guide for inspecting your apartment:

Neighborhood: Where you live can turn sour if things like transportation, shopping, and recreational facilities are not all they should be. A convenient location, for instance, would be at the end of a more-or-less straight line from work. Conversely, a commute that requires complicated changes from one highway to another—or bus transfers—might be rated "far out," even though the distance is not far. And you can be too close to wheezing buses, noisy (and nosy) neighbors, busy highways, and the local fire engine route. Nearby schools are important if you have children.

It is a good idea to psyche out the kind of people who are living in the building or complex—singles, families with young children, older people. Many places have become very specialized according to life situations.

Do not just look on the block. Travel a few miles to get a clear idea about shops and services and places to play. If these are missing or remote, the area hardly qualifies as a neighborhood.

Parking: Will you park your car on the street, in a lot, or in a garage? Are parking fees as much as the rent? Will parking be available to your guests?

Entrance: The way a landlord maintains the front door and lobby areas of the building is a good indication of what his attitude will be when you want more heat in the winter. Check for security: a good intercom system, adequate locks, and/or a doorman to fend off offenders. Well-lit entries make it easier for people with keys and harder for those without.

On the way up, check out things like the size of elevators and the width of stairways to see if you can get what you already own into the apartment. If there are stairs, how many will you have to climb everyday?

Floor plans: There are certain human factors to consider about how an apartment is laid out: Is the bathroom within stumbling distance of the bedroom? The dining area near the kitchen? Is there a place near the door where you can pull off boots? Can the kitchen be closed off from the living room if you need to do it?

Mentally move in your furniture and try to arrange it, estimating whether there is adequate wall space for the sofa and enough height for your bookcases. If you have an odd piece of furniture or if the apartment has a lot of nooks and crannies, it is a good idea to take along a tape measure.

General condition: Here is where you have to have a clear idea of what you are able and willing to do yourself. If things look a little shoddy and you do not mind doing a little work, you should expect a break on the rent. Try bargaining. You may at the very least get the management to supply materials.

Windows should operate smoothly, with no gaps for air or noise to leak through. To check out just how sound resistant a window or sliding glass door is, open it, wait for a large truck or other noisemaker to pass, then close the window. The din should substantially dim.

Peace and quiet: The more solid a wall, the quieter the apartment will be. So take time to thump on common partitions. Old-fashioned plaster and lath walls do a fairly good job of blocking noise if they are not badly cracked and pierced with holes. Middle-age buildings—built in the fifties and early sixties—frequently have nothing but flimsy dry-wall construction, which is notoriously noisy. Many newer buildings use double walls, staggered-stud construction, and a variety of other techniques to protect your ears from noise.

Kitchen: Investigate the stove, refrigerator, fans, dishwasher, and garbage disposal to see how well they work.

Make sure there is enough space in the kitchen and that it is well organized.

Bathroom: Make sure everything here works. Extra storage space is a bonus.

Storage: You will never have enough space to store everything but can this apartment at least neatly file away most of your belongings? Is a big closet or a locker in the basement available for bicycles, skis, barbecue grill, etc.?

Can you control heating and cooling precisely? Find out who pays for the heat and cool—you or the landlord. If the building is not air conditioned, does it at least have wiring adequate for window units? Check to be sure each room has at least one electrical outlet per wall (although you can add more with surface wiring). Is there an antenna on the roof for television?

Extras: Swimming pools, saunas, health clubs, and putting greens are nice but do not forget about the less flashy amenities. Do check out laundry facilities. (You can often tell how well run a building is by looking at the laundry room.) Is there a doorman or someone in the building who can accept packages and messages when you are out?

Apartment guides: Apartment hunting in a strange city is not necessarily the chore it used to be. Over the past year apartment guides—publications giving detailed information about available rental housing—have been started in most major cities.

The guides do not list every apartment in town, and they are not objective about the places they mention. (The cost of printing the booklets is paid by the complexes and a few other companies who want your business. It is a form of advertising usually dominated by the middle and upper income places.) But they give you more to go on than the classified ads. Complimentary copies are available through most chambers of commerce.

Who are you renting? If the manager is brusque or long-winded when you ask about the apartment, you can multiply that by fifty the day the furnace breaks down. When you arrive on the premises, size up the manager's own quarters. If he has been relegated to a former coal bin on the dark side of the furnace, you can be certain the owner does not care who is minding the building. If you are visiting a big complex, expect an office, not a corner of the manager's own apartment.

If the person who shows you the apartment is not the manager, ask for an introduction. Find out about the chain of command, who will give you answers and action after you have moved in, especially if you are being shown around by a real estate agent.

Flexibility is another mark of a manager who is in command of the job. If you suggest something out of the ordinary, he or she should be able to give you an answer within a reasonable time, or pose an alternative.

What to Look for in a Lease

Contracts between landlords and tenants are rooted in a tradition that has total regard for the owner of land, with little thought given for the well-being of tenants who lived on that land. Just the words *landlord* and *tenant* are indicative of that historically unequal relationship.

But in the last ten or so years, great strides forward have been made. Enlightened lawmakers, jurists, and fair-minded apartment owners are making the management of apartments more businesslike: Money is paid and services are rendered in return. But there are still landlords who offer you an apartment on a take-it-or-leave-it basis, complete with an archaic lease they bought at the corner stationery store. These leases are usually margin to margin with small type and contain clauses that discriminate against you as a consumer: They may severely restrict how you use your apartment, ignore the need for maintenance of your apartment, and even try to bluff you out of rights that you are given under the Constitution.

So the first step, after sizing up the management and property, is to examine the lease or rental agreement you are asked to sign.

HOW TO READ A LEASE

Read every word. It is good advice in any contract but especially in apartment leases—and for a very good reason: More often than not it is the sentence buried in the middle of a paragraph that tells you what you really need to know.

Most leases are divided by section titles that are supposed to make reading it easier; they are often no help. The sections seem to be thrown in at random. Read the lease with an eye for how the different sections relate to each other.

Be wary of a sentence that begins: "It shall be deemed a substantial violation..." A substantial violation is the legal term for something that could get you evicted. Although some judges have said that these rules are unreasonable in the context of the entire agreement, others stick to the letter of the lease. Beware of phrases and words in all capital letters, heavier print, and italics; some judges would consider them "substantial" also.

Before you sign, read over all apartment "Rules and Regulations." Most leases state that these rules are part of the lease agreement. Plus, they are the day-to-day rules you will have to live with.

A few states have regulations that leases must be written in plain English. But, until yours does, here are some of the most used "legalese" words demystified.

Lessee: The renter.

Lessor: That is the owner or one of his employees, such as a manager or rental agent.

Demised premises: It sounds foreboding, but it is the legal jargon for the property you are renting.

Term of the lease: Just the length of time the lease is in effect.

Ejectment: The "nice" word for eviction.

Notice to quit: This is a written order for you to get off the landlord's property.

Notice to vacate: That is your written statement that you are getting off the landlord's property.

Assign or sublet: You will see these words together but they have a little different meaning. Subletting is when you lease out your place for only part of the time you have signed for (for instance, just for the summer). Assigning is when you lease out your apartment for the remainder of the time your lease runs.

Indemnify and render the lessor harmless: This means to make the landlord free of any responsibility even to the point of your not suing him.

Arrears: Money not paid when it is due, such as overdue rent.

Distraint proceeding (or proceed by distress): If you owe the landlord money and do not pay up, he can "proceed by distress" against you—that is, take your personal property to force you to pay or eventually sell it to get his money.

Goods and chattels: That is your personal property—both animate and inanimate. It is usually what the landlord will threaten to take if you do not pay.

Replevin: That is the legal action you can take to get property back that was unlawfully seized (taken through "unlawful distress"). Watch out though—many leases say you agree not to take this action.

Inure (or enure): It simply means to "take effect." Most leases inure when you sign them.

Special lease sections to double-check:

Sublet or assign clauses: If you cannot sublet your place, find out if the lease stipulates that there is no penalty (loss of your deposit or the demand for entire lease's rent immediately due and payable) if your employer transfers you.

Security deposits: Make sure you will get your entire deposit back by a reasonable date if you fulfill your lease duties. Although the matter is still up in the air legally, many tenants are fighting landlords who automatically—no matter if the place is spotless—deduct cleaning fees from security deposits. Also, in some states, you will be able to get interest on your deposit.

What happens when you move: See how long in advance you will need to notify your landlord that you are moving. (The contract will most likely say "in writing"; even better, send the letter by certified mail.)

When the lease is up: See if the lease automatically renews if you take no action (like writing the landlord that you are leaving) or if it turns into a month-to-month tenancy.

Privacy: Is there a clause restricting your landlord from entering your place at will?

Repairs: Does the lease mention anything about your landlord keeping the place in shape?

It's a bluff: Some lease clauses are unconstitutional, and many landlords ask you to sign away your constitutional rights. There are lease clauses hidden in tiny type that would take away:

Your right to free speech
Your right to assembly and petition
Your right to a jury trial

These clauses are designed to intimidate you and make you believe you have no rights. For years, landlords—who either accepted the old form lease without question or who planned to use it against you—have perpetuated the myth that they have all the rights and you have all the obligations. The lawyers who wrote leases and judges who upheld them did their share to keep the myth going.

Your best way to fight these oppressive clauses is to strike them out of the lease before you sign. But that is not always possible, especially if you are faced with a take-it-or-leave-it situation.

If you have already signed a bad lease, there is hope. Today you will be hard pressed to find a judge who would uphold so flagrant a denial of your rights. These intimidating clauses are no more than that—a bluff that will not hold up in court.

Your rights to trial by jury: Your right to a jury trial is one of the most basic of your constitutional rights. Yet some leases state that both you and the landlord will waive your right to trial by jury. On the surface it may sound reasonable since *both* of you give up that right. But most landlords know that you are more likely to receive sympathy from a jury than he or she is—that is the *real* reason it is written into the lease.

Even if you have signed a waiver of jury trial in your lease, there are still some protections through state laws and court decisions. A number of state legislatures have passed laws that make any waiver of jury trial in residential leases completely void. Even where there is no protection by state laws, more and more judges are interpreting the lease waivers in a way that will give the tenant every possible opportunity for a trial by jury.

Your rights to free speech and assembly: It is hard to believe but some landlords will try to squash your rights to free speech and peaceful assembly. A typical lease clause might say that you will be evicted if you "approach other tenants for the purpose of organizing a group to take concerted action relative to the operation of the complex."

The First Amendment guarantees your right to free speech and assembly; the Fourteenth Amendment guarantees that no state will take away that right. That is big protection.

A number of states have laws that protect you from landlords who would evict you for griping. Even without those laws, a few courts are recognizing that sort of eviction denies your right to free speech.

In addition, you are protected by what is technically called "public policy." For instance, housing codes are written to protect people from substandard housing; and, after all, how will housing authorities know where problems exist if they do not hear from tenants? So, trying to shut you up is against "public policy" and would thwart the codes that are designed to protect you.

Your rights to sue a negligent landlord: In many leases you are asked to sign away your right to sue the landlord or hold him liable in any way, even if you are injured or your property is damaged and it is his fault. Recently, because of a number of new laws and court cases, it has been hard for landlords to enforce this type of clause.

One of the strongest (and most recent) protections given to tenants is a court decision that says a landlord (like any other business person selling or renting goods) must guarantee that the apartment he rents is fit to live in. On the surface that does not sound so earth shattering, but it reverses all the years of common law that said if you rent an apartment, you must accept it as is.

In a number of states, where there are not implied habitabil-

ity rulings, courts have protected tenants in three ways: (1) by ruling that "no-sue" clauses are void because the landlord has a duty (under housing codes and state statutes) to perform certain services. So, it is against "public policy" to relieve him of those duties—and your right to sue if he does not perform them. (2) by ruling that the tenant was forced to sign away his right not to sue because he was given a take-it-or-leave-it lease—and, so cannot be held to the waiver. Or (3) by interpreting the waiver not to sue *strictly* against the landlord. This last example does not make the waiver void but just allows a judge (who is enlightened on the subject of civil rights) to look out for the tenant.

Your rights to fix up your apartment: You are probably all too familiar with the clause in your lease that says you cannot make any "additions or alterations" in your apartment. Many landlords will tell you that means you cannot change anything— not even make nail holes for pictures. Do not buy that oppressive explanation. Of course, you cannot tear down a wall, take out the plumbing fixtures or lower the ceiling, but impermanent decorations or changes that do not alter the structure of the property are certainly within your rights.

There is another catchy little clause that says any changes you make stay with the land-

lord when you move. Taken to the extreme (the way some landlords want it), this means that the towel rack you put up stays behind when you move. It is still a gray area in the courts but more and more judges are interpreting the clause to mean only changes that are permanent. Also, judges interpret the clause by its "intent" in relation to the rest of the lease. For instance, if the landlord says you must leave behind all improvements and at the same time says you must restore the apartment to its original condition, a judge might rule that the intent was not for you to leave something behind, because the clauses are contradictory.

If your lease itemizes the "alterations" that are to become the landlord's property such as curtains, window shades, lighting fixtures, or wall decorations, do not meekly fill the landlord's hope chest. Get a lawyer and fight it. No reasonable judge would enforce such an oppressive clause.

Talk the landlord into a change? If you and the landlord agree to add or subtract anything from the lease or to make any special repairs before you move in, do not rely on verbal agreement. If you disagree later, it will be your word against the landlord's. To make it legal, both of you should initial the paragraph you change, delete, or add on all copies of the lease.

Moving

HOW TO MANAGE A DO-IT-YOURSELF MOVE

You can save a lot of money by moving yourself and, if you get your act together beforehand, you will not take all of that savings out of your own hide. Here's help:

1. Picking the right truck size is not as difficult as it sounds. Start by estimating the total cubic feet of your belongings because that is how truck capacity is measured.

First measure each piece of furniture. Multiply the length times the width times the depth to get the cubic measurement of each item. Then estimate the number of cartons you will need for other items such as dishes and clothing.

Wardrobe cartons, which will hold up to ten suits and are available from most moving companies, simplify things by allowing you to take clothes directly from the closet to the carton. Normally a small closet's worth of clothes requires only one such carton.

A wardrobe carton takes up to 19 cubic feet, and a medium-size carton fills four cubic feet of space. Add your furniture's total cubic feet to the estimated total carton cubic feet. Pick the truck that matches the resulting figure. You can find out about van sizes and capacities by asking any rental agency.

2. Smart packing means tight packing with lots of cushioning. Save newspapers and other materials in advance. If you use supermarket cartons, be sure to tape the bottoms.

Pack cartons tightly. Use towels and paper to fill all gaps and cushion breakable items. Since most cartons will be handled a number of times, do not pack in more than 50 pounds for your back's sake. Also, cartons are likely to break with anything heavier.

Mark each carton with its contents and which room you want it delivered to.

Folded clothing can be left in dresser drawers and moved that way. Pack books in small cartons—they are heavy.

Mirrors and picture frames demand special attention. Make your own cartons for them from large flattened cardboard boxes.

Lampshades damage easily and are difficult to repair. Box each separately and cushion with paper.

Rent at least two to three dozen furniture pads to wrap around your furniture and secure these with ropes.

3. Loading the truck is important. Pack the truck in four sections. Fill every section tightly from top to bottom by putting light cartons on top of heavy items. Use furniture pads to fill odd-shaped spaces.

There are metal rings along the interior sides of a moving truck. As each quarter of the truck is filled in, tie the load to these rings so the furniture will not shift in transit.

Place the heaviest items in the front quarter of the truck. Long pieces of furniture, like sofas and mattresses, should go along the sides of the van. Place dresser drawers facing the mattress so they will not tip during the trip. Do not load flammable items such as paints, turpentine, or gasoline.

When you get to your new apartment, unloading should be easier than loading. The worst is over—and you are home.

HIRING A MOVING COMPANY

Big van lines that handle interstate business are regulated by the government. So when it is time for a major move, figure that their charges are based on similar rates and they all do about the same job.

There is not much price competition, but just because the moving companies offer similar services does not mean they will all perform with equal finesse. The differences show up in scratched furniture, stained upholstery—little things that are hard to claim damages for—and in time-wasting aggravation. Whether you or your employer is picking up the tab, taking time to audition several carriers can pay off in a smoother move.

Start the screening process by picking at least three of the most reliable movers in your area; ask your friends for recommendations and check the Better Business Bureau for complaint records. Once you have picked the most likely candidates and scheduled their visits to your apartment, it helps to lead the movers' representatives through your questions instead of waiting for them to volunteer bits and pieces of information. You will want to know: 1) how much they estimate your move will cost, 2) what packing materials and procedures they will use, 3) insurance and contractor details, and 4) who you will be dealing with at the other end of the line.

Get detailed written estimates. The estimates for a long-distance move are based on the approximate weight of your shipment, the miles it will cover, the size and number of packing cartons, and other materials and services you will need. (For a local move, they will charge an hourly rate.)

Be picky about packing. Make sure the movers provide enough of the packing cartons. Let them know how you want things packed, and how much you will do yourself—and how the difference will be reflected in the cost.

No mover will assume liability for plants, pets, food, or aerosol cans. Also: Carry your documents, securities, jewelry with you. Insurance is pretty standardized but you might want to get special coverage on antiques and unusual pieces.

Discuss the terms of the contract. Get the name and address of each mover's agent nearest your new home. They are the people who may be unloading your belongings and will handle all problems or damage claims. Make sure you are getting experienced hands at both ends of the move.

MOVING PLANTS

It is not impossible to take them along—it is just extra work. Some things to know:

1. Just before you wrap the plants, water them thoroughly. Most will be okay for up to five days if they are well insulated with newspaper or plastic wrapping and sealed in a box. Do not worry about the lack of sunlight, but trim off any buds or blooms that might strain the plant while it is in limbo.

2. Smaller plants are easier to handle if you wrap them individually and box several together. Each pot can be tucked into a grocery sack or slipped into a funnel of newspaper that gently pushes the foliage up.

3. Plants should be the last thing on the truck and the first thing off. If your plants must spend several days on the road, untended, in either very hot or very cold weather, the risk of loss is high. For shorter hauls, you can ease the dangers of freezing or baking. In summer, use only paper for wrapping. A block of dry ice in the plants' vicinity (not on them or up against their wrapping) is an effective way to cool part of the truck, and it gives off carbon dioxide, which is good for plants. In extreme cold, extra newspaper will help, but if the truck makes an overnight stop and cools off to below 50 degrees, your plants will suffer. A straight-through trip would be better.

Securing Your Apartment

IS YOUR LANDLORD RESPONSIBLE?

No landlord can absolutely ensure your safety—a professional thief can get in no matter what. But it is reasonable to expect your landlord to maintain the security system that was installed. A landlord's negligence should not make you the victim of a crime.

What to do? If you see security in your building deteriorating, notify your landlord in writing. Give details—front door lock is broken, doorman takes three-hour coffee breaks. The object is to put the landlord on notice. If he is diligent, he will act. If not, and you sue him for negligence, he will have a hard time claiming that a crime was unforeseeable.

WHAT TO DO FOR YOURSELF:

Burglars who hit apartments are usually amateurs. Lacking talent, they rely on a high-volume approach; they try lots of doors and windows until they find an easy entry.

Here are some ways to thwart those beginners whose skills are often limited to "card jobs" (using a credit card to spring a lock), jumping sliding doors and windows out of their tracks, and occasionally using a wire on a window latch. Securing your place takes only about two hours of work. Here's how: Your first step is thinking like a burglar as you survey your apartment. Pay special attention to openings that cannot be seen from the hall or street and have flimsy latches that should be replaced. And do not underestimate a crook's agility and motivation to reach an unguarded balcony or window.

The door: If you do not have a dead bolt and cannot get the landlord to put one on, here is how to do it yourself.

With a plain, hollow-core door (no steel edging), the sim-

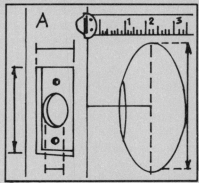

plest answer is to add a rim-type dead bolt (sometimes called the drop dead bolt, vertical dead bolt, or jimmy-proof lock) that is usually installed above the existing lock. You have to drill a hole in the door for the key mechanism and do a little wood gouging on the jamb for the strike (see drawing A).

Usually, it is easier to just replace the unsophisticated lock that came with your place. A lot of them are the vulnerable key-in-knob types with either no dead bolt or a short, ineffective one. You can substitute a tough cylindrical lock with a dead bolt ¾" to 1" long, and do little or no cutting on your door. There are no standardized sizes for locks; to avoid unnecessary wood gouging, get the measurements of your old lock before you buy a replacement.

Sliding glass door: There are three ways to secure sliding glass openings: 1) You can drop a piece of sawed-off wooden broomstick into the track so the door cannot slide (it can still be jumped). 2) Screw two metal (not wood) screws into the top center of the upper track (see

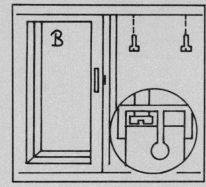

drawing B) and adjust their height so the door will barely slide under them. That way there is no extra space to lift the sliding section up into. Use a nail to start the screw holes; the job takes about ten minutes, and you cannot even see the screws when the door is closed. 3) This alternative leaves some visible holes but it is even easier than the screw-in-track method. Drill a hole in the top of the fixed part of the doorframe at the upper inside corner (see drawing C), and a second hole immediately behind the first, into the sliding frame while it is closed. Slide a three-penny nail into the lined-up holes and the door cannot be slid or lifted. (Tie a piece of monofilament line from the hole in the frame to the nail so it will not get lost.)

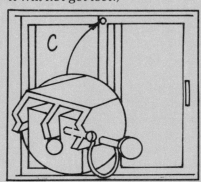

If you want to secure the door in a partially open position, get one of the friction-type track stops sold in hardware stores. A track stop will not keep the door from being lifted out of its track but the door cannot be opened wide.

Windows: The wooden sash, double-hung windows found in older apartments are the least challenging for a burglar and the easiest to burglar-proof. If they are even slightly warped, with a gap between the top and bottom sections, they are ideal for the crook who knows enough to force the latch with a knife blade or a piece of steel.

At the outside edge where the frames meet (see drawing

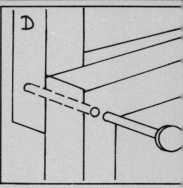

D), drill a hole in the bottom frame, then partway into the top frame. Slip a big nail or carriage bolt into the holes and the window cannot be moved. Another hole a few inches higher on the top frame, and the window is secure while open.

Take another look at any reachable casement window. Is it big enough for someone to climb through when it is open? Is there even the slightest gap where a thin flexible instrument could be used to dislodge the latch? If there is a crank, is it so freewheeling that the unlatched window could be pushed open? You don't trust it? Replace the simple pull latch with a locking-lever latch that has to be moved in two directions to open, or that has a lock button you hold down with one hand while you unlatch with the other. There are plenty of suitable latches around so look for one with screw holes to match the existing latch. The replacement is as simple as two screws-out . . . two-screws-in, and you can even put the old hardware back when you leave.

HARDWARE TALK FOR LOCK BUYERS

1. **Lock mechanism:** the part that fits through the door; knobs, keyhole, sometimes a decorative plate.

2. **Latch:** the part that comes through the edge of the door.

3. **Strike:** the metal plate that is screwed into the doorframe. The latch and/or dead bolt slip into it.

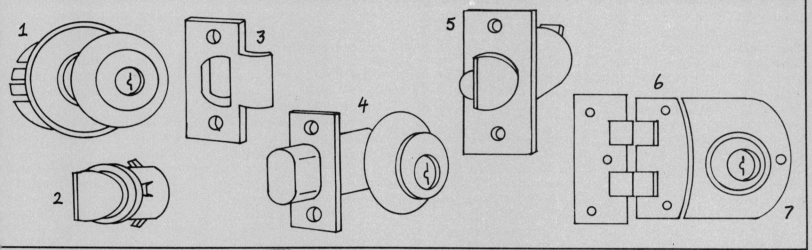

4. Dead bolt: a flat ended, steel plunger that is held locked into the doorframe and cannot be pushed back into the latch.

5. Deadlocking latch: a latch with an adjoining small plunger that deadlocks and makes the latch immune to card jobs.

6. Rim-type dead bolt: extra lock; puts bolt across surface of door and jamb.

7. Template: a paper pattern that comes with some locks. Shows what size holes are needed to put the lock in the door.

BURGLAR ALARM SYSTEMS

No matter what the burglar alarm salespeople say, no alarm system can give you foolproof protection against a cool, professional burglar. You still need good locks, solid doors and jambs to attach them to, and security-conscious people around you.

The burglar alarm's real value is that it can scare off a nervous, amateur crook, and the majority of burglars are those flappable types.

No matter what alarm you get, these generalities apply:

1. Simpler is better. The complicated systems usually have more breakdowns and cost more.

2. If you are getting a monitoring service with your system, check out the company with the Better Business Bureau or a consumer protection group. And make sure you get a warranty on the equipment as well as quick maintenance and service commitments.

3. Any alarm that uses electricity should have the UL tag for safety's sake.

4. Check to make sure the siren, bell, or other noisemaker is legal in your community.

You may not want to spend the time, money, and effort to wire up a complicated alarm system. But less expensive, portable, plug-in models are available. One of them is made up to look like a dictionary with a cord that plugs into any electrical outlet. Left on a shelf or table, it goes off if anyone comes within 10 feet and doesn't deactivate it within 10 seconds. The fact that they last for years and may be taken from one apartment to another with no fuss makes their cost just that much more reasonable.

Also, there is an inexpensive model that may be left against your door to topple and go off if someone forces it. Some people get one for their apartment and take another along on vacation to be propped against the motel door for the night.

PROPERTY INSURANCE FOR RENTERS:

Liability protection, under the usual tenant package, covers mishaps in your apartment, accidents you could be blamed for outside the apartment, and your legal fees if you are sued.

Most policies also cover loss of goods and damage in the event of fire, lightning, explosion, vandalism, and a number of other perils—17 in all. Any coverage on the building is up to the landlord.

Here are some things to know about apartment insurance:

Premiums for basic coverages will not vary much within your part of town but most companies offer extras at various prices. There are qualifications to most policies too. And since some of them run to ten or more pages, you might do better shopping the "disclaimers" and the extras instead of the basic price.

The basic renter's package is sold by most of the country's property and casualty insurance companies—directly, through licensed agents, or through brokers who sell for many companies.

An agent signs contracts with one or several insurance companies and represents only them. A broker, on the other hand, works independently, with no insurance company contract. He can offer whatever insurance he feels is best for you, right up to signing you with Lloyd's of London. Some people prefer the licensed agent's small, personal office; others, the broker's versatility or a company agent's direct line to his firm.

If you live in an inner city neighborhood that does not have a good crime record, there is still hope that you will be able to get coverage. One way is through what is called the FAIR (Fair Access to Insurance Requirements) Plan, a voluntary program by the insurance industry. A number of insurance companies in a state get together and agree that they will insure what would ordinarily be poor risks. You can find out if there is a FAIR Plan in your state and what its requirements are by writing the National Committee on Property Insurance, 800 Valley Forge Plaza, King of Prussia, Pennsylvania 19406.

Another route is to get coverage from the Federal Crime Insurance Program; it is set up in states where there is no FAIR Plan or where the government decides there is an inadequate one. For more information about Federal Crime Insurance and eligibility requirements, call (800) 638-8780 or write Federal Crime Insurance, P.O. Box 41033, Washington, D.C. 20014.

Your Rights as a Tenant

Tenant/landlord laws have evolved very quickly over the past decade. Many states are in the process of enacting legislation that is designed to treat the tenant in a more equitable way. Most of these laws are based on the same principles, but the specifics vary. For example: Most states put a maximum amount on the security deposit you pay to your landlord; it can range—depending on where you are—from one month's rent to two month's rent.

Laws vary greatly. Some states may provide for a slap on the landlord's hand while others make him pay off in triple damages, with attorney's fees and court costs included. One state's law may cover only security deposits while another covers every facet of tenant/ landlord agreement from painting requirements to unlawful eviction. So it is smart to know exactly what your own city and state laws say. It is not as difficult to find the laws as you might think. The answer is as close as your nearest law library (at government offices and law schools).

Then when your landlord swears that fixing a leaky pipe is not his job, call his bluff. The point: The informed consumer is the most effective one. Tell your landlord about a few laws and court cases. He will usually see your side of the story—fast. If not, you have got the information you need for Small Claims court.

THE LAWS THAT PROTECT YOU

Security deposit laws: Getting a security deposit back from your landlord used to be about as easy as walking out of Fort Knox with a load of gold. In the past, landlords have often stalled endlessly about refunds, or deducted large amounts for undocumented damages.

Now, thanks to security deposit laws in most states, you will have an easier time getting your money back. The laws are not identical but they do have some common safeguards:

Maximum security deposit: A ceiling is set on how much money the landlord can demand.

Interest: Many states require the landlord to pay you interest on your security deposit, although they allow him to keep some portion for bookkeeping services.

Use of the deposit: A deposit can be used only for legitimate purposes such as covering unpaid rent, cleaning expenses and repairs caused by negligence or abuse—but never the cost of ordinary wear and tear.

No more waiting for refund: All laws set a deadline for returning the deposit.

Itemized bill: If the landlord deducts any expenses, he must send you an itemized statement, usually by the same deadline that is set for refunds.

Penalties: You can sue your landlord for wrongfully withholding part or all of your deposit beyond the deadline. Under some laws you can get up to three times the deposit plus attorney's fees and court costs.

Some tips: Before moving in, inspect every inch of the apartment and make a list of the defects; get the landlord to sign the list. Then when you leave, you should not be charged for the leftover sins of former tenants. On moving day, send your landlord a certified letter, including the list of defects, and request a prompt refund on your deposit. (Be sure to include your new mailing address.)

If the landlord does not refund your money on time, or if you think his deductions are wrong, tell him—in writing— that you plan to sue him for the penalty, as provided for under

your state's law—unless, of course, the matter can be straightened out to your satisfaction. If you sue, your best bet is to take the case to a judge in your local Small Claims or Housing Court. It is an inexpensive, fast way to sue, and you do not need to hire a lawyer.

Under repair-and-deduct laws, you can have repairs made yourself and take the money out of your rent. The rent check is great leverage but you will have to follow some rules to make it work:

You must warn your landlord before you act—it is best by certified letter. After notification, the landlord is entitled to adequate time to make the repairs. Some states set a deadline such as 20 days while others say the landlord must have "reasonable time." If water is flooding through your ceiling, reasonable could mean 24 or less hours; on the other hand, for nonemergencies, it could mean a few weeks. A judge would make that interpretation.

There is a limit on how much you can deduct out of one month's rent. In your state it might be as little as $50, an entire month's rent, or "a just and reasonable amount" (the judge decides here).

Of course, it is unlikely that your landlord will stand idly by when you are not paying full rent. He may try to evict you on the grounds of nonpayment of rent. But if you can prove that you properly followed the law, you should have a good defense. You might have to prove that you did not negligently cause the defects, that you gave adequate notice and time for repairs to be made, and that the repairs were both appropriate in cost and necessary to the apartment's habitability.

Rent-withholding laws have the same purpose as repair statutes: They direct your rent

money into repairs, not the landlord's pocket. But instead making the repairs yourself, you let a court do it. First you have to petition a court to let you withhold your rent mone and put it into the hands of th court. Then the judge will usually appoint an administra tor to use the money to make repairs.

Privacy laws: In many state there are renters' privacy laws that say your landlord cannot enter your apartment withou good reason. There are varia tions in how strict the state laws are, but there are instances under most laws wher you can ask your landlord to return another time.

In most states, the landlord must announce a visit at least 24 hours in advance (in some states it is 48 hours) unless there is an emergency.

Laws on apartment upkeep: In an apartment you want mo than just a good buy; you wan a buy that stays good. In a growing number of states a landlord can no longer say tha there is no guarantee on repairs. These laws recognize th if rent is paid, services must be rendered; often, that rent is th leverage to get a landlord to make needed repairs.

There are three different laws—implied warranty of hab itability, repair-and-deduct an rent withholding. Some are no formally in the statute books, although they have the effect law because they come from court cases that have set precedents.

Essentially, the basis of the implied warranty of habitabili is that the landlord must guar antee that your apartment is f to live in. And he must keep it that way—the warranty never expires. In essence, your landlord warrants to keep your apartment and the common areas (such as halls, stairways lobby) in "habitable" condition

In most places it is up to a judge to decide what is habitable or uninhabitable. Some have strictly ruled that it means the bare essentials and nothing else —such as heat, water, unbroken windowpanes. Others, however, have broadened the warranty to include things that the tenant could "reasonably expect" when the lease was signed—such as elevator service.

The repair-and-deduct and rent-withholding laws are based on a similar principle: You ought to get what you are paying for; namely, a fit place to live. These two laws are simply different means for arriving at the same goal—to force your landlord to make repairs.

Implied warranties of habitability provide for varying remedies, depending on what the precedent or law in your state allows. Some say you can repair and deduct from your rent; others allow you to hold out on your rent.

Discrimination laws: Despite recent laws and guidelines, housing discrimination still exists across the country in the form of jacked-up rents, extra charges, and choosing one prospective tenant over another. But the 1968 Civil Rights Act and city and state fair housing laws are on your side. Title VIII of the 1968 Civil Rights Act prohibits discrimination on the basis of race, color, religion, sex, and national origin. Some state and city fair housing codes are even tougher, also including marital status, age, or the fact that you have children.

If you believe you have been discriminated against, you will need evidence. Proving that the landlord would rent to someone else is the best way to support your claims. And such tests stand up in court. The evidence also gives you the bargaining power to settle out of court.

To set it up find someone to apply for the same apartment as soon as possible after you have been turned down. This substitute must be someone who will not be rejected for the same reason you think you were. Your friend should offer the same information you did—income, marital status, and so on—and make sure he gets a commitment from the person showing the apartment, saying that the apartment is still available. Then your friend should stall and promise to call back later. Be sure that each of you immediately writes down what happened. Include the name of the person you spoke to, apartment number, address, and every detail you can remember.

If you are being discriminated against, you can also call the U.S. Department of Housing and Urban Development. The local office will be listed under "U.S. Government" in the phone book or call HUD's toll-free number, (800) 424–8590.

HOW TO FIGHT BACK
Form a Tenant's Union:
There is power in numbers. More and more, landlords are recognizing the power and consumer clout tenant organizations wield—and are correcting the problems they point out.

If you think you need a tenant group in your building, here is how to get one organized:

You and other organizers need to tell fellow tenants that you are having a meeting to take action on a particular problem. Door-to-door and personal contact is the best way, followed up with reminder notices. At the first meeting spend some time getting acquainted, then select leaders. Form two committees: one for publicity, the other for finances. Ask for volunteers to canvas the building again to get more tenants involved.

Draw up a list of grievances from the tenants and set priorities on those complaints. Keep the list at a moderate length. One that is too long will make you sound unreasonable and put the landlord on the defensive. A short list with only major points leaves you with nothing negotiable—and your landlord with no "victories" at the bargaining table. Then decide strategy. Negotiation is the first step. Write the landlord a letter that 1) informs him that you have organized, 2) explains your purpose in general terms and in specific complaints, 3) invites him to set up a meeting, and 4) asks him to answer your invitation within a certain number of days.

Some general rules: 1) Meet on a neutral ground. 2) Make it clear that you want to meet with the landlord or his representative—not the building manager. 3) Have only a small negotiating committee represent the entire group. 4) Clearly define your complaints and what you want done about them. 5) Get the landlord to put all agreements in writing; add penalties if he does not carry out his promise (rent strike, legal action, etc.).

If negotiations fail: Get a lawyer. 1) You can sue if the conditions in the building are bad enough. 2) You can harass the landlord (picket lines). 3) Make the necessary repairs and deduct the cost from your rent but only if your state law recognizes this remedy. 4) Go on a rent strike.

Arbitration: Half the battle in arbitration is getting the other party to arbitrate once a dispute starts. You can save yourself a lot of grief by putting a clause right in your lease that says you and your landlord will use arbitration. It is less expensive than a long court battle and less time consuming. When and if you need arbitration, you and your landlord can contact Community Dispute Services of the American Arbitration Association, 140 West 51st Street, New York, N.Y. 10020, or one of its regional offices. There is no problem getting an impartial arbitrator to hear the case in your area. Usually both parties split the fee (often several hundred dollars).

Either you or the landlord submits a written statement outlining the basic dispute and calling for arbitration. When the case is heard, it usually takes about 18 days for settlement.

Hire a lawyer, coop style: Your tenant group raises money to put a lawyer, law firm, or panel of lawyers with experience on a partial retainer. The annual fee gets each member a chunk of the lawyer's time, plus a big discount if you need serious help. Of course, the range of services and fees will vary according to the number of people in your group and the program you work out with your lawyer(s). There is no "model plan" that works for all groups because each group has special needs. The best way is to find a sympathetic lawyer and make your own deal.

Take it to court: There are two types of courts that cover most landlord/tenant problems: Small Claims and Housing courts.

Small Claims Court: All states have Small Claims courts. The rules governing them vary from state to state so your best source of accurate information is the court clerk. Look up "Small Claims Court" in the Yellow Pages under the heading for your city or county. Talk with the court clerk, briefly explain whom you want to sue and for how much, and ask what steps you must take to file suit. Here are some things to know:

The court clerk will usually tell you the day your case will be heard, not a specific hour.

Keep the entire day open.

You have to pay a small amount to cover the expenses of the court. You will also have to pay to have the summons delivered.

You can only sue for so-called money damages, the value of what you have lost.

The maximum amount of damages you can sue for as "small claims" varies, most often between $500 and $1,000.

There are some tricky rules about where you must file your lawsuit. You have to sue in the court that has what lawyers call the "proper venue," frequently the court located in the district where the defendant lives, works, or maintains a place of business.

Make sure you have the correct legal name of any business you are suing. Ask the court clerk how you can locate the true name of the business.

Lawyers are not required. You can do it yourself.

Bring to the trial any documents—warranties, bills, leases, letters—that support your side of the story. Make arrangements with the clerk if you want to subpoena witnesses or documents.

The defendant will be notified by the court of any judgment you win. If he does not pay up, remind him of his obligation by certified mail. You may even have to return to the court and enlist the services of a sheriff or marshal. The court clerk can best explain the alternatives.

Housing Court: This is a relatively new type of court that operates much like a cross between arbitration and Small Claims court. Few cities have them yet.

Call in your complaint to the city's Housing Violation Bureau. If the matter is not settled in 30 days, go down to Housing Court, deposit $10, and you will be assigned a trial date not more than ten days away. You will also be given a summons for delivery to your landlord by anyone but you. On the trial date the judge will assign you to a small hearing room, presided over by special housing judges. Then—some-times in just two sessions only a few weeks apart—the housing dispute is settled.

An alternative that has been growing in numbers and usefulness is the Neighborhood Court, which deals in conflict resolution. Trained mediators help people learn techniques to work out their differences.

For more information about mediation centers, write to Community Mediation Center, 356 Middle Country Road, Coram, New York 11727. By sending $4 to the Superintendent of Documents, U.S. Government Printing Office, Washington, D.C. 20402, you can receive a copy of *Neighborhood Justice Center: An Analysis of Potential models* (#027-000-0598-5).

THE APT SOURCE GUIDE

Having moved in and out of dozens of apartments every year over the years, we have learned some shortcuts for finding furnishings, accessories, and wares that make life easier and make rooms better looking. These sources come in two varieties—the retail store where you can walk in and buy what you need and the others which include wholesalers, manufacturers, importers and to-the-trade-only showrooms. The wholesale sources will usually answer all written queries so that you can find out where in your area the products are available. Occasionally, you will be able to buy direct from wholesale sources. Do not count on it but it does not hurt to try. This source guide is broken down into categories that will make it faster for you to find exactly what you are looking for.

CONTEMPORARY FURNISHINGS

Retail

The Chair Store
1694 Union St.
San Francisco, CA 94123
Butcher block tops.

Conran's
160 East 54th St.
New York, NY 10022
One of the largest selections of furnishings and accessories under one roof.

Cost Plus Imports
2552 Taylor St.
San Francisco, CA 94133

The Door Store
210 East 51st St.
New York, NY 10022
A classic mix of finished and unfinished furnishings.

H.U.D.D.L.E.
10918 Kinross Ave.
Los Angeles, CA 90024
Innovative furniture, fabrics, and sono tube kids' systems.

Storehouse
2737 Apple Valley Rd.
Atlanta, GA 30319
High-quality furnishings.

The Workbench
470 Park Ave. So.
New York, NY 10016
Good solid furniture at good prices.

Other

Beylerian Limited
225 Fifth Ave.
New York, NY 10016
High-styled Italian design furnishings in plastic at reasonable prices.

Boling Chair Co.
Box 409
Siler City, NC 27344
Manufacturers of a light wood windsor chair.

Bremshey
International Products Trading, Inc.
380 Franklin Turnpike
Mahwah, NJ 07430
Unusual and functional pieces.

Design Institute of America
815 Park Ave.
New York, NY 10021
Laminated tables and rattan furnishings.

Directional Industries, Inc.
979 Third Ave.
New York, NY 10022
Very modern.

Domani
A Division of Burris Industries
Lincolnton, NC 20802
Good-looking European styles.

Founders of Thomasville
Furniture Industries, Inc.
Box 339
Thomasville, NC 27360
Quality furniture.

Furniture To Go, Inc.
2535 Metropolitan Dr.
Trevose, PA 19047
Well-designed seating at exceptional prices.

Gold Medal Inc.
1700 Packard Ave.
Racine, WI 53403
The new director's chair.

Kinnovations, Inc.
2444 Walnut Ridge St.
Dallas, TX 75223
Simple canvas and steel furniture.

The Lane Co, Inc.
Altavista, VA 24517
Wide variety of furnishings.

Moreddi
734 Grand Ave.
Ridgefield, NJ 07657
Well-priced imports, especially seating.

Otto Gerdau Co.
82 Wall St.
New York, NY 10005
Good chairs and desks in chrome, glass and butcher block.

Overman U.S.A., Inc.
200 Lexington Ave.
New York, NY 10016
European style seating.

Primitive Artisans
Route 10 and N.W. Dr.
Plainville, CT 06062
Baskets, ornaments and seating pieces.

Raymor/Richards
Morgenthau, Inc.
41 Madison Ave.
New York, NY 10010
Contemporary accessories.

Scandinavian Design, Inc.
117 East 59th St.
New York, NY 10022
Interesting imports.

Telescope Folding Furniture
Co, Inc.
Granville, NY 12832
The classic director's chair.

Thayer Coggin, Inc.
High Point, NC 27262
Well-designed and well-constructed pieces.

Thonet Industries, Inc.
305 East 63rd St.
New York, NY 10021
The original bentwood chair.

Trend Pacific
507 Towne Ave.
Los Angeles, CA 90013
Light wood and canvas furniture.

TRADITIONAL FURNISHINGS

These furnishings are widely available at retail stores across the country. If you write to the main offices, you can find the outlet in your area.

American-Drew Co., Inc.
200 Lexington Ave.
New York, NY 10016
Specializes in Early American.

Basset Furniture Industries, Inc.
Basset, WV 24055
Good prices, availability and a range of styles.

Burlington House Furniture
1345 Avenue of the Americas
New York, NY 10019
A broad selection of many styles.

Chapman Manufacturing Co.
21 East 26th St.
New York, NY 10010
Lamps, furniture and accessories.

Davis Cabinet Co.
Box 60444
Nashville, TN 37206
Good range of styles and finishes.

Drexel Heritage Furnishings,
Inc.
Drexel, NC 28619
Selection of styles and pieces, especiall the Et Cetera collection.

Ethan Allen, Inc.
Danbury, CT 06910
Good Early American as well as othe periods.

Henredon Furniture Industries
Inc.
Morganton, NC 28655
Tasteful, expensive reproductions.

Kroehler Mfg. Co.
222 East Fifth Ave.
Naperville, IL 60540
Good comfortable upholstery and furnishings by Angelo Donghia.

Riverside Furniture Corp.
Drawer 1427
Fort Smith, AR 72901
Oak reproductions.

Sarreid, Ltd.
Box 3545
Wilson, NC 27893
Country pine furniture.

Thomasville Furniture
Industries, Inc.
Thomasville, NC 27360
Stylish reproductions from many eras.

White Furniture Co.
Mebane, NC 27302
Quality reproductions.

WICKER AND RATTAN FURNITURE

Retail

Cost Plus Imports
2552 Taylor St.
San Francisco, CA 94133

Fran's Basket House
Route 10
Succasunna, NJ 07876

Kreiss Ports of Call
8445 Santa Monica Blvd.
Los Angeles, CA 90069

The Patio
550 Powell St.
San Francisco, CA 94108

ther

California Asia
Brown Jordan Co.
360 Gidley St.
El Monte, CA 91734

Ficks Reed Co.
4900 Beacon St.
Cincinnati, OH 45230

Kreiss Corp.
139 Figueroa
Los Angeles, CA 90012

The McGuire Co.
Rotaling Place at Jackson Sq.
San Francisco, CA 94111

Pan-Asian Designs, Inc.
321 Aviation Blvd.
Inglewood, CA 90301

Tropi-Cal
731 Alba
Los Angeles, CA 90058

Walter's Wicker Wonderland
191 Second Ave.
New York, NY 10009

DESIGNER SOURCES

Retail

Habitare
12 East 57th Street
New York, NY 10022
Slick Italian designer furnishings.

Ambienti
92 Madison Ave.
New York, NY 10021
Italian modern furnishings and accessories.

Other

Atelier International
595 Madison Ave.
New York, NY 10022
Modern Italian furnishings and some accessories.

Castelli Furniture, Inc.
950 Third Ave.
New York, NY 10022
Modern Italian furnishings.

Herman Miller
600 Madison Ave.
New York, NY 10021
Modern classics.

ICF, Inc.
145 E. 57th St.
New York, NY 10022
Slick imports, great storage systems.

Knoll International
745 Fifth Ave.
New York, NY 10022
Good selection of modern pieces.

Stendig
410 East 62nd St.
New York, NY 10021
Lush leather and innovative seating.

UNFINISHED FURNITURE

Retail and Mail Order

Country Workshop
95 Rome St.
Newark, NJ 07105

Furniture-in-the-Raw
1021 Second Ave.
New York, NY 10022

The Unpainted Place
1601 Hennepin Ave.
Minneapolis, MN 55403

BEDS

Retail

Loftcraft
Primark International Corp.
200 Madison Ave.
New York, NY 10016
Solutions for space problems.

Murphy Bed and Kitchen Co.
40 East 34th St.
New York, NY 10016
Old standard.

Other

Simmons U.S.A.
One Park Ave.
New York, NY 10016
Sleep sofa specialists.

RECLINERS

Other

Barca-Lounger
Hayes-Williams, Inc.
261 Madison Ave.
New York, NY 10016

The Berkline Corp.
One Berkline Dr.
Morristown, TN 37814

La-Z-Boy Co.
1284 Telegraph Rd.
Monroe, MI 48161

OUTDOOR INDOOR

Other

Cottage Shops, Inc.
101 S. La Cienega
Los Angeles, CA 90048

Gentle Swing
156 Calle Cresto
San Juan, Puerto Rico 00901
Beautiful hammocks.

The Hammock Shop
Box 308
Pawleys Island, SC 29585
The classic rope hammocks.

Meadowcraft, Div. of Birmingham Ornamental Iron Co.
Box 1357
Birmingham, AL 35201
Contemporary and traditional indoor-outdoor furniture.

Medallion Industries, Inc.
Box 427
Taimanii Station
Miami, FL 33144
Very contemporary and stylish pieces in a great range of colors.

Molla, Inc.
110 State St.
Westbury, NY 11590

Tropitone Furniture
Box 3197
Sarasota, FL 33578

Woodward Furniture
Owosso, MI 38867

GIANTS

Retail and Mail Order
A surprisingly good variety for all the basics. Time-saving sources found in every city.

J. C. Penney Co., Inc.
1301 Avenue of the Americas
New York, NY 10019

Montgomery Ward
619 W. Chicago Ave.
Chicago, IL 60607

Sears, Roebuck and Company
40-15 Sears Tower
Chicago, IL 60684

Spiegel
1040 W. 35th St.
Chicago, IL 60609

FABRIC

Retail

Black Sheep
The Cannery
2801 Leavenworth
San Francisco, CA 94133
Bright contemporary cottons.

Calico Corners
Mt. Kisco, NY 10549
Barn full of choices at good prices.

Fabric Barn
2839 North Broadway
Chicago, IL 60613
Big retail outlet with many contemporary fabrics.

Fabrications
146 East 56th St.
New York, NY 10022
Wide selection of many styles.

Far Eastern Fabrics
171 Madison Ave.
New York, NY 10016
Thai silk, scarves, batik and authentic antique oriental fabric.

Jensen-Lewis Co., Inc.
156 Seventh Ave.
New York, NY 10009
Canvas by the yard.

Laura Ashley, Inc.
714 Madison Ave.
New York, NY 10021
English prints in a variety of colors.

Liberty of London
108 W. 39th St.
New York, NY 10018
Famous for the Liberty Lawn and William Morris cotton prints.

Pierre Deux
369 Bleeker St.
New York, NY 10014
The spirit of the south of France in fabrics.

Other

Bloomcraft
295 Fifth Ave.
New York, NY 10003
Fabrics for everything at good prices.

Central Shippee
Bloomingdale, NJ 07403
The source for felt.

Covington Fabrics
267 Fifth Ave.
New York, NY 10016
Traditional prints, checks and Kanvastex.

Cyrus Clark Co., Inc.
267 Fifth Ave.
New York, NY 10016
Traditional prints.

F & F Tergal Importers
252 W. 40th St.
New York, NY 10018
Laces for every purpose.

International Printworks, Inc.
100 Wells Ave.
Newton, MA 02159
Post Marimekko and European cotton prints.

Quaker Lace
24 West 40th St.
New York, NY 10018
Laces of every description.

Riverdale
295 Fifth Ave.
New York, NY 10016
Well-priced, widely distributed range of styles.

Schumacher
939 Third Ave.
New York, NY 10022
Huge collection of traditional textures and prints.

Waverly Fabrics
58 West 40th St.
New York, NY 10018
Traditional prints and contemporary fabrics.

LIGHTING

Retail

George Kovacs
831 Madison Ave.
New York, NY 10021
Home of the best contemporary lighting.

Light, Inc.
1162 Second Ave.
New York, NY 10021
Designer lighting in many styles.

Thunder 'N Light, Inc.
171 Bowery
New York, NY 10002
Industrial lighting.

Other

Basic Concepts, Ltd.
135 Lawrence St.
Hackensack, NJ 07501
Inexpensive contemporary lighting.

Halo Lighting
Div. of McGraw-Edison Co.
400 Busse Rd.
Elk Grove, IL 60007
Good track lighting systems.

Koch and Lowy
940 Third Ave.
New York, NY 10022
Contemporary fixtures.

Laurel Lamp Manufacturing
Inc.
111 Rome St.
Newark, NJ 07105
Brass pharmacy lamps, green glass cone lamps and many favorites at realistic prices.

Lighting Associates
351 East 61st St.
New York, NY 10021
Selection of contemporary designs.

Lightolier
346 Claremont Ave.
Jersey City, NJ 07305
Makers of the track lighting system.

Luxo Lamp Corp.
Port Chester, NY 10573
The classic work lamp.

Stiffel Co.
700 N. Kingsbury St.
Chicago, IL 60610
Wide range of traditional styles.

FLOORING

Retail

Central Carpet Cleaning Co.,
Inc.
426 Columbus Ave.
New York, NY 10024
Good used orientals and other styles.

La Chambre Perse
347 Bleecker St.
New York, NY 10014
Beautiful orientals.

Other

American Olean Tile Co.
Lansdale, PA 19446
Classic ceramic tiles.

Armstrong Cork Co.
Lancaster, PA 17604
Large selections of good, practical floor coverings in many materials.

Bigelow-Sandford, Inc.
Box 3089
Dept. BJA
Greenville, SC 29602
Good choice of carpetings in many colors.

Concepts International
919 Third Ave.
New York, NY 10022
Designer area rugs at good prices.

Congoleum Corp.
Resilient Flooring Division
195 Belgrove Dr.
Kearny, NJ 07032
Hard surface flooring.

Country Floors
300 East 61st St.
New York, NY 10021
Beautiful ceramic tiles in all shapes and colors.

Couristan
The Carpet Center
919 Third Ave.
New York, NY 10022
Good selection of quality reproduction Indian and oriental rugs.

Flintkote
480 Central Ave.
East Rutherford, NJ 07073
Vinyl tiles.

Hoboken Wood Flooring Corp
100 Willow St.
East Rutherford, NJ 07073
Wide selection of wood strip flooring.

Import Specialists
83 Wall St.
New York, NY 10005
Sisal and the sisal look.

Karastan, a division of
Fieldcrest Mills
919 Third Ave.
New York, NY 10022
Good variety and great quality.

Lee Carpets
Valley Forge Industrial Park
Morristown, PA 19401
Good selection in various colors.

Regal Rugs, Inc.
819 Buckeye St.
North Vernon, IN 47265
Designer area rugs at good prices.

INDUSTRIAL SUPPLY SOURCES

Retail

Abstracta Structures, Inc.
101 Park Ave.
New York, NY 10017
Flexible chrome tube display and storage system.

Art et Industrie
132 Thompson St.
New York, NY 10012
The best and most innovative retail collection of old and new industrial designs.

Manhattan Ad Hoc
Housewares
842 Lexington Ave.
New York, NY 10021
The source for the slickest industrial look.

Other

Able Steel Equipment Co., Inc.
50-02 23rd St.
Long Island City, NY 11101
Industrial shelving and storage.

Albert Cayne Equipment Co.
93 Mercer St.
New York, NY 10012
Industrial lockers and shelving.